Taxcafe.co.uk Tax Guides

How to Save Property Tax

By Carl Bayley BSc ACA

D0293389

Important Legal Notices:

Taxcafe®
TAX GUIDE – "How to Save Property Tax"

Published by:
Taxcafe UK Limited
67 Milton Road
Kirkcaldy
KY1 1TL
United Kingdom
Tel: (01592) 560081

Eighteenth Edition, June 2014

ISBN 978-1-907302-85-5

Disclaimer
Before reading or relying on the content of this Tax Guide, please read the disclaimer.

Disclaimer

1. Please note that this publication is intended as **general guidance** only and does NOT constitute accountancy, tax, financial or other professional advice. The author and Taxcafe UK Limited make no representations or warranties with respect to the accuracy or completeness of the contents of this publication and cannot accept any responsibility for any liability, loss or risk, personal or otherwise, which may arise, directly or indirectly, from reliance on information contained in this publication.

2. Please note that tax legislation, the law and practices of government and regulatory authorities (e.g. HM Revenue and Customs) are constantly changing. Furthermore, your personal circumstances may vary from the general information contained in this tax guide which may not be suitable for your situation. We therefore recommend that for accountancy, tax, financial or other professional advice, you consult a suitably qualified accountant, tax specialist, independent financial adviser, or other professional adviser who will be able to provide specific advice based on your personal circumstances.

3. This guide covers UK taxation only and any references to 'tax' or 'taxation', unless the contrary is expressly stated, refer to UK taxation only. Please note that references to the 'UK' do not include the Channel Islands or the Isle of Man. Foreign tax implications are beyond the scope of this guide.

4. Whilst in an effort to be helpful this tax guide may refer to general guidance on matters other than UK taxation, Taxcafe UK Limited and the author are not expert in these matters and do not accept any responsibility or liability for loss which may arise from reliance on such information contained in this guide.

5. Please note that Taxcafe UK Limited has relied wholly on the expertise of the author in the preparation of the content of this tax guide. The author is not an employee of Taxcafe UK Limited but has been selected by Taxcafe UK Limited using reasonable care and skill.

About the Author

Carl Bayley is the author of a series of 'Plain English' tax guides designed specifically for the layman and the non-specialist. Carl's particular speciality is his ability to take the weird, complex and inexplicable world of taxation and set it out in the kind of clear, straightforward language that taxpayers themselves can understand. As he often says himself, "my job is to translate 'tax' into English".

Carl enjoys his role as a tax author, as he explains: "Writing these guides gives me the opportunity to use the skills and knowledge learned over almost thirty years in the tax profession for the benefit of a wider audience. The most satisfying part of my success as an author is the chance to give the average person the same standard of advice as the 'big guys' at a price which everyone can afford."

Carl takes the same approach when speaking on taxation, a role he frequently undertakes with great enthusiasm, including his highly acclaimed annual 'Budget Breakfast' for the Institute of Chartered Accountants.

In addition to being a recognised author and speaker on the subject, Carl has often spoken on taxation on radio and television, including the BBC's 'It's Your Money' programme and BBC Radio 2's Jeremy Vine Show.

Carl began his career as a Chartered Accountant in 1983 with one of the 'Big 4' accountancy firms. After qualifying as a double prize-winner, he immediately began specialising in taxation.

After honing his skills with several major international firms, Carl began the new millennium by launching his own tax and accounting practice, Bayley Miller Limited, through which he provides advice on a wide variety of taxation issues; especially property taxation and tax planning for small and medium-sized businesses.

Carl is a member of the governing Council of the Institute of Chartered Accountants in England and Wales, Deputy Chairman of the Institute's Tax Faculty, and a former President of ICAEW Scotland. He has co-organised the annual Peebles Tax Conference for the last twelve years.

When he isn't working, Carl takes on the equally taxing challenges of hill walking and creative writing – his Munro tally is now 73, but his first novel remains firmly in the planning stage!

Carl lives in Scotland with his partner Isabel and has four children.

Dedication

For the Past,

Firstly, I dedicate this book to the memory of those I have loved and lost:

First of all, to my beloved mother Diana – what would you think if you could see me now? The memory of your love warms me still. Thank you for making it all possible;

To my dear grandfather, Arthur - your wise words still come back to guide me; and to my loving grandmothers, Doris and Winifred;

Between you, you left me with nothing I could spend, but everything I need.

Also to my beloved friend and companion, Dawson, who waited so patiently for me to come home every night and who left me in the middle of our last walk together. Thank you for all those happy miles; I still miss you son.

For the Present,

Above all, I must dedicate this book to the person who stands, like a shining beacon, at the centre of every part of my life: Isabel, my 'life support system', whose unflinching support has seen me through the best and the worst. Whether anyone will ever call me a 'great man' I do not know, but I do know that I have a great woman behind me.

Without her help, support and encouragement, this book, and the others I have written, could never have been.

For the Future,

Finally, I also dedicate this book to four very special young people: Michelle – who is well on her way to being a 'great woman' in her own right; Louise – the kind-hearted; James – the intellectual of the family; and Robert – the 'chip off the old block'.

I am so very proud of every one of you and I can only hope that I, in turn, will also be able to leave each of you with everything that you need.

Thanks

First and foremost, I must say an enormous thank you to Isabel: for all her help researching everything from obscure points of tax legislation to popular girls' names in Asia; for reading countless drafts; for making sure I stop to eat and sleep; and, most of all, for putting up with me when I'm under pressure. She is truly the other (and probably better) half of 'Carl Bayley'. I simply cannot ever thank her enough for everything that she does for me, but I intend to spend the rest of my life trying!

Thanks to the Taxcafe team, past and present, for their help in making these books far more successful than I could ever have dreamed.

I would like to thank my old friend and mentor, Peter Rayney, for his inspiration and for showing me that tax and humour can mix.

Thanks to Rebecca, Paul and David for taking me into the 'fold' at the Tax Faculty and for their fantastic support at our Peebles conference over many years.

Thanks are also due to Gregor for giving me a chance to see theory put into practice.

And last, but far from least, thanks to Ann for keeping us right!

C.B., Roxburghshire, June 2014

Contents

Contents

Contents

Contents

Contents

Introduction

This guide was first published in 2002, as a response to the huge demand for advice on property taxation issues which we had been experiencing at Taxcafe.co.uk. That demand continued to grow at a phenomenal pace and is responsible for the fact that now, twelve years on, this guide is in its eighteenth edition, and has expanded to the nine chapters which you have here.

People in the UK have invested in property for centuries, but substantial increases in personal wealth and disposable income over a number of decades prior to the recent banking crisis combined with difficulties in other areas of investment and the pensions industry to make this a significantly important area of personal financial planning.

The first few years of this century, in particular, saw phenomenal growth in the property sector, not just in the amount of property investment activity but also in the sheer numbers of people entering the property market as investors, developers and dealers. Whilst the big flotations of the 1980s acted to spread investment in stocks and shares into all sectors of society, the late 1990s and early years of this century witnessed a similar spreading of property investment.

'Property Investment' itself is a very wide term. A few years ago, the majority of new investors tended to be purely interested in the 'Buy-to-Let' market. As the property sector grew larger and more sophisticated, however, many other types of activity began to proliferate more widely, including 'Buy-to-Sell', 'Let-to-Buy' and, of course, a great deal of renovation, conversion and development activity. Beyond these, there also lie the fields of property trading and management.

When increasing property prices raised the barrier to entry, people found other ways to invest in property, such as investing abroad, or clubbing together to invest through syndicates or special purpose vehicles (often called 'SPVs').

All of these different types of activity are subject to different tax regimes and establishing the correct tax classification for each property business can be quite tortuous. One of our first tasks in this guide is therefore to help you understand how your own business will be treated for tax purposes and this is something which we will consider in depth in Chapter 2.

There are also many different reasons for becoming a property investor. Some fall into it by accident, finding themselves with a second property through marriage, inheritance or other changes in personal circumstances.

Others move into the property sector quite deliberately, seeing it as a safe haven providing long-term security and perhaps an income in retirement. Still others see the property market as a means to generate a second income during their working life.

An ever-growing proportion of landlords are choosing to enter the property business as a professional career.

In fact, given the ever-increasing volume of rules and regulations which the private rented sector has to contend with, a professional approach to property investment has now become essential: whatever reasons you may have for entering the property market in the first place.

This is no bad thing: a professional approach to property investment has always been desirable. Those who are prepared to devote substantial time and resources to their business are generally rewarded with better results – including those who plan their tax affairs carefully.

The last few years have, of course, seen enormous changes in the property market and in the economy as a whole and previously held views on the certainty of capital growth and the whole philosophy of 'you can't lose' have been questioned and found wanting.

Whilst these changes have been disastrous for some, they have created opportunities for others and the lower level of interest rates enjoyed by many investors over the last few years often mean that rental profits have been making up for the relatively poor levels of capital growth in many areas.

In effect, the recent economic difficulties can be seen as part of an evolutionary process. The fittest property businesses have survived to become part of a stronger property sector.

So, despite recent difficulties, I personally believe that the property investment sector as we know it today is here to stay. Naturally, the sector will have its ups and downs, as any other business sector does, but the philosophy of property investment as a 'career move' is now so well entrenched that it has become impossible to imagine that it could ever disappear altogether.

The recent changes in both the economy and in tax legislation have dramatically altered the tax planning landscape for property investors. A few years ago, Capital Gains Tax was most investors' biggest concern. Then, as capital growth slowed and interest rates fell, Income Tax became increasingly important.

2

Now, with modest capital growth returning to most areas, and Capital Gains Tax rates having been increased again, planning for both of these taxes together has become more important than it has been for many years. Tax and tax planning are a vital part of every business's strategy. Property businesses are no exception.

Whatever reasons you may have for entering the property investment market, and whatever type of property business you may have, my aim in this guide is to give you a better understanding of how the UK tax system affects you and to show you how to minimise or eliminate your potential tax liabilities.

In the first two chapters of the guide, we will set the scene by looking at the different UK taxes which you will meet as a property investor and then looking at how they apply to the various different kinds of property business.

Chapters 3 to 7 are then devoted to explaining in detail how the UK tax rules currently apply to property investment and other types of property business and how you can minimise your own tax burden.

In Chapters 8 and 9 we will examine some more advanced tax planning strategies which you, the investor, can employ to reduce your tax burden. Chapter 8 is devoted to strategies available to individuals investing directly in property themselves. Chapter 9 then goes on to cover some of the other main investment structures and techniques available.

There are plenty of **'Tax Tips'** along the way to help you minimise or delay your tax bills, as well as **'Wealth Warnings'** designed to keep you away from some of the more treacherous pitfalls awaiting the unwary, and **'Practical Pointers'** which will make the whole process of meeting your tax obligations as painless as possible.

I believe that this guide is comprehensive enough to meet the needs of almost every property investor based, or investing, in the UK and I hope that, with its help, you will be able to enjoy a much larger proportion of the fruits of your endeavours.

Finally, I would just like to thank you for buying this guide and wish you every success with your property investments.

Scope of this Guide

This guide aims to help you understand the current UK tax system applying to property and also to help you plan for the future.

In this guide, we aim to cover as much as possible of the UK tax implications of investing in property, or running some other kind of property business. There are three different types of property investor for whom UK tax will be an issue. These three types of investor may be summarised as follows:

(i)   UK residents investing in UK property
(ii)   UK residents investing in overseas property
(iii)   Non-UK residents investing in UK property

Obviously, the same person might have investments falling under both (i) and (ii) and we will cater for that situation also.

Non-UK residents may also have overseas property investments, but these should generally be outside the scope of UK taxation.

For tax purposes, the UK does not include the Channel Islands or the Isle of Man, but comprises only England, Scotland, Wales and Northern Ireland.

Wealth Warning

It is important to remember that both UK residents investing in property overseas and non-UK residents investing in UK property may also face foreign tax liabilities on their property income and capital gains. Each country has its own tax system, and income or gains which are exempt in the UK may nevertheless still be liable to tax elsewhere.

Additionally, in some cases, citizens of another country who are resident in the UK for tax purposes may nevertheless still have obligations and liabilities under their own country's tax system. The USA, for example, imposes this type of obligation on its expatriate citizens.

It is only when talking about taxpayers who are both UK residents and UK citizens, and who are investing exclusively in UK property, that we can be absolutely certain that no other country has any right to tax the income or gains arising.

4

The tax-planning strategies outlined in this guide represent a reasonably comprehensive list of the main techniques available to all classes of individual property investor with UK tax obligations.

Most of this guide is aimed primarily at those who are running a property business personally, jointly with another individual, or through a partnership. Whilst many of the principles will remain the same where another type of legal entity or investment vehicle is used, it should be noted that many of the points covered in Chapters 1 to 8 of this guide will not apply (except where specifically stated to the contrary).

In Chapter 9, however, we will be looking at some of the tax advantages, disadvantages and other implications of investing in property through other investment vehicles, such as limited companies, limited liability partnerships, property trusts or pension schemes. A great deal more detailed guidance on the implications of using a property company is contained in the Taxcafe.co.uk guide *'Using a Property Company to Save Tax'*.

Those who have the benefit of being non-UK resident or non-UK domiciled may be able to employ some more specialised tax-planning techniques which are covered in further detail in the Taxcafe.co.uk guide *'Non-Resident & Offshore Tax Planning'*.

Finally, the reader must bear in mind the general nature of this guide. Individual circumstances vary and the tax implications of an individual's actions will vary with them. For this reason, it is always vital to get professional advice before undertaking any tax planning or other transactions which may have tax implications. The author cannot accept any responsibility for any loss which may arise as a consequence of any action taken, or any decision to refrain from action taken, as a result of reading this guide.

A Word about the Examples in this Guide

This guide is illustrated throughout by a number of examples.

Unless specifically stated to the contrary, all persons described in the examples in this guide are UK resident and domiciled for tax purposes.

Furthermore, and again unless stated to the contrary, it is also assumed for the purposes of the examples in this guide that the High Income Child Benefit Charge (see Section 3.3) does not apply.

In preparing the examples in this guide, we have assumed that the UK tax regime will remain unchanged in the future except to the extent of any announcements already made at the time of publication, including the Budget on 19ᵗʰ March 2014.

It is, however, important to understand that the Budget proposals are not yet law and may undergo some alteration before they are formally enacted.

Furthermore, if there is one thing which we can predict with any certainty, it is the fact that change **will** occur. The reader must bear this in mind when reviewing the results of our examples.

All persons described in the examples in this guide are entirely fictional characters created specifically for the purposes of this guide. Any similarities to actual persons, living or dead, or to fictional characters created by any other author, are entirely coincidental.

Chapter 1

What is Property Tax?

1.1 KNOWING YOUR ENEMY

We will begin this guide with an explanation of how the UK tax system applies to property investment and other types of property business.

This is essential because you cannot begin to consider how to save property tax until you actually understand what property tax is. In other words, you must 'know your enemy' in order to be able to combat it effectively.

It is important to understand that there is no single 'property tax', but rather a whole range of taxes which can apply to property. There is no point in avoiding one of these taxes only to find yourself paying even more of another!

Horror stories of this nature happen all too frequently, such as the taxpayer who managed to avoid 1% Stamp Duty on part of his new house, only to find that he was stuck with a 17.5% VAT charge instead!

Worse still was the taxpayer who undertook some Inheritance Tax planning on the advice of his lawyer only to find himself with a £20,000 Capital Gains Tax bill without any cash sale proceeds from which to pay it.

If only they'd spoken to a <u>real</u> tax expert first!

In this introductory chapter we will therefore take a brief look at the taxes which can affect the property investor and give some consideration to the relative importance of each.

Later, when we begin to consider tax-planning strategies, it is vital to bear in mind that it is the overall outcome which matters most, not simply saving or deferring any single type of tax.

In fact, I would go even further than that...

Bayley's Law

The truly wise investor does not seek merely to minimise the amount of tax payable, but rather to maximise the amount of wealth remaining after all taxes have been accounted for.

If this seems like no more than simple common sense to you, then all well and good. However, in practice, I am constantly amazed at how often people lose sight of this simple fact and, in trying to save tax at any price, actually end up making themselves worse off in the long run!

1.2   WHAT TAXES FACE A PROPERTY INVESTOR?

The only UK taxes which are specific to property are Council Tax (for residential property), Business Rates (for commercial property), Stamp Duty Land Tax, and the Annual Tax on Enveloped Dwellings (for residential property owned by companies and other 'non-natural persons').

However, the investor should not for a moment think this means that property investment gets off lightly under the UK tax system.

Far from it! Property investment is exposed to a huge range of UK taxes.

Tax is levied when property is purchased (Stamp Duty Land Tax), rented out (Income Tax) and sold (Capital Gains Tax). Property investors have to pay tax when they need to buy goods or services (VAT), when they make their investments through a company (Corporation Tax) and even when they die (Inheritance Tax).

Those who are classed as property developers or property traders will pay Income Tax and National Insurance on the profits derived from their property sales (or Corporation Tax if they use a company). Property developers must also operate and account for tax under the Construction Industry Scheme when using sub-contractors for even the most routine building work.

When the successful investor needs to employ help in the business, he or she will have to pay PAYE and employer's National Insurance. Doubtless, the investor will also be paying Insurance Premium Tax, as well as Road Tax and duty on the petrol they buy as they travel in their business. They may even be paying Air Passenger Duty if their business takes them far.

Faced with this horrifying list, investors might be excused for turning to drink: only to find themselves paying yet more tax!

1.3   WHICH TAXES ARE MOST IMPORTANT?

For most property investors, two taxes comprise the vast majority of the actual or potential tax burden which they will face during their lifetime. These are Income Tax and Capital Gains Tax and they are covered in detail in Chapters 3 to 6.

The exact way in which these two very important taxes will actually be applied to your property business will depend on exactly what type of property investor you are.

For tax purposes, there are a number of different categories into which a property business might fall and it is crucial that you understand how your business is likely to be classified before you can attempt to plan your tax affairs. I will return to this question in more detail in Chapter 2.

For some classes of investor, National Insurance will form what is effectively an additional layer of Income Tax and we will examine this extra tax burden in Chapter 5.

Other taxes which may also have a significant impact include Stamp Duty Land Tax and VAT. These are covered in Chapter 7.

For those investors using a company, Corporation Tax will become of equal, if not greater, importance to the two main taxes and Inheritance Tax is also likely to be a major concern for most property investors. These two important taxes are covered in the Taxcafe guides *'Using a Property Company to Save Tax'* and *'How to Save Inheritance Tax'*.

1.4 HOW DOES PROPERTY TAX COMPARE WITH TAX ON OTHER TYPES OF INCOME?

Property income might reasonably be described as 'middle-ranking' in terms of the level of tax which is levied on it in the UK.

On the one hand, property income is treated less favourably than dividends – basic rate taxpayers have no liability on most dividends and most higher rate taxpayers usually suffer an effective rate of only 25%.

On the other hand, however, one saving grace is that property rental income is not regarded as 'earnings'. This means that most property rental income does not give rise to any liability for National Insurance (but see Section 4.16 regarding some recent developments in this area).

This, in turn, means that the effective tax burden on rental income received is usually much less than for:

   a) Self-employment or partnership trading income – most taxpayers have to pay an additional 9% in Class 4 National Insurance on the majority of their profits, plus £2.75 a week in Class 2 National Insurance. (The Class 4 rate drops to 2% for annual profits over £41,865, giving an overall effective rate of 42% in combined Income Tax and National Insurance on income between £41,865 and £100,000 in most cases.)

b) Employment income – the combined National Insurance burden for employers and employees on most earnings is 25.8%, giving an overall effective rate of 45.8% in combined Income Tax and National Insurance on most employment income. (The effective rate of combined Income Tax and National Insurance on income between £41,865 and £100,000 is generally 55.8%!)

One can therefore readily see the massive advantage which rental income has over employment income with a lesser, but still significant, advantage over other forms of self-employment. Consider the following by way of illustration:

For a basic rate taxpayer with annual income of less than £41,865 to get an extra £100 in his or her pocket net of all taxes will require:

a) Their tenants to pay an extra £125.00 in rent (as a landlord),
b) Their customers to pay an extra £140.85 (as a self-employed trader), or
c) Their employer to pay an extra £167.35 in salary and National Insurance (as an employee).

Similarly, for a higher rate taxpayer with annual income between £41,865 and £100,000 to get an extra £100 in his or her pocket net of all taxes will generally require:

a) Their tenants to pay an extra £166.67 in rent (as a landlord),
b) Their customers to pay an extra £172.41 (as a self-employed trader), or
c) Their employer to pay an extra £196.21 in salary and National Insurance (as an employee).

Furthermore, most self-employed traders with gross annual sales income over £81,000 will also need to charge VAT on the figure given at (b) above, bringing the total extra charge required up to £206.89.

Naturally, however, the property market is not just about rental income and there are other forms of property income to be considered. The profit which property dealers or property developers make on the sale of their investments is treated as trading income and is subject to National Insurance, just like any other trade.

Property management fees will also generally be treated as trading income subject to both Class 2 and 4 National Insurance.

Note
The effective tax rates on income between £50,000 and £60,000 will be higher where the High Income Child Benefit Charge applies. The additional charge applies equally to all forms of income, so the

differential in rates between property income and other forms of income remains unaffected. See Section 3.3 for further details.

1.5   WHAT ABOUT CAPITAL TAXES?

Unfortunately, this is where property investment really can suffer in comparison to other forms of investment.

The rates of Stamp Duty Land Tax on property are quite prohibitive (see Section 7.2), especially when compared with the single 0.5% rate of Stamp Duty which still applies to shares and securities.

In Chapter 6 we will be looking at the current system of Capital Gains Tax reliefs and exemptions. These can work well for the wiser and better prepared property investor, but it is nevertheless somewhat disappointing to note that the most popular forms of property investment fail to attract many important reliefs, including entrepreneurs' relief and rollover relief.

Worse still, if you are classified as a property dealer or property developer, the profits arising on the sale of your properties will be taxed as income, rather than capital gains. Generally speaking, this will be highly disadvantageous, although, as with most things in tax, there are exceptions (as we shall see later in the guide).

Finally (in more ways than one), there is the fact that Inheritance Tax will most likely be payable in full on most property investments if the investor fails to plan effectively during his or her lifetime.

1.6   DEALING WITH REVENUE AND CUSTOMS

At various points in this guide, you will see me refer to your 'Tax Office'. This is the HM Revenue and Customs office which sends you a notice to deliver a tax return or, if you are not yet in the self-assessment system, the office which your employer or private pension provider deals with.

Failing either of these, contact details for HM Revenue and Customs can be found in the telephone directory, or by visiting www.hmrc.gov.uk.

Chapter 2

What Kind of Property Investor Are You?

2.1 INTRODUCTION

Before we begin to look in detail at exactly how property businesses are taxed in the UK, we must first consider what type of property business we are looking at. This is an essential step, as the tax treatment of a property business will vary according to the type of business activities involved.

While it would be possible to come up with a very long list of different 'types' of property business, I would tend to regard the following four categories as the definitive list as far as UK taxation treatment is concerned:

a) Property investment (including property letting)
b) Property development
c) Property trading (or dealing)
d) Property management

Wealth Warning

Care must be taken here, because a great deal of what the layman would tend to call 'property investment' is, in fact, likely to be categorised as property development or property dealing for tax purposes.

Before we go on to look at the detailed tax treatment of these different types of property business, it is perhaps worth spending a little time to explain exactly what these different terms mean in a taxation context.

It is also important to understand that these different types of property business are not exclusive to individual property investors and that these different categorisations may also be applied to a property company, a partnership, or any other kind of property investment vehicle.

The reason that we need to consider these different types of property business here is the fact that an understanding of what type of property business you have is crucial in determining which taxes will apply to your business and when.

The most fundamental issue is whether you are carrying on a property investment business (type (a) above), or a property trade (types (b), (c) and (d) above).

Whilst each type of property business has its own quirks, the 'trading or investment' issue is by far the most important and I will be examining this in more detail in Sections 2.8 and 2.9.

To complicate matters still further, however, there is also a strange 'no-man's land' lying somewhere between a property investment business and a property trade, which is not regarded as a business at all and is taxed neither as a capital investment nor as a trade. For want of a better term, I will refer to this as 'casual property income' and we will look at it further in Section 2.7.

Further out, on the periphery of the property sector, there are other property-based trades such as hotels, guest houses, nursing homes and hostels, as well as activities in the commercial property sector such as serviced offices and warehousing.

These trades involve the provision of services far beyond that which the normal property investor would provide. We will look briefly at the tax treatment of these property-based trades in Section 2.11.

A property investor may, of course, be carrying on more than one type of property business, which could result in a mixture of tax treatments. We will look at the possible consequences of this in Section 2.10.

You will see that there is no mention of Stamp Duty Land Tax in the remainder of this chapter. This is for the simple reason that this tax is generally unaffected by what kind of property business you have. The Stamp Duty Land Tax rules outlined in Chapter 7 apply equally to almost everyone.

2.2   DOES IT MATTER WHAT KIND OF PROPERTY YOU INVEST IN?

For tax purposes, there are two main types of property: residential and commercial.

Residential property, naturally, means people's homes, and covers flats, houses, apartments, bungalows, cottages, etc, etc. Also counted in this category are holiday homes, as we shall see later on in Chapter 4.

Commercial property covers a wide range of properties, including shops, offices, restaurants, pubs, doctors', dentists' and vets' surgeries, hotels, sports centres, warehouses, factories, workshops, garages, schools, hospitals, prisons... anything which isn't residential, basically.

Practical Pointer

It is important here to distinguish between:

a) Owning commercial property and renting it out to other businesses, (which is generally an investment activity), and,
b) Actually occupying and using the commercial property yourself, which is generally a trade.

Example

Basil owns a string of hotels which he does not run himself, but rents to a number of other businesses. Basil is therefore a property investor and is taxed as outlined in Section 2.3.

Sybil rents one of Basil's hotels and runs it as her own business. Sybil is therefore operating a hotel trade, which is taxed as outlined in Section 2.11. She is not a property investor.

Developing, or dealing in, commercial property is also a trade, but a very different one to occupying and using that property in your own trade. Naturally, it follows that the tax treatment of such trades is also very different.

How Does This Affect What Type of Business You Have?

Assuming that you are not actually occupying and operating a trade from your properties, the type of property in which you invest has absolutely no bearing on which of the four main types of property business you have.

The guidelines set out in the remainder of this chapter therefore apply equally to both residential and commercial property investors. The question of what type of property business you have depends purely on the way in which you behave as an investor and not on the nature of the properties which you own.

Naturally, though, there are many other important differences between the tax treatment of residential property and commercial property and, indeed, in the tax treatment of different types of residential and commercial property. We will examine these differences as we progress through the following chapters. Note also that it is quite possible to have both commercial and residential property within the same property business.

2.3   PROPERTY INVESTMENT (OR PROPERTY LETTING)

These are businesses which predominantly hold properties as long-term investments. The properties are the business's fixed assets, which are held to produce income in the form of rental profit, long-term capital growth or, most commonly, a combination of both.

Whilst capital growth will be anticipated, and will form part of the investor's business plan, short-term property disposals should usually only take place where there is a strong commercial reason, such as an anticipated decline in value in that particular geographical location or a need to realise funds for other investments.

In general, properties will be held for a long period and rapid sales for short-term gain will be exceptional.

Having said that, where unexpected opportunities for short-term gains do arise, it would be unreasonable to suggest that the investor should not make the most of them.

Example

Fletcher purchases three properties 'off-plan', intending to hold them as long-term investments. On completion of the properties, however, he sells one of them in order to provide funds for a new investment which he now wishes to make. Nevertheless, the other two properties are retained and rented out for a number of years.

Although Fletcher sold one of the properties very quickly, there was a good commercial reason for doing so. Hence, he may still be regarded as having a property investment business.

Management

In many cases, the owner has a minimal level of involvement in the day-to-day running of the business and pays an agent to manage his or her property affairs. This is the model operated by many buy-to-let investors: who are thus generally regarded as having a property investment business.

There are also, however, many more 'hands on' property letting businesses where the landlord is much more involved in the management of the business on a day-to-day basis. For larger property letting businesses, the landlord's job even becomes a full-time one.

As long as the business still meets the overall long-term investment criterion outlined above, it remains a property investment business for tax purposes regardless of the level of the landlord's involvement on a day-to-day basis. Managing your own properties does not, in itself, mean that you have a property management trade.

Where the landlord begins to provide services way beyond mere management, the business could eventually become a property-based trade of the type examined in Section 2.11. Generally, this does require some fairly extreme steps but we will return to this issue and, in particular, some instances in which it may be beneficial, later in the guide.

For tax purposes then, we can generally regard 'property investment businesses' and 'property letting businesses' as one and the same. The only real difference lies in the level of administrative expenses which may justifiably be claimed, as we shall see in Chapter 4.

Tax Treatment

An investor with a property investment business must account for their rental profits under the specific rules applying to property income (see Chapter 4).

Property disposals are dealt with as capital gains. Property held on death is usually fully liable to Inheritance Tax (subject to the 'nil rate band' and the spouse exemption).

National Insurance should not generally be payable on any property investment business, but we will return to this point in Section 4.16.

Is there any advantage in having a property investment business rather than one of the other types of property business?

Yes, there is often quite an advantage for an individual property investor (or a partnership, trust, etc.) in having a property investment business instead of one of the other types of property business which are classified as trades for tax purposes.

The main reason for this is the fact that property disposals are treated as capital gains, taxed under the Capital Gains Tax regime, and not income which is taxed under the Income Tax regime.

This, in turn, enables the investor to benefit from Capital Gains Tax rates of just 28% at most, as well as providing the opportunity to utilise the many different Capital Gains Tax reliefs available (see Chapter 6).

However, this is far from the end of the story and we will return to the comparative advantages and disadvantages of property investment or property trading in Section 2.8.

Wealth Warning

It is always important to remember that it is the way in which you carry on your business which determines the tax treatment – it is not a matter of choice!

Comparing the top Capital Gains Tax rate of 28% with effective combined Income Tax and National Insurance rates on trading profits of up to 62% (or even more in some cases) means that we can sometimes have differences of 34% or more between the tax applying to a capital gain and the tax applying to a trading profit. The tax on the profit on a property disposal could be over *twice as much* for a property developer or property dealer as for a property investor.

This makes it extremely important to take care that your business is classified correctly. With such a large differential applying to the tax at stake, you can be sure that HM Revenue and Customs is going to be extra vigilant!

In Section 2.9 we will return to this issue and examine the borderline between investment and trading in greater detail.

2.4   PROPERTY DEVELOPMENT

These are businesses which predominantly acquire properties or land and carry out building or renovation work with a view to selling developed properties for profit.

The term 'property development' covers a very wide range of activities, from major building companies that acquire vacant land and construct vast new property developments, to amateur property investors who acquire the occasional 'run-down' property to 'do up' for onward sale at a profit. No one would doubt that the former are correctly categorised as property developers, but not everyone realises that the latter type of activity also means that the investors are actually trading as property developers.

It is vital to understand here that even the most minor of conversion or renovation projects can lead to the investor being treated as a property developer if the property concerned was clearly acquired with the sole or main intention of realising a quick profit. This is what many of the characters we see on morning television these days are actually doing.

Generally speaking with this type of business, a property will be disposed of as soon as possible after building or renovation work has been completed. It is the profit derived from this work which produces the business's income and the owners do not usually look to rent properties out other than as a matter of short-term expediency.

Example

Godber purchases three old barns in February 2014 and converts them into residential property. The work is completed in August 2015 and he then sells two of the former barns immediately.

The third barn, unfortunately, proves difficult to sell. In the meantime, in order to generate some income from the property, Godber lets it out on a short six-month lease. The property is never taken off the market during the period of the lease and a buyer is found in January 2016, with completion taking place in March.

Although Godber let one of the properties out for a short period, his main business activity remained property development. His intention was clearly to develop the properties for sale at a profit. This was reinforced by the fact that the property remained on the market throughout the lease. Godber therefore has a property development business.

Tax Treatment

A property development business is regarded as a trade.

The profits from property development activities, i.e. the profits arising from development property sales, are taxed as trading profits. Trading profits are subject to both Income Tax and National Insurance (see further in Chapter 5).

Where, as in the example above, there is some incidental short-term rental income, it should be dealt with under the specific rules applying to property income. In practice, however, this is sometimes accepted as incidental trading income. Whether this is beneficial to the taxpayer or not will depend on a great many factors, as we shall see in Section 2.8.

The great disadvantage of being classified as a property developer is the fact that all profits are dealt with under the Income Tax regime and not the Capital Gains Tax regime. This means that reliefs such as the annual Capital Gains Tax exemption, principal private residence relief and private letting relief will not be available.

More importantly, it also means that effective combined Income Tax and National Insurance rates of up to 62% (or even more in some cases) will apply instead of Capital Gains Tax at no more than 28% at the most.

On the other hand, the business itself, if it has any value (e.g. goodwill), may be eligible for both entrepreneurs' relief for Capital Gains Tax purposes (see Section 6.28) and business property relief for Inheritance Tax purposes. The latter relief would even apply to any properties held as 'trading stock' at the time of death.

Capital gains treatment would apply to any disposals of the business's long-term fixed assets, such as its own offices, for example.

We will take a more detailed look at the comparative advantages and disadvantages of having a property trade, rather than being a property investor, in Section 2.8.

The Construction Industry Scheme

Property developers who utilise sub-contractors for any building work, even quite minor plumbing, decorating or electrical work, are required to operate the Construction Industry Scheme for tax purposes. This may involve having to deduct tax, at a special rate particular to the Construction Industry Scheme, from payments made to sub-contractors and then account for it to HM Revenue and Customs, rather like PAYE.

The tax deduction rate currently applying to payments to registered sub-contractors under the Construction Industry Scheme is 20%. Payments to unregistered sub-contractors are subject to deduction at the higher rate of 30%.

2.5   PROPERTY TRADING (OR PROPERTY DEALING)

This type of property business used to be fairly rare, but has grown in popularity in recent years. A property trader generally only holds properties for short-term gain. Properties are bought and sold frequently and are held as trading stock. Such traders may sometimes also be known as property dealers.

Properties will not usually be rented out, except for short-term financial expediency. These investors derive their income simply by making a profit on the properties they sell. Property traders differ from property developers in that no actual development takes place on the properties. Profits are made simply by ensuring a good margin between buying price and selling price.

To be a trade, however, there does need to be some degree of serious intent involved. The investor must be undertaking the property trading activity in a reasoned and methodical manner. There is an important distinction, therefore, between a professional property trader and a casual investor. To be 'professional' in this context does not necessarily mean that it must be a full-time activity; merely that it is more than casual. I will explain this concept further in Section 2.7.

Example

Over the last two years, Mr McKay has bought 30 different properties 'off-plan'. He has sold each property within a few months of completion.

Since Mr McKay has neither developed any of the properties, nor held on to them as investments for any appreciable length of time, he is clearly neither a property developer nor running a property investment business. Furthermore, the frequency and scale of his activities clearly indicates that he is a professional property trader.

Tax Treatment

A property trader's profits from property sales should be taxed as trading profits within the Income Tax regime. Once again, these profits are also subject to National Insurance (see Section 5.5).

As with a property developer, any incidental letting income which does arise should be dealt with under the specific rules applying to property income (see Chapter 4).

The value of this type of business is specifically not eligible for business property relief for Inheritance Tax purposes.

As for Capital Gains Tax, the theory is that a property trading business is still a 'trade' and hence the long-term assets of such a business (e.g. goodwill or office premises) should be eligible for entrepreneurs' relief (see Section 6.28).

Wealth Warning

The major difference between property investment and property trading lies in the treatment of the profit arising on property disposals. In essence, the question is whether such 'profits' are capital gains or trading profits.

This is very much a 'grey area' and hence HM Revenue and Customs can be expected to examine borderline cases very carefully and to argue for the treatment which produces the most tax – usually property trading.

As discussed in Section 2.3, the effective total tax rate on property trading profits could be 62% or more: over *twice* the top Capital Gains Tax rate of 28%. We can therefore expect to see a significant number of HM Revenue and Customs enquiries on this issue.

Furthermore, where an investor is potentially exempt from Capital Gains Tax (e.g. on a former principal private residence), HM Revenue and Customs will have even more to gain by arguing that there is a trading activity in order to be able to levy Income Tax on that investor instead. We will look at this issue further in both Section 2.9 and in Chapter 6.

Is it always disadvantageous to be a property trader rather than a property investor?

No, not always; there are some situations where trading status is actually more beneficial overall, even despite the higher tax rates potentially applying.

We will take a more detailed look at the advantages and disadvantages of trading status in Section 2.8.

Always remember, however, that it is the way in which you conduct your business which determines its status and not a matter of choice.

2.6   PROPERTY MANAGEMENT

These businesses do not generally own properties at all (except, perhaps, their own offices). Instead, they provide management services to property owners. If you have a property letting agent taking care of the day-to-day running of your properties, the chances are that it is probably a property management company.

A property management business's income is derived from the management or service charges which it charges to the actual owners of the property.

Tax Treatment

A property management business is a trade for all tax purposes.

The long-term assets of a property management business are usually eligible for both entrepreneurs' relief for Capital Gains Tax purposes (see Section 6.28) and business property relief for Inheritance Tax purposes.

The profits arising from property management activities will be treated as trading profits, subject to both Income Tax and National Insurance.

Any incidental letting income should, as usual, be dealt with under the specific rules applying to property income.

2.7   CASUAL PROPERTY INCOME

Somewhere between property investment and property trading there lies a 'no-man's land' which I will term 'casual property income'.

As we have seen already in previous sections, property investment businesses hold their properties as long-term capital assets, whereas property trades hold properties as short-term trading stock.

In this strange intermediate 'twilight zone' however, lie the property transactions which are neither long-term investments nor part of a trading activity.

The key features of casual property income are as follows:

    i)   Transactions are entered into with the expectation of short-term profit.

    ii) Profit is derived from a disposal of the investment, or an interest therein, rather than an income stream such as rent.

    iii) The investor plays a passive role in the transactions.

An 'investment' for this purpose may include an existing property, or interest in property, which becomes the subject of a 'casual property income' transaction. This, in fact, is the most likely scenario for 'casual property income'. In these cases, the existing property effectively ceases to be a long-term asset as soon as the 'casual property income' transaction is entered into.

Example

Mr Barraclough is having a quiet drink in his local one night when he is approached by Mr Grout, a local builder.

"That's a pretty big garden you've got there Barraclough; big enough for another house. Ever thought of developing it?"

22

"Well, I don't know really", replies Barraclough, "Mrs Barraclough is very fond of her garden you know."

Groutie won't take no for an answer, however, and eventually persuades Mr Barraclough to give him half of his garden in exchange for a quarter of the sale proceeds for the new house.

The part of the garden used for the development was worth £20,000 before construction of the new house began and the new house sells for £200,000, so Mr Barraclough makes a profit of £30,000 (£200,000 x ¼ - £20,000). Because Mr Barraclough's profit was dependent on the eventual sale price of the new house, this profit will be treated as income in nature, rather than a capital gain.

On the other hand, however, Mr Barraclough's role was totally passive. Mr Grout sought him out. Barraclough did not have to 'get his hands dirty' in any way and did not participate directly in the development or sale of the new house. There is no way, therefore, that Mr Barraclough could be regarded as having a property trade and his £30,000 profit represents casual property income.

Most people in Mr Barraclough's position would tend to prefer this profit to be treated as a capital gain, rather than as income, as the first £11,000 of 'profit' would be covered by their annual Capital Gains Tax exemption and the remainder would be taxed at just 18% or 28%. However, because Mr Barraclough effectively took a share in the development profit on the new house, his £30,000 profit cannot be treated as a capital gain and is taxed as 'casual property income'.

This type of transaction is the most common source of 'casual property income' as the 'investor' (i.e. Mr Barraclough in our example) has a totally passive role but does profit indirectly from another person's trading activities.

It is worth noting that, if Mr Barraclough had simply sold his surplus land for a fixed price of £50,000, this would have been a capital gain. Furthermore, as we shall see in Section 8.12, if he had structured the sale correctly it may well have been completely tax free! We will see some more examples of how to benefit from the existing development potential of your own property tax efficiently in Chapter 8.

Tax Treatment

Casual property income is 'other income' for tax purposes. It is not taxed under the special rules applying to property income (as outlined in Chapter 4) and neither is it treated as trading income (as detailed in Chapter 5). It is, however, still subject to Income Tax at normal rates.

Any income of this nature should be entered in Boxes 16 to 18 of your tax return with a suitable description in Box 20.

Where, as in our example, an existing property becomes the subject of a 'casual property income' transaction, any existing increase in the value of that property prior to that date will usually be a capital gain.

Hence, for example, if the original cost of the land which Mr Barraclough gave to Mr Grout when it was worth £20,000 had been £8,000, then Mr Barraclough would have had a capital gain of £12,000 in addition to his 'casual property income' of £30,000. (See Section 6.16 for details of how such a gain would be treated for Capital Gains Tax purposes.)

Any underlying assets held in the course of producing casual property income will not be eligible for business property relief for Inheritance Tax purposes or entrepreneurs' relief for Capital Gains Tax purposes (see Section 6.28). Casual property income should not generally give rise to any VAT liabilities or any obligation to register for VAT.

The best thing about casual property income though is the fact that, since it is not a trade, it does not attract National Insurance. For many people this means a saving of 9%. For most others there is still a saving of 2% - not much, but still better than a 'poke in the eye with a sharp stick'!

The only drawback, of course, is that to be 'casual income', there must be an absence of any serious trade-like intent. In other words, once you set out to make the income in any organised manner, it inevitably ceases to be casual and you will have a property trade. For this reason, this type of income is fairly rare. Nevertheless, if you do meet a 'Harry Grout' in the pub and do decide to participate in his venture, then at least you know you can avoid National Insurance.

Any property rental income, no matter how transient or casual, will always be subject to the special rules for 'property income', as outlined in Chapter 4, and will never form 'casual property income'.

2.8 ADVANTAGES AND DISADVANTAGES OF INVESTMENT OR TRADING

As we have seen already, the most important issue is whether your property business is classed as investment or trading. The major difference is in the treatment of profits arising on property disposals, but there are many other differences which need to be taken into account. In this section, therefore, I thought it might be useful to set out a brief summary of the tax advantages and disadvantages of each type of property business.

Tax Advantages of Property Investment Businesses

- 'Profits' arising on property disposals are treated as capital gains. This means:
  - Tax rates of no more than 28% at the most
  - Ability to claim Capital Gains Tax exemptions and reliefs, including:
    - The Annual Exemption
    - Principal Private Residence relief
    - Private Letting relief
  - Most non-UK residents will enjoy:
    - Total exemption from UK tax on gains arising on commercial rental property
    - Exemption on gains arising up to 5ᵗʰ April 2015 on residential property

Tax Tip

For a non-UK Resident investing in commercial rental property, capital gains are usually completely exempt from UK tax. For these investors, treatment as a property investment business rather than any other type of property business is therefore an enormous advantage and they would be well advised to take care to arrange their affairs accordingly (but see the 'Wealth Warning' in Section 3.7).

- No National Insurance on rental income (but see Section 4.16 for recent developments) or on capital gains
- No compulsory VAT registration of the business (in most cases)

Tax Disadvantages of Property Investment Businesses

- All business assets are usually fully exposed to Inheritance Tax on death
- Abortive expenditure on property purchases (e.g. surveys), or sales (e.g. advertising), may sometimes not be allowed for tax purposes
- Interest and other finance costs may only be set against rental income and cannot be set against capital gains
- Very limited scope for loss relief (both for capital losses and for rental losses)
- Accounting periods ended 5ᵗʰ April each year are generally necessary
- Difficulty in transferring business without incurring tax charges

Tax Advantages of Property Trades

- Greater scope for claiming indirect or abortive expenses relating to property purchases and sales
- Full relief for interest and other finance costs
- Long-term assets of the business may be eligible for entrepreneurs' relief or rollover relief for Capital Gains Tax purposes
- Losses can be set off against any income arising in the same tax year or the previous tax year (subject to the limitations explained in Section 5.10)
- Any date may be chosen for the accounting year end
- The value of a property development or property management business will usually be exempt from Inheritance Tax on death
- Businesses may usually be transferred (e.g. to a company or to another individual) without any significant tax charges

Tax Disadvantages of Property Trades

- Profits arising on property sales are subject to both Income Tax and National Insurance
- Non-UK residents are fully taxable on all profits derived from a property trade based in the UK
- VAT registration will become compulsory if annual turnover from taxable activities for VAT purposes exceeds £81,000

2.9 THE BOUNDARY BETWEEN INVESTMENT AND TRADING

After reading the previous section, you've probably got a fair idea of how you would *like* your property business to be treated for tax purposes. However, as I have already pointed out, it is not a question of choice, but is determined by how you conduct your business.

Furthermore, not only is it a matter of how you actually behave, very often it will hinge on what your intentions were at the beginning of any particular project.

There are two things which the examples I gave in Sections 2.3, 2.4 and 2.5 had in common:

i) In each case the taxpayer's intentions were clear.
ii) They were all chosen to illustrate a position which quite definitely fitted the type of business in question.

In reality, a taxpayer's intentions may not be so clear. When I ask my clients to tell me their plans for their property investments, I often hear answers like these:

"I might sell it, or I might hang on to it for a while if I can't get a good price."

"We think we'll rent it out for a few years, but we might sell if we get a good offer."

"We'll probably sell a few and rent the rest out."

Naturally, any investor is going to do whatever produces the best result and if an unexpected opportunity comes along they would be foolish not to take it while they can.

For tax purposes though, what we have to do is to establish what the investor's main intention was, at the outset, when the investment was made.

The trouble with intentions, of course, is that they can be very difficult to prove. Who but you can possibly know exactly what was in your mind when you purchased a property?

Looking at it from HM Revenue and Customs' point of view, the only evidence which they generally have to go on is what actually transpired and this may be very different to what was intended.

Tax Tip

Document your intentions for your property business.

This could take many forms. Some of the most popular are a business plan, a diary note, a letter to your solicitor, or notes of a meeting with your accountant.

Remember to make sure that your documentary evidence is dated.

Expect the Unexpected

A business plan which says "we will rent the properties out for five years and then sell them" may not ring true if you actually sell all the properties very quickly.

In other words, merely having a business plan (or other internal documentation) which purports to support your intention to hold properties as long-term investments may not be very persuasive if you actually start behaving blatantly like a property trader.

Example

McLaren buys ten commercial properties off-plan in August 2014. He finances part of the purchase through a loan from a High Street bank. To support his loan application he draws up a business plan which states "I intend to hold commercial properties in prime rental sites for a period of five to ten years".

Despite his business plan, in May 2015 McLaren sells all of the properties; after having emigrated to Australia in March.

Any reasonably competent Tax Inspector is going to question McLaren's motives here and it is highly likely that they would argue that he was, in fact, a property trader, despite his business plan.

But what if there is more to the story?

Example Part 2

McLaren protests that he had no intention of emigrating to Australia until the sudden and unexpected death of his great aunt Bunny in February 2015.

Bunny left McLaren a vast estate in Queensland and he had to move to Australia as quickly as possible in order to look after his new inheritance. Running a UK property business now appeared impractical so McLaren sold the UK properties as soon as he could.

Now we can see that McLaren's behaviour was merely the result of an unexpected change in circumstances. His original business plan therefore regains more credence and might be sufficient to persuade HM Revenue and Customs that he did indeed have a property investment business and not a property dealing trade.

An occurrence as dramatic as the one in the example probably speaks for itself, but more often it is some more subtle shift in circumstances which causes an investor to change their mind.

Tax Tip

In such cases, documenting the reasons behind your change of plans is again the most sensible way to proceed. A diary note to the effect of "Johnny got a place at Glasgow University instead, so we sold the flat in St Andrews and bought one there", for example, could save you thousands of pounds one day!

Acceptable reasons for changing your mind could include:

- An unexpected shortage of funds
- An unexpected and exceptionally good offer
- Relocation due to work, family or other reasons
- Divorce or separation
- Bereavements and inheritance
- Health problems (yourself or a family member)
- Concerns over the property market in a particular location
- Funds are required for an investment opportunity elsewhere

But Life Isn't Always That Simple

The second common denominator in my examples was the fact that they each fell so obviously into one type of business or another. Somewhere between these extremes though there is the 'grey area' where investment meets trading. It's not always so easy to be sure which side of the line you're on.

It is almost impossible to give you a definitive answer to explain exactly when investment becomes trading. Here, however, are some useful guidelines:

Renovation and Conversion Work

Activity such as building, conversion or renovation work may sometimes be indicative that there is a trading motive behind the purchase of land or property. However, the mere fact that this work takes place does not, in itself, necessarily make it a property development trade.

If you continue to hold the property for several years after the completion of your building work, it is likely that you still have an investment property.

On the other hand, however, if you sell the property immediately after completing the work, you may well be regarded as a property developer **unless** your original intention had been to keep the property and rent it out, but some change in circumstances led you to change your mind.

Frequency of Transactions

If you only sell a property once every few years, you are likely to be carrying on a property investment business. If you make several sales every year, representing a high proportion of your portfolio, you may be a property trader or developer.

Number of Transactions

As well as their frequency, the number of property transactions which you have carried out can be a factor in deciding whether you are trading.

Many people like to buy a house, 'do it up', then sell it and move on. If you do this once then you're probably nothing other than a normal homeowner in the eyes of HM Revenue and Customs.

If you do it every six months for ten years, then I would suggest that somewhere along the way you have become a property developer.

Finance Arrangements

Long-term finance arrangements, such as mortgages or longer term personal loans are generally indicative of an investment activity.

Financing your business through short-term arrangements, such as bank overdrafts will be more indicative of a development or dealing trade. Short-term finance tends to indicate short-term assets.

Length of Ownership

There is no definitive rule as to how long you must hold a property for it to be an investment rather than trading stock. Like everything else, length of ownership is just one factor to consider. For example, many property developers hold land stocks for many years before commencing development (known as a 'land bank') but this does not alter the trading nature of their activities.

Where there is no obvious trading activity, however, I have heard it suggested that an ownership period of three years or more is generally regarded as being beyond any challenge, although there is no legal basis for this.

This is not to say that ownership for any lesser period cannot represent an investment where the facts of the case otherwise support it and we have seen several examples of this already.

In practice, the longer the period that you generally hold your properties, the more likely they are to be accepted as investments.

Renting the Properties Out

Renting properties out provides a pretty good indication that they are being held as investments and not part of a property trade.

Like everything else on this list though, it may not be conclusive on its own (see the example in Section 2.4).

Living in a Property

Living in the property is another useful way to evidence your intention to hold it as a long-term asset. Once again though, this may not be enough if the other facts of the case prove to be contrary to this idea. We will explore this area of planning in a great deal more detail later in the guide.

'Hands On' Involvement

Being actively involved in the renovation or development of a property makes you look like a property developer. Contracting all of the work out looks more like property investment.

Property Management

As I mentioned in Section 2.3, managing your own properties does not mean that you have a property management trade. Managing other unconnected investors' properties would, however, almost always be a trade.

Managing a mixture of your own and other people's properties might, in some circumstances, amount to a trade. To be more certain of this treatment, the property management activities are better carried out through a separate entity, such as a company or partnership.

In Summary

Remember that everything that I have discussed in this section is merely one factor in determining what kind of property business you have.

Ultimately, it is the overall picture formed by your intentions, your behaviour and your investment pattern which will eventually decide whether you have a property investment business, a property trade, or both (see Section 2.10).

In many cases, this 'overall picture' will point to a fairly clear answer and the correct treatment of the business will be obvious.

In some cases, however, the position may be more borderline and the correct treatment will not be clear. In these cases, it may often be beneficial to adapt your behaviour a little, bearing the guidelines set out above in mind, in order to produce a clearer picture of the nature of your business and therefore secure a more beneficial treatment for tax purposes.

In Section 6.5, I have given some more detailed examples of cases which may be regarded as investment or as trading.

2.10 'MIXED' PROPERTY BUSINESSES

"What if my business doesn't happen to fit neatly into one of these categories?" you may be asking.

If you have a 'mixed' property business, involving more than one of the different types of property business described in this chapter, to a degree which is more than merely incidental, then, for tax purposes, each of the business types should be dealt with separately, in the usual manner applicable to that type.

However, having said that, there is a great danger that any property development or property trading may effectively 'taint' what would otherwise be a property investment business, with the result that HM Revenue and Customs might attempt to deny you Capital Gains Tax treatment on all of your property transactions. (Property management will generally stand alone without too much difficulty, as it does not involve any property ownership.)

Tax Tip

To avoid the danger of a property investment business being 'tainted' by development or trading activities, you should take whatever steps you can to separate the businesses, such as:

i)   Drawing up separate accounts for the different businesses.
ii) Using a different business name for the different activities.
iii) Reporting the non-investment activities as a different business in your tax return.
iv) Consider a different legal ownership structure for the non-investment activities (e.g. put them in a company or a partnership with your spouse, partner or adult children).

(On the other hand, it is also worth noting that combining a property investment business with a property development business may produce Inheritance Tax savings: see the Taxcafe.co.uk guide *'How to Save Inheritance Tax'* for further details.)

2.11 OTHER PROPERTY-BASED TRADES

As discussed previously, there are a number of trades which are inextricably linked with the business's underlying property but which are quite distinct from simple property investment. Such trades include:

- Hotels and Guest Houses
- Nursing Homes and Private Hospitals
- Hostels
- Serviced Offices
- Warehouses
- Holiday Parks

The key difference between these trades and the property businesses which we have examined previously in this chapter is the fact that the property's owners actually occupy the property for use in their own trade.

Tax Treatment

The profits derived from running these business activities are treated as trading profits subject to Income Tax and National Insurance.

Most of these businesses will need to be registered for VAT when their gross annual sales income exceeds £81,000.

Gains arising on disposal of the properties held by these businesses will be subject to Capital Gains Tax, with the full range of attendant reliefs available to business property, including entrepreneurs' relief and rollover relief (see Sections 6.28 and 8.28 respectively).

Most properties used in these types of business will also be eligible for business property relief for Inheritance Tax purposes. Dangers arise, however, where the business confers some long-term rights of occupation to its customers, as is sometimes the case with nursing homes or caravan parks, for example.

2.12 SPOUSES AND CIVIL PARTNERS

Throughout this guide, you will see me refer many times to 'married couples', spouses, or husbands and wives. In each case, the tax treatment being outlined applies equally to:

- Married couples of opposite sexes,
- Married couples of the same sex, and
- Registered civil partners

Hence, any references to 'married couples' throughout this guide should be taken to also include registered civil partnerships; any reference to the taxpayer's 'spouse' will also include their civil partner where relevant; and any reference to 'husbands' or 'wives' will include spouses of the same gender and civil partners.

However, it remains important to remember that, unless specified to the contrary, the tax treatment being outlined applies to legally married couples and legally registered civil partners only. Unmarried couples are subject to entirely different rules.

2.13   JOINT OWNERSHIP & PROPERTY PARTNERSHIPS

Before we move on to look at the detailed tax treatment of property businesses, it is worth pausing to think about the potential impact of joint ownership.

The first point to note is that joint ownership itself does not alter the nature of your property business.

In England and Wales, joint ownership comes in two varieties:

- Joint Tenancy, and
- Tenancy in Common.

Do not be confused by the word 'tenancy' here, this is terminology only and does not affect the fact that you jointly own the freehold, leasehold, etc.

In Scotland, joint ownership of property comes predominantly in one major form called 'Pro Indivisio' ownership and, as far as the tax position is concerned, this is more or less the same as a Tenancy in Common.

Joint Tenancy

Under a joint tenancy the ownership of each person's share passes automatically on death to the other joint tenant. This is known as 'survivorship'. Furthermore, neither joint owner is normally able to sell their share of the property without the consent of the other.

Each joint owner under a joint tenancy is treated as having an equal share in the property.

In effect, joint tenants are regarded as joint owners of the whole property.

Tenancy in Common

Under a tenancy in common, the joint owners are each free to do as they wish with their own share of the property and there is no right of survivorship.

The joint owners' shares in the property under a tenancy in common do not necessarily have to be equal.

In effect, tenants in common each own their own separate share in the property.

The same considerations apply equally to joint 'Pro Indivisio' owners in Scotland.

Tax Tip

A tenancy in common provides far more scope for tax planning than a joint tenancy. We will see much more on the potential benefits of tenancies in common in the following chapters.

Property Investment & Joint Ownership

When it comes to a property investment business, all that joint ownership means is that each individual has their own property investment business and is taxed on their own share of rental profits and capital gains accordingly. The joint ownership does not affect the nature of the underlying business.

Joint owners carrying on a property investment business will not generally constitute a business partnership unless they also formally create such a partnership.

Property Development

Joint owners engaged in property development will generally form a business partnership under basic legal principles. This is because two or more individuals engaged in the mutual pursuit of commercial trading profits are, in law, generally deemed to constitute a partnership.

Example

Ingrid and Lenny buy an old barn and some disused farm land as tenants in common.

They convert the barn into a pair of semi-detached dwellings and build two new houses on the disused land. They then sell all of the newly developed properties and share the profit equally.

Ingrid and Lenny are in a trading partnership.

It nevertheless does remain possible for joint owners of a property used in a property development trade to be engaged in a 'joint venture', rather than a business partnership, if the terms of the arrangements between the parties do not amount to the mutual pursuit of profit.

Example

Luke owns an old farm. At the edge of the farm there is a small field which Luke is no longer able to farm profitably.

Ives comes to Luke with a proposition which goes like this: "If you sell me a half interest in your small field for its current agricultural value, I'll get planning permission to build some houses and then, after I've built and sold them, I'll pay you the residential use value for your remaining half interest."

Whilst this proposition does involve joint ownership of some development land, it does not amount to a trading partnership as Luke is not participating in Ives' development profit.

A property trading partnership may also exist without joint ownership.

Example

Norman holds a piece of land on which he has planning permission to build ten houses. Unfortunately, however, he does not have the funds or the expertise to carry out the development.

Norman approaches Stanley, a wealthy property developer and suggests that they carry out the development jointly and share the profit equally.

Whilst Norman is the sole owner of the land, his arrangement with Stanley may constitute a trading partnership.

In practice, the boundary between a partnership and a joint venture can be quite blurred and this is a subject which could easily take up a whole book on its own. Usually, in reality, the issue is resolved by the nature of the agreements drawn up between the parties.

The best principle which I can provide is that a partnership usually exists where both parties share, whether equally or not, in the same risks and rewards. Where, however, one party's income is fixed or determined without reference to the other party's overall net profit then this is more akin to a joint venture.

Where a joint venture exists, each party has their own business and it is even possible for one of them to have a property investment business whilst the other has a property development business. In fact, as we saw in Section 2.7, it is also possible for one of them to have no business at all, but to be merely receiving 'casual property income'.

Property Partnerships

In England and Wales, a partnership is not recognised as a separate person with its own legal status (like a company): except for Limited Liability Partnerships.

This means that traditional style partnerships in England and Wales cannot own property in their own name.

This is reflected in the fact that it is not the partnership which has any capital gain on the sale of a property, but the individual partners themselves.

The problem of legal ownership is generally circumvented through the use of nominees. Between two and four of the partners will usually own the partnership's property as nominees for the partnership. For legal reasons, it is wise to ensure that there are at least two nominee interests, as a single nominee could claim to own the property outright!

In Scotland, a partnership does have its own legal status and can own property in its own name.

The tax position remains the same, however, with the partners themselves being taxed on any capital gains made by the partnership.

The nature of the business carried on by a property partnership is determined under exactly the same criteria as we have already examined earlier in this chapter.

For tax purposes, the partnership income is allocated to the individual partners in whatever shares have been established between them and continues to be treated as investment income or trading income, as appropriate.

Hence, a partner may be in receipt of partnership trading income subject to both Income Tax and National Insurance or partnership property rental income subject to Income Tax only. Or both!

The calculation of the amount of tax due on each partner's share of the partnership income is exactly the same as if they had received an equal amount of the same type of income directly from their own individual business.

The way in which the income must be reported does, however, get a little more complicated and we will return to this in the next chapter.

Chapter 3

How to Save Income Tax

3.1 INTRODUCTION TO INCOME TAX

Income Tax will probably not be the first tax which you will encounter as a property investor. No, before you've even installed your first tenant or sold your first property you will most likely have had to pay some Stamp Duty Land Tax and some VAT on your legal and professional fees.

However, Income Tax is nevertheless still the first tax which causes the property investor any real concern. It was originally introduced by William Pitt (the Younger) in 1799 as a 'temporary measure' to enable the Government to raise the revenue required to fight the Napoleonic Wars. Bonaparte may have met his Waterloo in 1815, but it seems that the British taxpayer is still paying for it!

The tax was initially charged at a single rate of two shillings in the pound (10% in today's terms). The top rate rose to a (previous) all-time high of 95% under Harold Wilson's Labour Government in the 1960s. Rates remained fairly high (with a top rate of 60%) until Nigel Lawson's tax-cutting Budget of 1987 established 40% as the top rate.

This remained the top rate for 23 years until Alistair Darling introduced the 'super tax' rate on income over £150,000 in 2010 (originally at 50%, but reduced to 45% from April 2013). At the same time, the withdrawal of personal allowances for those with income over £100,000 also created an effective rate of 60% (currently on income between £100,000 and £120,000).

From January 2013, George Osborne has gone even further, with additional tax charges which have created even higher effective tax rates for many parents with income between £50,000 and £60,000: over 100% in a few cases!

The long history of Income Tax may go some way towards explaining some of its quirks. Badly needed modernisation is often slow in coming. It was only as recently as 1998 that 'the expense of keeping a horse for the purposes of travel to the taxpayer's place of work' ceased to be allowable.

The roots of how Income Tax affects the property investor lie in the so-called 'schedular' system of Income Tax introduced in the 19ᵗʰ Century. Under the schedular system, each type of income was classified separately and taxed under a different 'Schedule'.

From 1970, income derived from land and property investments was designated as Schedule A. This Schedule gave us the rules governing rental income and also some other property based income, such as premiums received on the grant of a short lease.

The rules governing rental income under Schedule A were, until relatively recently, somewhat archaic and hence rather restrictive. Fortunately, however, in 1995 the system underwent something of an overhaul producing the rather more sensible rules we have today which, quite rightly, treat property investment as a business. (But not as a trade, which does lead to some fundamental differences in tax treatment, as we shall see to both our frustration and our delight later in this guide.)

From 2005, the old term 'Schedule A' is no longer applied for Income Tax purposes and, under the Income Tax (Trading and Other Income) Act 2005 we now refer simply to 'Property Income'.

The new tax act's rather lengthy name is often shortened to 'ITTOIA 2005', which, as a fan of Ms Wilcox, I refer to as 'I Toyah' – sounds like an early 1980s album doesn't it?

Anyway, despite the recent name changes, the basic principles of how property income is taxed in the UK have remained the same since 1995 and we will examine these in detail in Chapter 4.

Where the taxpayer is deemed to be trading, the income falls under a different set of rules which we will be looking at in Chapter 5.

Other major changes in recent years have included the introduction of 'separate taxation' for husbands and wives in 1990 (before which a wife's 'unearned' income was treated as her husband's for tax purposes); self-assessment, which came into force in 1996; and the recognition of the legal status of registered civil partners in 2005.

Despite recent reforms, however, Income Tax has passed its bicentenary with some of its greatest peculiarities still intact. Indeed, in recent years, the Government has seemed incapable of avoiding adding to them!

Perhaps the greatest oddity of all, the UK's peculiar tax year-end date of 5[.] April, has surprised many of us by surviving well into the 21[.] Century.

3.2   BASIC PRINCIPLES OF INCOME TAX

The UK tax year runs from 6 April each year to the following 5 April. The year ending 5 April 2015 is referred to as '2014/15' and the tax return for this year is known as the '2015 Return'.

Since 1996/97, individuals, partnerships and trusts have been subject to the self-assessment system for UK Income Tax. Under this system, the taxpayer must complete and submit a tax return for each tax year. The return is normally due for submission to HM Revenue and Customs by:

a) 31 October if completed on paper, or
b) 31 January following the tax year when filed online.

The taxpayer must also calculate the amount of tax he or she is due to pay, although HM Revenue and Customs will do the calculation for you if the return reaches them by the due date. Frankly, however, I would not recommend relying on HM Revenue and Customs' calculations.

The Income Tax due under the self-assessment system is basically the taxpayer's total tax liability for the year less any amounts deducted at source or under PAYE.

All Income Tax due under the self-assessment system, regardless of the source of the income or rate of tax applying, is payable as follows:

- A first instalment or 'payment on account' is due on 31 January during the tax year.
- A second payment on account is due on 31 July following the tax year.
- A balancing payment (where appropriate) is due on 31 January following the tax year.

Where the payments on account exceed the final self-assessment tax liability for the year, no balancing payment will be due and the taxpayer will receive a repayment of the excess (or may set it off against the first payment on account due for the next year).

Each payment on account is usually equal to half of the previous tax year's self-assessment tax liability. However, payments on account need not be made when the previous year's self-assessment liability was either:

a) No more than £1,000, or
b) Less than 20% of the individual's total tax liability for the year.

Hence, where an individual's self-assessment liability for 2013/14 is no more than £1,000, no payments on account will be due on 31 January or 31 July 2015.

Applications to reduce payments on account may be made when there are reasonable grounds to believe that the following year's self-assessment tax liability will be at a lower level.

Individuals in employment, or in receipt of a private pension, may apply to have self-assessment tax liabilities of up to £3,000 collected through their PAYE codes for the following tax year. This produces a considerable cashflow advantage.

The self-assessment system is also used to collect Class 4 National Insurance on self-employed or partnership trading income and certain student loan repayments.

3.3   INCOME TAX RATES

The current UK Income Tax rates and main allowances are set out in Appendix A. Property income forms part of the 'non-savings' or 'other' element of an individual's income and is currently taxed at three rates, namely 20%, 40% and 45%. These same rates also apply to any trading income arising from property development, trading or management.

Individuals with total income in excess of £100,000 also lose £1 of their personal allowance for every £2 by which their income exceeds this level. This creates an effective rate of Income Tax of 60% on any property or trading income falling into the band between £100,000 and £120,000.

The High Income Child Benefit Charge

From January 2013, an additional Income Tax charge is levied on the highest earner in any household where:

- Any member of the household has annual income in excess of £50,000, and
- Child Benefit is being claimed

The additional tax charge is equivalent to 1% of the Child Benefit claimed in the same tax year for every £100 by which the highest earner's income exceeds £50,000. Once the highest earner's income reaches £60,000, the whole of the Child Benefit will effectively have been withdrawn and the charge will have reached its maximum.

For 2012/13, the charge only applied to Child Benefit claimed during the period from 7ᵗʰ January to 5ᵗʰ April 2013. In subsequent years, the charge applies to all Child Benefit claimed during the year.

Those affected by the charge for 2014/15 will have an overall effective Income Tax rate on income between £50,000 and £60,000 as follows:

No. of Qualifying Children	Effective Tax Rate
1 Child	50.66%
2 Children	57.71%
3 Children	64.75%
4 Children	71.80%
Each additional child	+7.05%

As an alternative to the Income Tax charge, the claimant can choose not to claim Child Benefit.

The highest earner's total annual income for the purpose of the charge is their 'adjusted net income'. This means taxable income less 'grossed up' gift aid and personal pension contributions, making these reliefs extremely valuable to individuals who are subject to the High Income Child Benefit Charge.

We will look at some other ways of avoiding, or at least mitigating, the High Income Child Benefit Charge in Section 8.31.

In all other sections of this guide, however, unless expressly stated to the contrary, it is assumed for the purpose of all examples, tables, and other calculations, that the High Income Child Benefit Charge does not apply.

3.4   CALCULATING THE INCOME TAX DUE

The best way to explain how Income Tax due under self assessment is calculated is by way of an example. For Income Tax purposes, the profits could equally be rental profits or property trading profits. Note, however, that property trading profits would also be subject to National Insurance which is not taken into account in this example, but will be examined later in Chapter 5.

The example will also demonstrate the impact that beginning to receive untaxed income, such as rental or trading profits, may have on the timing of an individual's tax liabilities.

Example

In the tax year 2014/15, Meera receives a gross salary of £40,000 and gross interest income of £1,000. She has already suffered Income Tax deductions totalling £6,000 under PAYE on her salary as well as Income Tax deducted at source on her interest of £200.

If Meera had no other income during 2014/15, she would have no self-assessment tax liability: as the tax deductions made at source would cover all of her Income Tax for the year. Many people are in this sort of situation before commencing a property business.

However, for the first time in 2014/15, in addition to her salary and interest income, Meera also has profits of £10,000 from a property business.

Her Income Tax calculation for 2014/15 is therefore as follows:

Employment Income:	£40,000
Property Income:	£10,000
Less: Personal Allowance:	(£10,000)
Total 'Other' Income Taxable:	£40,000
Income Tax @ 20% on £31,865:	£6,373
Income Tax @ 40% on balance (£8,135):	£3,254
Interest Income:	£1,000
Income Tax @ 40% on £1,000:	£400
Total Tax For The Year:	£10,027
Less: Tax paid under PAYE	£6,000
Tax deducted at source from interest	£200

Tax Due under Self Assessment   **£3,827**

Not only does Meera have a considerable amount of tax to pay for 2014/15, her liability is too great for her to be eligible to pay her tax through her PAYE coding and she must make payments on account in respect of 2015/16. Hence, unless Meera has reasonable grounds for claiming that her 2015/16 tax liability will be less than that for 2014/15, she will have to make tax payments as follows:

By 31· January 2016:
Tax due for 2014/15:	£3,827.00
First Instalment for 2015/16:	£1,913.50
Total payment due:	£5,740.50

By 31· July 2016:
Second Instalment for 2015/16:	£1,913.50

By 31· January 2017:
Balancing payment (or repayment) for 2015/16
First Instalment for 2016/17

And so on, every six months thereafter for as long as her self-assessment tax liability exceeds £1,000 per annum.

The example has also demonstrated another very important fact. When you begin to receive any significant level of income that is not taxed at source, such as property rental or trading profits, the tax liabilities arising in the first year can be quite severe. You will need to find the tax on two years' worth of profits within the space of only six months – most of it on one single day. This is what I call the 'double whammy' effect of self assessment!

Of course, once you are 'in the system' and things settle down a bit, you should just be paying fairly similar levels of tax every six months.

Nevertheless, every time your rental or trading income increases significantly, you will be hit by this 'double whammy' effect again!

Wealth Warning

Where an individual is already paying tax under PAYE and also has property rental income, HM Revenue and Customs often attempts to collect the tax due on the property business through the PAYE system.

At best, this vastly accelerates the date of collection of the tax due, at worst it can lead to overpayments. Whilst such overpayments may eventually be reclaimed, there will be no compensatory payment of interest.

Fortunately, taxpayers have the right to appeal against any PAYE codings which attempt to include their rental income in this way and hence continue to pay the tax on this income via the self-assessment system.

Turn to Section 5.5 to see the example in this section revisited where Meera has a property trade and is thus also subject to National Insurance on her profits.

3.5 TAX RETURNS

Rental income from UK land and property should be detailed on pages UKP1 and UKP2 of the tax return. This is referred to as the 'UK Property Supplement'.

Page UKP1 begins with a few general questions, including the number of UK rental properties which you had during the relevant tax year (Box 1).

This may seem like a pretty trivial and innocent question, but it is important to get it right as HM Revenue and Customs will compare this figure with the details of the properties you hold at the land registry.

When completing Box 1, remember to include:

i)   UK properties only (subject to point (iii) below).

ii)   Rental properties that you hold jointly with another person.

iii)   UK properties and other properties within the European Economic Area let as qualifying furnished holiday accommodation (see Section 8.15 for details).

iv)   Properties not let on arm's length commercial terms (see Section 4.15).

v)   Any property on which you are claiming 'rent-a-room relief' (see Section 4.10).

vi)   All your UK rental properties (see Section 4.3), including any properties from which you actually received no rental income during the year.

If you hold any of these properties jointly with another person you should put an 'X' in Box 3. (We will look at joint lettings and some of their potential benefits in more detail in Section 8.2.)

We will deal with the significance of Boxes 2 and 4 later, in Chapter 4.

The rest of page UKP1 deals with income from the commercial letting of furnished holiday accommodation in the UK or elsewhere in the European Economic Area (see Appendix D). See Section 8.15 for further details.

Details of all other UK property rental income should be entered on page UKP2.

Income from land and property located overseas is treated as a different source of income. With the exception of income from qualifying furnished holiday accommodation in the European Economic Area, this income should be detailed on pages F4 and F5 which form part of the 'Foreign Supplement'.

Any foreign tax suffered on this income should also be detailed on pages F4 and F5.

Any foreign tax suffered on qualifying furnished holiday accommodation within the European Economic Area should be detailed on page F6.

To claim relief for the foreign tax suffered on all of your overseas property income, you should include the total eligible amount in the sum entered at Box 2 on page F1.

Where your property business is deemed to be a trade for tax purposes, you will instead need to complete the 'Self-Employment Supplement'.

A short, two page version of this supplement can be completed in certain restricted circumstances. In most cases, however, you will need to complete the full six page version, including any cases where gross sales income exceeds the VAT registration threshold for the relevant tax year (the current threshold for 2014/15 is £81,000; see Section 7.9 for further details), or you are claiming any capital allowances (see Section 3.10).

If you have both investment and trading activities then you will need to complete both the UK Property Supplement (and/or the Foreign Supplement, as appropriate) and the Self-Employment Supplement.

Where property is held jointly, but not as a partnership (see Section 2.13), each joint owner must include their own share of property income and expenses on their own tax return each year, as appropriate.

For any form of income received from a partnership, the Partnership Supplement should be used. The full version of this supplement will be required where there is partnership rental income but the short version can be used where there is only partnership trading income.

A separate partnership tax return must also be completed on behalf of the partnership in addition to each of the partners' own tax returns.

Short Returns

HM Revenue and Customs issues short returns to selected taxpayers. These short returns are only four pages long and may, in some circumstances, detail all of a taxpayer's sources of income rather more concisely than the usual full tax return of six pages plus supplements.

Some property investors whose tax affairs are relatively simple may receive a short return.

Wealth Warning

If you receive a short return, it remains your legal obligation to ensure that all of your income and capital gains are reported to HM Revenue and Customs, as appropriate.

In some cases, this will mean that you should revert to the normal full return and it is your responsibility to ascertain whether this is the case. In particular, you cannot use a short return if:

- Your gross business income exceeds the VAT registration threshold for the relevant tax year (see Section 7.9), or
- You have any income from furnished holiday lettings.

Completing a short return (if you are issued with one and remain eligible to use it) will make no difference whatsoever to your actual tax liability, nor its due date for payment.

3.6 REGISTERING A NEW PROPERTY BUSINESS

Guidance issued by HM Revenue and Customs suggests that anyone starting up a new property business should register with them within three months. In the case of a new property trade, this is quite correct and we will take a closer look at the relevant reporting requirements in Section 5.5.

The guidance also states that landlords should "contact Revenue and Customs for a self assessment and a land and property form, or register as self-employed".

> **Wealth Warning**
>
> Landlords starting a property letting business should **not** register as self-employed. Self-employment income is subject to National Insurance. Rental income is not. (See Section 4.16 regarding recent developments on this issue)
>
> By registering as self-employed, landlords may incur National Insurance liabilities which, by rights, they should not have to pay.

It is, however, advisable to follow HM Revenue and Customs' first suggestion and notify them of the start of your property business by requesting a self-assessment tax return with either a UK property supplement or a foreign supplement, as appropriate (see Section 3.5). This can be done online at www.hmrc.gov.uk.

The law actually only requires you to do this by 5ᵗ October following the tax year in which the letting business commences rather than within three months, as suggested by HM Revenue and Customs. Generally, however, it is probably better to get it done sooner rather than later, but:

> **Practical Pointer**
>
> Some taxpayers registering a new business with HM Revenue and Customs within the same tax year as they commenced their business have been issued a notice to deliver a tax return for the previous year. Once a notice has been issued, there is an obligation to complete a tax return, and hence unnecessary extra work has been created.

In such circumstances, it may be better to write to your Tax Office making it clear that the business only commenced during the current tax year. Better still, for property letting businesses, I would suggest waiting until after 5ᵗʰ April in order to avoid the inevitable misunderstanding (but see Section 5.5 regarding new property trades).

HM Revenue and Customs can withdraw a notice to deliver a tax return where it has been issued unnecessarily: but requesting them to do this will also require unnecessary extra work (although perhaps not as much), so it is still best avoided in the first place!

Strictly speaking, a taxpayer is always required to notify HM Revenue and Customs of any new source of income by 5ᵗʰ October following the tax year in which the 'new source' commences.

A 'new source' for this purpose means the commencement of a property business, rather than a new property within an existing business. It is not necessary to advise HM Revenue and Customs every time you rent out a new property!

However, as explained in Section 4.3, when someone with a UK property business rents out their first overseas property, this does amount to a new source. The same is true for anyone renting out their first UK property, including non-UK residents.

Furthermore, commencing a property trade when you already have a property investment business, or vice versa, will also constitute a new source of income. (See Section 5.5 for further requirements for new property trades)

In practice, there are not usually any penalties for a delay in reporting a new property investment business, as long as the tax return includes the new source of income, and is completed and submitted by the normal due date.

However, for anyone not already within the self-assessment system, it is essential to report the new source of income by the 5ᵗʰ October deadline so that a 'Unique Taxpayer Reference' ('UTR') number can be issued in time for them to complete and file their tax return by the due date.

It is now almost impossible to file a tax return without a UTR and there is a considerable delay in issuing new numbers. If you have not reported your new source of income by the 5ᵗʰ October deadline, you will have no legitimate excuse for filing your tax return late just because you did not receive your UTR in time.

In Summary

In summary, to avoid any unnecessary penalties, additional paperwork, or other aggravations, my advice is to notify HM Revenue and Customs of the commencement of a new property business as follows:

- New property trades: within three months (following the procedure detailed in Section 5.5).
- New property investment businesses where you are **not** already within the self-assessment system: as soon as possible after the end of the tax year in which the business commenced.
- New property investment businesses where you **are** already within the self-assessment system: by 5ᵗʰ October after the end of the tax year in which the business commenced or by simply including the new source of income in your tax return.

3.7   NON-RESIDENTS, ETC

Non-UK residents remain liable for UK Income Tax on rental income receivable from property situated in the UK. Generally speaking, however, they are not liable for UK Income Tax on property situated abroad.

The UK Income Tax liability of non-residents may extend to both UK rental income and to other profits from UK-based property businesses, such as property developing, property management or property trading.

Wealth Warning

Where a non-UK resident investor (who is therefore currently exempt from UK Capital Gains Tax) is investing substantially in UK property, HM Revenue and Customs may argue that there is a trading activity, in order to be able to levy Income Tax on that investor instead.

The taxation of non-residents will be subject to the terms of any double taxation agreement between the UK and their country of residence. Most double taxation agreements, however, still allow the UK to tax non-residents on income, profits or gains derived from property situated in the UK (although the UK generally does not currently impose Capital Gains Tax on non-residents – but see Section 6.3 regarding forthcoming changes and other important exceptions).

Certain classes of non-resident individuals with taxable income in the UK are entitled to the same personal allowances as UK residents (see Appendix A), and may set these off against that income. These include British nationals resident abroad, nationals of states within the European Economic Area (see Appendix D), Crown servants, residents of the Isle of

Man or the Channel Islands and residents of other countries which have a suitable double taxation agreement with the UK.

UK residents who are also UK domiciled are liable for UK Income Tax on all worldwide income as it arises.

UK resident but non-UK domiciled individuals may choose to only pay UK Income Tax on income from property situated abroad as and when they remit it back to the UK. This option, known as the 'remittance basis', comes at a price, however. We will look at the taxation of these individuals in more detail in Section 8.23.

From 6ᵗʰ April 2013, a new statutory definition of residence for UK tax purposes has been introduced. We will look at this in Section 8.32.

The tax concept of domicile can sometimes be fairly complex and is examined in detail in the Taxcafe.co.uk guide *'How to Save Inheritance Tax'*.

Broadly, though, in most cases:

- You are resident in the country in which you live.
- You are domiciled in the country where you were born or where your nationality lies.

Your residence can change throughout your life from year to year. Few people will ever change their domicile.

For the vast majority of people, the situation is quite straightforward and it is safe to say that, if you have British parents and have lived in the UK all of your life, then you are most probably UK resident and domiciled.

3.8   CLAIMING DEDUCTIONS

Whatever type of property business you have, there will usually be expenses which may be claimed as a deduction from your business profits.

Some deductions are very much dependent on the type of business which you have and we will therefore examine some of the specific types of deductible expenditure in the next two chapters.

Firstly, however, it is worth dealing with some of the basic principles which will apply to deductions claimed in any type of property business.

Accruals versus Cash

The general rule under UK tax law is that expenses are deductible when they are incurred: known as the 'accruals basis'; rather than when they are paid for: known as the 'cash basis'.

For example, if a landlord has some roof repairs carried out on a rental property in March 2015, they may deduct the cost in their accounts to 5ᵗ April 2015, even if the roofer doesn't invoice them until May and they do not pay the bill until July.

By exception, it is sometimes possible to prepare accounts and tax returns on a 'cash basis'. This has long applied to landlords with annual rental income of £15,000 or less (see Section 4.1).

Additionally, from 2013/14 onwards, small trading businesses are permitted to elect to use a new 'cash basis'. We will examine this in Section 5.11.

It is important to note that the existing 'cash basis' for small landlords and the new 'cash basis' for small trading businesses are not the same thing. Indeed, the new 'cash basis' examined in Section 5.11 is not available to landlords in respect of their property rental income.

Although we will examine the use of the two available 'cash bases' in Sections 4.1 and 5.11, it is assumed throughout the rest of this guide (unless specifically stated to the contrary) that accounts and tax returns are being prepared on an 'accruals basis'.

Wholly and Exclusively

All expenses must be incurred wholly and exclusively for the purposes of the business and, naturally, must actually be borne by the taxpayer themselves.

The term 'wholly and exclusively' is enshrined in tax law but it is not always interpreted quite as literally as you might think.

Example

Saleema pays £50 per week for gardening services. This covers the upkeep of her own garden and that of the house next door, which she also owns and rents out. This is what we call 'mixed use'. The gardening costs are partly private expenditure and partly incurred for Saleema's property business. This does not mean that all of the gardening expenditure falls foul of the 'wholly and exclusively' rule. The correct interpretation is to say that part of the gardening expenses are incurred wholly and exclusively for business purposes and to claim an appropriate proportion.

Nevertheless, any expenditure incurred for the benefit of the taxpayer or their family will not be allowed as a business deduction. Where there is a 'dual purpose' to the same expenditure (i.e. both business and private elements exist), the strict position is that none of the expenditure is allowable.

This contrasts with 'mixed use' expenditure, as in our example above, where a reasonable apportionment between the business and private elements is possible so that the business element may still be claimed.

The distinction between 'dual purpose' and 'mixed use' is a difficult one. The best explanation I can give you is that with 'dual purpose' expenditure, the business and private elements generally take place simultaneously. This is why most office clothing is not allowable, since it performs the personal functions of providing warmth and decency at the same time as giving the wearer the appropriate appearance for their line of work.

The 'Revenue versus Capital' Issue

As well as being incurred 'wholly and exclusively' for the purposes of the business, expenditure must usually also be 'revenue expenditure' if it is to be claimed for Income Tax purposes (except for small trading businesses operating the 'cash basis' – see Section 5.11 for details).

The term 'revenue expenditure' refers to expenditure which is incurred on an ongoing basis in order to earn revenue (i.e. income) in the business.

In the tax world, all business expenditure will be either 'revenue' or 'capital'. Capital expenditure may not usually be claimed for Income Tax purposes, but will often be deductible in Capital Gains Tax calculations (though not always!) Some Income Tax relief for certain types of capital expenditure is, however, given in the form of 'Capital Allowances' or the 'Wear and Tear Allowance'. We will examine these allowances further in Sections 3.10 and 4.9 respectively.

Whether expenditure is capital or revenue depends not only on the nature of the expenditure itself, but also on the type of business which you have.

Capital expenditure is a particularly significant issue in a property investment or property letting business as a great many of your expenses will be deemed to be capital for tax purposes. We will therefore cover some more specific examples relevant to property investment businesses in the next chapter.

Before that, however, let's look at a simple example to illustrate the difference between capital and revenue expenditure.

Example

Willie runs a chain of sweet shops. As part of his expansion programme, he opens two new shops, one in Midchester and one in Normingham. He buys the freehold of the Midchester shop, but rents the premises in Normingham.

The Midchester shop is a long-term capital asset of Willie's business. The cost of buying the freehold is therefore a capital expense, deductible only for Capital Gains Tax purposes if and when Willie decides to sell the property.

This treatment also extends to all costs incurred in the purchase, such as legal fees and Stamp Duty Land Tax. (But see Section 4.4 for the treatment of interest and other finance costs.)

The Normingham shop, however, is only rented and Willie does not own any long-term asset. The rent paid is a direct cost of making sales of sweets in Normingham and thus represents a revenue cost which Willie may deduct against his profits for Income Tax purposes.

Practical Pointer

Many capital expenses which you incur will be deductible in the event of a sale of the underlying property. That sale may take place many years from now.

It is useful, therefore, to keep the receipts and other documentary evidence of this expenditure in a safe and sensible place as it may save you a significant amount of Capital Gains Tax one day.

Grants & Insurance Claims

Any grants or insurance claims received should be deducted from the underlying expense.

Tax Tip

If you incur deductible expenditure which is also the subject of an insurance claim, you may claim the expenditure as and when it is incurred and need only credit the insurance claim (as a 'negative expense') back into your accounts when it is actually received.

This could be in a later tax year, thus giving you a tax cashflow advantage to partly compensate you for the cashflow disadvantage you suffer whilst waiting for your insurance claim to be sorted out.

VAT On Expenses

If you are unable to recover the VAT on any expense then, as long as the underlying expense itself is deductible, you may also include your irrecoverable VAT cost in the deduction claimed. This is a simple reflection of the fact that, in such cases, the business expense incurred is the VAT-inclusive cost. We will return to the question of when VAT may be recoverable in Chapter 7.

Commencement & Pre-Trading Expenditure

You may incur some expenses for the purposes of your property business before it even starts. Such expenses incurred within seven years before the commencement of your business may still be allowable if they would otherwise qualify under normal principles. In such cases, the expenses may be claimed as if they were incurred on the first day of the business.

3.9   ADMINISTRATIVE EXPENSES

One category of expenses which is pretty common to any type of property business is administrative expenses. This heading is very broad, and can extend to the cost of running an office, motor and travel costs and support staff's wages. As usual, the rule is that any expenditure must be incurred wholly and exclusively for the purposes of the business. Sadly though, most entertaining expenditure is specifically excluded.

Motor Expenses

The cost of running any vehicles used in your business may be claimed as a business expense. Generally, the vehicle will also have some private non-business use, so an appropriate proportion only is claimed. (Or a proportion is disallowed, depending on how you look at it and how you want to draw up your accounts.)

The appropriate proportion to claim will vary from one taxpayer to the next. Typically, for a self-employed taxpayer with a property business, it will fall in the range 25% to 50%. The specific facts of your own case must, however, support your claim.

If, on the other hand, you were to buy a van purely for use in your business then a 100% claim might be justifiable.

Mileage Rates

As an alternative to claiming a proportion of actual running costs, you could instead make a claim for business mileage at the approved rates.

For cars and vans, the rate is 45p per mile for the first 10,000 business miles travelled in each tax year, and 25p per mile thereafter.

For motorcycles, a single flat rate of 24p per business mile may be claimed.

If claiming fixed mileage rate deductions, it is essential to keep a mileage log (although a mileage log is advisable in any case).

This method has the advantage of simplicity, but it does have some drawbacks. If claiming business mileage rates, then you cannot also claim any running costs or capital allowances (see Section 3.10) for the vehicle; although you could still claim a suitable proportion of any finance costs, where relevant.

Furthermore, once you have chosen one method or the other (i.e. either fixed mileage rates, or a proportion of actual running costs and capital allowances), you must stick to that method throughout your ownership of the vehicle.

Home Office Costs

Many people with a new property business will begin by handling their business administration from a room in their own home, just like many other new small businesses. In these cases, the taxpayer may claim an appropriate proportion of their household bills as a business expense.

Generally, the proportion to be used is based on the number of rooms in the house, excluding bathrooms, toilets, kitchens, landings and hallways. The claim should be further restricted where there is also some private use of the part of the house which is used in the business.

Example

Shakira runs her property business from a small room in her house. The house also contains a living room, a kitchen, a bathroom and two bedrooms. Shakira's house therefore has four rooms which count for the purposes of our calculation.

The room which Shakira uses for business also has some private use which she estimates to amount to around 10% of the room's total use.

Shakira may therefore claim 90% of one quarter, or 22.5%, of her household bills as a business expense.

In practice, where the private use of the part of the house used in the business is negligible, HM Revenue and Customs has not usually sought a further reduction in the <u>proportion</u> of household expenses which may be claimed.

Wealth Warning

Exclusive business use of part of your home can have a detrimental effect on your Capital Gains Tax position, as we shall see in Chapter 6.

The household expenses which may be included in the office cost calculation would generally comprise:

- Heating and lighting (electricity, gas, oil, coal, etc.)
- Cleaning (cleaners' wages and/or cleaning materials)
- Council tax
- Water rates
- General repairs to the fabric of the building
- Insurance
- Mortgage interest or rent

Sections BIM 47800 to BIM 47825 of HM Revenue and Customs' own Business Income Manual provide instructions to tax inspectors telling them to accept reasonable claims for an appropriate proportion of the above costs. (It may be useful to refer to these sections if you encounter any resistance to a claim for a proportion of household expenses.)

HM Revenue and Customs' instructions acknowledge that there are a variety of acceptable methods for apportioning household expenses where there is business use of the home and that no particular method is mandatory.

The instructions do, however, draw a distinction between running costs (heating, lighting and cleaning) and fixed costs (all of the other items listed above). They then go on to suggest that running costs should be apportioned according to actual use, whereas fixed costs should be apportioned according to the room's availability.

In practice, the key point is to be reasonable.

Where the business use is quite extensive (say 20 hours or more per week) it will generally be reasonable to claim the same proportion of all household costs (as in Shakira's example above).

Where there is only moderate business use, however, (say less than 20 hours per week) it will usually be reasonable to restrict the claim for fixed costs to a lower proportion.

One potential method for doing this is illustrated by the following example.

Example

Rhodri has five rooms in his house excluding the kitchen, bathrooms and hallway. One of these is his study which he uses for business purposes just nine hours per week. The study is also used privately for an average of just one hour per week.

Rhodri's total household costs for the year are:

Running costs: £2,500
Fixed costs: £8,000

Rhodri uses his study for business purposes for nine hours per week out of total actual usage of ten hours per week on average. He therefore claims the following proportion of his running costs:

£2,500 x 1/5 x 9/10 = £450

Rhodri also considers that his study is available for use 16 hours per day (it has no bed so cannot be used at night). This equates to 112 hours per week. He therefore claims the following proportion of his fixed costs:

£8,000 x 1/5 x 9/112 = £129

This gives him a total claim in respect of his household expenses of £579.

The 'number of rooms' allocation method is not compulsory and any other method which produces a reasonable result may be applied instead. Some consistency in the allocation method used would generally be expected, however.

Minimal Use

HM Revenue and Customs' instructions also suggest that small claims not exceeding £2 per week, or £104 per year, will be acceptable for even the most minimal amounts of business use.

Flat Rate Deductions

From 2013/14 onwards, a new system of flat rate deductions for business use of the taxpayer's home is available for trading businesses. (See below regarding property letting businesses.)

The flat rate deductions are an alternative method which is available **instead of** the proportionate calculation discussed above.

The amount of the deduction is calculated on a monthly basis according to the number of hours spent wholly and exclusively working on business matters. The rates applying are:

Hours worked in the month	Deduction allowed for the month
25 to 50	£10
51 to 100	£18
101 or more	£26

Example

Sofia runs a property management business from her home. She draws up accounts to 31ᵗ March each year. From April to July 2014 she spends 40 hours per month working at home. She takes a holiday in August and does no work at home. She has some catching up to do in September and spends 110 hours working at home that month. She then spends around 55 hours per month working at home from October 2014 to March 2015 – except in December when she only manages to work about 20 hours.

If Sofia chooses to use the flat rate deduction for her 'use of home', she will be able to claim:

4 months at £10 =	*£40*	*(April to July)*
1 month at £26 =	*£26*	*(September)*
5 months at £18 =	*£90*	*(October, November and January to March)*
2 months at £0 =	*£0*	*(August and December)*
Total claim:	*£156*	

Laughingly, this incredibly complex calculation, which produces a deduction of a mere £156 in this case, is brought to us under a regime called 'Simplified Expenses'!

Strictly speaking, this new flat rate deduction regime is only available to trading businesses. Whether, in practice, HM Revenue and Customs will permit landlords with property rental income to use the regime remains to be seen. However, their own manuals do tell their inspectors that where "there is only minor business use of the home you may accept a reasonable estimate". It is hard to see what grounds they could have for not accepting the use of the same flat rate deductions which are available to other businesses as a reasonable estimate.

Having said all that, the new flat rate deductions are not exactly generous, so I find it difficult to believe that many property business owners working from home at least 25 hours per month will want to use them anyway.

Anyone who feels that it is not worthwhile performing complex calculations to arrive at a suitable proportion of household expenses can still claim a simple deduction of £2 per week under existing guidance from HM Revenue and Customs. (See above – there does not seem to be any reason to suppose that this existing guidance cannot still be relied upon.)

In our example above, Sofia could have claimed a 'use of home' deduction of £104 for the year ending 31· March 2015 without having to carry out **any** calculations. Even if she is a higher rate taxpayer, using the so-called 'simplified expenses' regime will only save her a mere £22. She would almost certainly be better off carrying out a proper calculation and claiming a suitable proportion of her actual household running costs.

Telephone, Fax & Internet

The cost of business calls and other business use of telephone lines, broadband, etc, may be claimed. Strictly, a detailed analysis of business and private use should be carried out but, in practice, a reasonable estimated allocation will usually be acceptable.

A suitable proportion of line rental and other service charges may also be claimed.

Business Premises

If your property business grows to the point where you need to rent premises from which to run it, the rent, business rates and other running costs which you incur will generally be an allowable expense.

Expenditure on purchasing or improving your own business premises will always be treated as capital in nature, whatever type of business you have.

If you buy a property from which to run your business, you will be able to claim any interest and other finance charges incurred as a result in exactly the same way as if you'd bought a rental property (see Section 4.4). The property's running costs, including business rates, may also be claimed as annual overheads.

Travel and Subsistence

Travel costs incurred for business purposes should generally be allowable. This might include the cost of:

- Visiting existing rental properties or development sites.
- Scouting for potential new properties or sites.
- Visiting your bank, your solicitor, or your accountant.

Where your trip necessitates an overnight stay, you will additionally be able to claim accommodation costs and subsistence (meals, etc.).

Care needs to be taken here, however, in the case of any travel which has a 'dual purpose'. Travel, subsistence and accommodation costs will only be allowable if your trip was purely for business purposes, or if any other purpose was merely incidental.

If you travel to Brighton for a day to view some properties, for example, the fact that you spend a spare hour at lunchtime sunbathing on the beach will not alter the fact that this was a business trip.

If, on the other hand, you take your whole family to Brighton for a week and spend just one afternoon viewing a few properties, then the whole trip will be private and not allowable for tax purposes.

Strictly speaking, subsistence costs may only be claimed where connected with an overnight stay whilst travelling on business. However, in practice, reasonable expenditure incurred whilst some distance away from your own home and business base is usually accepted.

Staff Training

Any costs you pay to train your employees should be allowable. Different rules apply to your own training costs, however, and we will return to these in Chapters 4 and 5.

Staff Entertaining

At the beginning of this section, I pointed out that most entertaining expenditure is not allowable for Income Tax purposes. The only exception, for any business large enough to have employees, is staff entertaining.

Please don't take this as carte blanche to have continual parties and meals out 'on the business', as such expenditure represents a benefit in kind for the employees on which they will have to pay Income Tax and you will have to pay employer's National Insurance at 13.8%.

There is, however, an exemption for one or more annual staff parties or similar functions costing no more than £150 per head. For most businesses, this is sufficient to ensure that no-one gets taxed on the annual Xmas party.

Naturally, before you can make use of this exemption, you need to have some employees!

3.10 CAPITAL ALLOWANCES

As explained in Section 3.8, capital expenditure is not usually directly eligible for an Income Tax deduction claim. Some capital expenditure is, however, eligible for a form of Income Tax relief known as 'capital allowances'.

Capital allowances on property expenditure are dependent on both the type of business and the type of property. We will therefore return to these in Chapters 4 and 5.

In this section, however, we will look at the basic principles of the capital allowances regime applying both to 'plant and machinery' and to motor vehicles used wholly or partly in a property business.

Using This Section

In this section, as in the rest of this guide, I will be concentrating predominantly on property businesses run by individuals or partnerships.

Whilst I will refer to companies occasionally, most of the details given in this section relate to other property businesses rather than companies.

Having said that, the capital allowances regime for companies is broadly the same: the principal difference in most cases being that allowances and rates for companies are usually changed with effect from 1ˢᵗ April, rather than 6ᵗʰ April.

For further details of the capital allowances regime applying to property companies, see the Taxcafe.co.uk guide *'Using a Property Company to Save Tax'*.

The capital allowances regime has undergone several changes in recent years. To keep this section to a manageable size, and focus on current planning issues, I will largely ignore capital allowances on expenditure incurred prior to 6ᵗʰ April 2012 throughout this edition of this guide. (Except in a few cases where some of the old rules remain relevant.)

More details on the capital allowances regime in general, and capital allowances on expenditure within property in particular, can be found in the Taxcafe.co.uk guide *'Capital Allowances'*.

Plant and Machinery

The term 'plant and machinery' covers qualifying plant, machinery, furniture, fixtures, fittings, computers and other equipment used in a business.

What qualifies as 'plant and machinery' for capital allowances purposes depends on the nature of the business, so we will look at this again in Sections 4.8 and 5.8, when the practical application of the rules set out in this section will become more apparent.

The Annual Investment Allowance

The annual investment allowance provides 100% tax relief for qualifying expenditure on plant and machinery up to the maximum amount of the allowance available for each accounting period.

The allowance is available to sole traders, partnerships and companies alike. Some restrictions apply to companies in groups and also to other companies or businesses which are closely related to each other.

The maximum amount of annual investment allowance available depends on the business's accounting period, as follows:

Accounting periods falling into the period:
- 6 April to 31 December 2012:   £25,000
- 1 January 2013 to 5 April 2014:   £250,000
- 6 April 2014 to 31 December 2015:   £500,000
- 1 January 2016 onwards: £25,000

Transitional rules apply to determine the maximum amount of annual investment allowance available where an accounting period straddles one of the above dates.

The annual investment allowance is also restricted where there is an accounting period of less than twelve months' duration. This will often apply to a new business's first accounting period.

Example

Rebecca commences business by letting out her first rental property on 1 December 2014. Her maximum annual investment allowance for the period to 5 April 2015 will be: 126/365 x £500,000 = £172,603

Periods Straddling January 2013

For accounting periods straddling 1 January 2013, the maximum annual investment allowance is calculated on a pro rata basis. For example, a landlord with an accounting year ended on 5 April 2013 will be entitled to a maximum annual investment allowance for the whole year of:

270/365 x £25,000 =   £18,493
95/365 x £250,000 =   £65,069
Total: £83,562

But, an additional rule also applies to any expenditure incurred before 1 January 2013: the maximum annual investment allowance which can be claimed on this expenditure is £25,000.

Further transitional rules apply to accounting periods which also straddle 6 April 2012. See the previous (seventeenth) edition of this guide for full details.

Periods Straddling April 2014

Another set of transitional rules applies to accounting periods which straddle 6 April 2014.

The maximum annual investment allowance available for the whole period is again determined by a simple pro rata calculation. For example, in the case of a property developer with a twelve month accounting period ending 31 December 2014, the maximum annual investment allowance available will be:

95/365 x £250,000 =   £65,069
270/365 x £500,000 =   £369,863
Total: £434,932

However, the maximum annual investment allowance available in respect of expenditure incurred during the part of the period which precedes the increase in the limit on 6 April 2014 is restricted to £250,000 (the old limit).

Periods Straddling January 2016

Yet another set of transitional rules will apply to accounting periods which straddle 1 January 2016: when the current temporary increase in the annual investment allowance is scheduled to come to an end and the maximum amount of the allowance is set to reduce back to just £25,000.

This time, the maximum annual investment allowance for the year as a whole, in the case of an accounting year ending on 5ᵗʰ April, will be:

270/366 x £500,000 =   £368,852   (2016 will be a leap year)
96/366 x £25,000 =   £6,557
Total: £375,409

Again, there will be an additional rule, this time applying to expenditure incurred after 31ˢᵗ December 2015. In this case, the taxpayer will be eligible to claim an annual investment allowance of just £6,557 on qualifying expenditure incurred between 1ˢᵗ January and 5ᵗʰ April 2016.

Other Accounting Periods

As explained in Section 4.1, landlords generally use accounting periods ending on 5ᵗʰ April each year. The impact of the transitional rules on accounting periods ending on 5ᵗʰ April 2013 and 5ᵗʰ April 2016 is illustrated above. The transitional rules do not affect twelve month accounting periods ending on 5ᵗʰ April 2014 or 2015.

Those with property trades may have different accounting periods. The maximum annual investment allowances applying for some other popular accounting periods are as follows:

Year ended	31-Mar	30-Apr	30-Jun	30-Sep	31-Dec
2013					
For the year as a whole	£81,507*	£98,973	£136,575	£193,288	£250,000
Before 1/1/2013	£26,027*	£25,000	£25,000	£25,000	n/a
2014					
For the year as a whole	£250,000	£267,123	£308,904	£371,918	£434,932
Before 6/4/2014	n/a	£250,000	£250,000	£250,000	£250,000
2015					
For the year as a whole	£496,575	£500,000	£500,000	£500,000	£500,000
Before 6/4/2014	£250,000	n/a	n/a	n/a	n/a
2016					
For the year as a whole	£381,899	£342,964	£263,798	£144,399	£25,000
After 31/12/2015	£6,216	£8,265	£12,432	£18,716	n/a

* of which, at least £1,370 would need to be incurred between 1ˢᵗ and 5ᵗʰ April 2012.

Tax Tip

Careful timing of qualifying expenditure over the next couple of years may produce significant tax savings.

Year end planning is discussed in Section 8.29 but, as well as your own accounting year ends, the other key date to be aware of is 31 December 2015. Accelerating qualifying expenditure so that it falls before this date will, in many cases, enable you to obtain immediate tax relief at 100% instead of writing down allowances at just 8% or 18%.

Enhanced Capital Allowances

In addition to the annual investment allowance, certain categories of expenditure are eligible for 'enhanced capital allowances' of 100%. These include:

- Qualifying energy-saving equipment - see www.etl.decc.gov.uk
- Environmentally beneficial equipment - see www.wrap.org.uk

In each case, the equipment must be new and unused in order to qualify for this allowance.

Enhanced capital allowance claims do not use up any of the claimant's annual investment allowance and are not generally subject to any monetary limit.

For further details see the Taxcafe.co.uk guide *'Capital Allowances'*.

Writing Down Allowances

Expenditure on qualifying plant and machinery which is neither eligible for the annual investment allowance, nor for enhanced capital allowances, is eligible for 'writing down allowances'.

The rate of writing down allowances on most plant and machinery is now 18%, having been reduced from 20% with effect from 6 April 2012. (Transitional rules applied to accounting periods spanning 6 April 2012 with the result that such periods benefited from a writing down allowance somewhere between 18% and 20%.)

Expenditure qualifying for writing down allowances is pooled together with the unrelieved balance of qualifying expenditure brought forward from the previous accounting period. This pool of expenditure is known as the 'main pool' (or sometimes the 'general pool').

The writing down allowance of 18% is calculated on the total balance in the main pool. The remaining balance of expenditure is then carried forward and 18% of that balance may be claimed in the next accounting period. And so on.

However, where the balance in the main pool reduces to less than £1,000, the full balance may then be claimed immediately.

Example

During the year ended 31 December 2014, Margaret spent £300,000 on qualifying plant and machinery for her property development business, of which she spent £251,800 during the period between 1 January and 5 April.

£298,200 of her expenditure is covered by the annual investment allowance and she therefore obtains immediate tax relief for the whole of this sum.

The remaining £1,800, however, is not eligible for the annual investment allowance: this is the amount by which her expenditure during the period from 1 January to 5 April 2014 exceeds the restricted annual investment allowance limit for that period of £250,000 (see above).

This further sum of £1,800 is eligible for a writing down allowance of £324 (18%). The 'unrelieved' balance of this expenditure, £1,476, is carried forward to the year ending 31 December 2015.

Margaret's total capital allowances for the year ending 31 December 2014 are:

Annual investment allowance:	*£298,200*
Writing down allowance:	*£324*
Total allowances claimed:	*£298,524*

Margaret's qualifying capital expenditure in each of the next three years is fully covered by the annual investment allowance.

In the year ending 31 December 2015, she is also able to claim an 18% writing down allowance on the £1,476 balance of unrelieved expenditure brought forward from the previous year: i.e. £266. A balance of £1,210 is then carried forward again to the year ending 31 December 2016 when Margaret is able to claim a writing down allowance of 18%, or £218.

This leaves a balance of £992 carried forward. As this is less than £1,000, Margaret will be able to claim this balance in full in the year ending 31 December 2017.

Note that, for the sake of illustration, I have assumed throughout this example that Margaret did not have any balance on her main pool brought forward from the year ended 31 December 2013.

Note also that, if Margaret had spent more than the maximum amount of the annual investment allowance on qualifying plant and machinery in any future year, the excess would be added to the main pool and the process of claiming 18% of the remainder each year would be further prolonged, perhaps indefinitely.

The Special Rate Pool

Certain types of expenditure must be allocated to a 'special rate pool' instead of the main pool. These include:

- Certain defined categories of 'integral features' (see Section 4.8).
- Expenditure of £100,000 or more on plant and machinery with an anticipated working life of 25 years or more.
- Expenditure on thermal insulation of an existing building used in a qualifying trade.

Expenditure in the special rate pool is currently eligible for writing down allowances at just 8%, instead of the usual 18%. This is particularly relevant to property investors letting out commercial property or qualifying furnished holiday accommodation and we will therefore return to this issue in Section 4.8.

It is worth noting, however, that the annual investment allowance may be allocated to any such expenditure in preference to expenditure qualifying for the normal rate of writing down allowance.

Where the balance on the special rate pool reduces to less than £1,000, the full balance may then be claimed immediately in the same way as for the main pool.

The rate of writing down allowances on the special rate pool was also reduced with effect from 6ᵗ April 2012. In this case, the old rate was 10%. Transitional rules again applied to determine the rate for accounting periods spanning the date of change.

Motor Vehicles

Capital allowances are also available on motor vehicles used in the business.

Vans and motorcycles will generally be eligible for the same allowances as plant and machinery, as described above.

Most cars are not eligible for the annual investment allowance, but do have their own system of writing down allowances.

There are now effectively two different capital allowances regimes for cars which are used in a business. These two regimes apply to:

a)   Company cars and other cars with no private use.
b)   Business owner's cars with some private use.

The first regime is actually broader than one might think and applies to:

i)   Cars provided to employees,
ii)   Cars owned by a company, and
iii)   Other cars which are wholly used for business purposes.

Cars falling under heading (iii) are pretty rare as this means that the car is owned and used by the owner of the business and there is absolutely no private use of the vehicle. In almost thirty years as a tax adviser, I have never encountered such a car.

For the rest of this section, we will therefore concentrate purely on the second regime: i.e. cars owned and used by the business owner themselves which have some element of private use. For details of the capital allowances regime applying to company cars, see the Taxcafe.co.uk guide *'Using a Property Company to Save Tax'*.

Cars owned by a business owner and used for business purposes, which also have some element of private use, must each be put in their own individual pool for capital allowances purposes.

For cars purchased after 5· April 2009, the rate of writing down allowances available depends on the car's CO_2 emissions.

For cars purchased from April 2013 onwards, the emissions levels which determine the rate of writing down allowances available have been tightened up.

- Cars with CO_2 emissions over 130g/km (160g/km for cars purchased before 6· April 2013) attract writing down allowances of just 8%.

- Cars with CO_2 emissions over 95g/km (110g/km for cars purchased before 1· April 2013) but not over 130g/km (160g/km for cars purchased before 6· April 2013) attract writing down allowances of 18%.

As with other expenditure, these writing down allowances were reduced from 10% and 20% respectively with effect from 6· April 2012. Transitional rules again applied to determine the rate of writing down allowances for periods spanning that date.

The allowances must then be restricted to reflect the element of private use. For example, a car purchased during 2014/15 for £20,000 which has 140g/km of CO2 emissions and 75% private use will be eligible for an allowance of £400 (8% x £20,000 = £1,600 less 75%).

A car purchased during 2014/15 for £10,000 which has 120g/km of CO2 emissions and 75% private use will be eligible for an allowance of £450 (18% x £10,000 = £1,800 less 75%).

Note that the unrelieved balance of expenditure to be carried forward to the next period is calculated before the deduction in respect of private use.

For cars purchased before 6ᵗʰ April 2009, the annual capital allowances available are the lower of 18% of the unrelieved balance of expenditure, or £3,000. A suitable proportion must again be deducted from the allowance to reflect the vehicle's private use.

'Green' Cars (I'm talking about environmentally friendly cars here, not the colour of the paintwork!)

Cars with CO2 emissions of 95g/km or less (110g/km or less for cars purchased before 1ˢᵗ April 2013) attract a 100% first year allowance. The usual restriction for private use still applies and a balancing charge (see below) will continue to apply on disposal of the car.

The threshold for this first year allowance is to be reduced to 75g/km for cars purchased after 31ˢᵗ March 2015. It is currently expected to then apply for a further three years with this reduced threshold.

Cars with CO2 emissions of more than 75g/km purchased after 31ˢᵗ March 2015 will not be eligible for the first year allowance and will, instead, only attract writing down allowances at 18% (or 8% where the car's CO2 emissions exceed 130g/km).

Balancing Allowances and Charges

When a car with private use is sold (or otherwise disposed of), a balancing allowance, or charge, will arise, reflecting the difference between the sale price (or other disposal proceeds) and the unrelieved balance of expenditure.

A balancing allowance, like any other capital allowance, is a deduction from taxable income. A balancing charge is added to taxable income. Balancing allowances and charges on cars with private use are subject to the same restriction in respect of private use as writing down allowances.

Summary of Capital Allowances on Cars with Private Use

To summarise the position, let's look at an example.

Example

In May 2014, Kenneth buys a car for £20,000 and uses it 40% for his property business and 60% privately. The car has 142g/km of CO2 emissions.

In his accounts for the year to 5 April 2015, Kenneth claims a writing down allowance of £640 (£20,000 x 8% x 40%). However, the unrelieved balance carried forward to the next year is just £18,400 (£20,000 – 8%).

For the year ending 5 April 2016, Kenneth is able to claim a writing down allowance of £589 (£18,400 x 8% x 40%). The unrelieved balance carried forward this time is £16,928 (£18,400 – 8%).

In February 2017, Kenneth sells the car for £12,000. This gives rise to a balancing allowance of £1,971 (£16,928 - £12,000 = £4,928 x 40%).

Note that, if Kenneth had sold the car for more than £16,928 (the unrelieved balance of expenditure), he would have been subject to a balancing charge. The charge in this case would have been 40% of the excess of the sale price over £16,928.

Other Assets with Private Use

The capital allowances regime for cars is echoed to some extent in the case of other assets with any element of private use.

Where an asset is purchased and used by a business owner, capital allowances remain available but, as with cars, a suitable deduction must be made in respect of the private use of the asset.

All such assets must also each be placed in their own capital allowances pool, or 'puddle', as I like to call them.

The writing down allowances on these 'puddles' will be at either 8% or 18%, as appropriate, less the deduction for private use. As usual, these allowances were reduced from 10% and 20% respectively with effect from 6 April 2012 and are subject to transitional rules where the accounting period spans that date.

As with cars, the unrelieved balance on the 'puddle' carried forward to the next period is calculated before the deduction for private use.

The great advantage (or occasional disadvantage) of the 'puddle' is that a balancing allowance (or charge) will arise when each asset is disposed of.

These balancing allowances or charges are calculated in exactly the same way as for a car with private use, as explained above.

Balances under £1,000 in 'puddles' cannot be written off like similar small balances in the main or special rate pools.

The annual investment allowance is available on assets (other than cars) with an element of private use. The allowance must, however, be restricted to reflect the private use, so the annual investment allowance should be allocated to other expenditure first whenever possible.

Assets purchased for a business proprietor's own use can only attract allowances if genuinely used in the business.

Other Points on Capital Allowances

Both the annual investment allowance and all writing down allowances, including allowances on motor cars, are restricted if the business starts part-way through the year or, in the case of a trading business, if accounts are drawn up for a period of less than twelve months.

The annual investment allowance is not available on used assets which the taxpayer introduces into the business or on assets acquired from connected persons (see Section 6.9).

None of the usual allowances are available in the year that a business ceases. A balancing allowance or charge will apply instead, based on the difference between the unrelieved balance of expenditure and the total value of the remaining business assets at the date of cessation.

Assets bought on hire purchase continue to be eligible for capital allowances as normal but must be brought into use in the business before the end of the accounting period.

Subject to the above points, the full allowance due is available on any business asset purchased part-way through the year – even on the last day.

Prior to 2008, balancing charges did not generally arise on disposals of plant and machinery used wholly in the business. This is because any sale proceeds received were simply deducted from the balance on the main pool. Hence, no balancing charge could arise on these assets unless the business ceased or one or more of the assets were sold for a sum in excess of the balance on the pool.

So, what's changed?

Well, the principle that any sale proceeds are deducted from the unrelieved balance of expenditure in the pool remains true, albeit slightly complicated by the fact that we now have the special rate pool to consider as well as the main pool.

What has changed, however, is the fact that, due to the annual investment allowance, most small businesses now have little or no balance of unrelieved expenditure left. Hence, whenever any asset used in the business is sold, there will probably be a balancing charge.

Capital Allowance Disclaimers

It is worth pointing out that, apart from balancing allowances and charges, capital allowances are not mandatory. The amount of allowance available is effectively a maximum which may be claimed and the taxpayer may claim any amount between zero and that maximum each year.

Why claim less than the maximum?

Tax Tip

If your total taxable income is less than your personal allowance, any capital allowances which you claim may effectively be wasted.

Instead, it will generally be better to claim a lower amount of allowances in order to fully utilise your personal allowance against your income (or as much as possible).

The unrelieved balance of expenditure carried forward will then be greater, giving you higher capital allowances next year when, hopefully, they will actually save you some tax!

Some possible exceptions to the above 'tax tip' may arise where your property business is making losses and you are able to obtain tax relief for your capital allowances in a different period. See Sections 4.11 and 5.1 for further details.

3.11 THE TAX RELIEF 'CAP'

From 2013/14 onwards, there is an annual limit on the total combined amount of Income Tax relief available under a number of different reliefs.

The limit applies where the loss, or other source of the relief, arises in 2013/14 or a later tax year (regardless of which year the relief is claimed for).

The total amount of relief which any individual may claim under all of these reliefs taken together in any one tax year is now limited to the greater of:

- £50,000, or
- 25% of their 'adjusted total income' (see below)

Hence, for anyone with total income of no more £200,000, the limit is £50,000.

The Affected Reliefs

Ten different reliefs are affected. The most important ones for property investors to be aware of are:

- Property loss relief
- Relief for trading losses against other income
- Qualifying loan interest
- Share loss relief

'Property loss relief' refers to an individual's ability to set capital allowances within UK rental losses or overseas rental losses against their other income for the same tax year or the next one (see Sections 4.11 and 4.14).

Individuals with trading losses can set them off against their other income in the same tax year or the previous one. Additional relief applies in the early years of a trade. (See Section 5.10 for further details.)

'Qualifying loan interest' is the relief which is given for interest on personal borrowings used to invest funds in a qualifying company (or partnership). This relief will often be claimed by property investors who invest via a company and is covered in detail in the Taxcafe.co.uk guide *'Using a Property Company to Save Tax'*.

'Share loss relief' applies in certain limited circumstances and allows owners of some private companies to claim Income Tax relief for losses on their shares. Sadly, it is not usually available to property company owners.

Adjusted Total Income

Broadly speaking, 'adjusted total income' means an individual's total taxable income for the tax year in which relief is being claimed; after deducting gross pension contributions (including tax relief given at source); but before deducting any other reliefs.

Chapter 4

Saving Income Tax on a Property Investment Business

4.1 THE TAXATION OF RENTAL INCOME

In many respects, property letting is treated very much like any other business for Income Tax purposes, but it also has many quirks which set it apart!

The first point to note is that, for tax purposes, property letting needs to be divided into four categories:

- 'Normal' UK property letting
- 'Normal' overseas property letting
- UK furnished holiday letting
- Other furnished holiday letting within the European Economic Area (see Appendix D)

'Normal' in this context simply means anything other than furnished holiday letting in the UK or elsewhere in the European Economic Area.

Each of these four categories is effectively treated as a separate business. Most of the rules which we will examine in this chapter apply equally to each category, but there are a few variations applying to overseas property (see Section 4.14) and furnished holiday letting (see Section 8.15).

Each of the four categories described above needs to be accounted for and reported on your tax return separately. Hence, you will need to draw up accounts for each category which detail all your income as well as all relevant expenses.

However, all of the properties within each category are effectively regarded as a single business.

'Normal' UK property letting is generally referred to as a 'UK property business' and 'normal' overseas property letting is generally referred to as an 'overseas property business'.

So, for example, if you are letting a number of UK properties on a commercial basis (none of which are furnished holiday lets), this will be treated as a single UK property business and one set of accounts will usually suffice (although many landlords prefer to have a separate set of accounts for each property).

Separate accounts will, however, be required for any non-commercial lettings (see Section 4.15) within any of the four categories.

All rental income must be included within the appropriate category, no matter how modest the source, unless it is fully covered by the 'rent-a-room' scheme (see Section 4.10).

Technically, landlords may draw up accounts for any period. Unlike other types of business, however, landlords must generally be taxed on the rental profits arising for the tax year running from 6ᵗʰ April to the following 5ᵗʰ April.

Hence, whilst landlords could draw up accounts for a different period and then 'time apportion' the results in order to produce appropriate figures for the tax year, this would seldom produce any significant advantages and it is far simpler to just produce accounts for the year ending 5ᵗʰ April. This, therefore, is what most landlords do.

Generally, your accounts have to be drawn up on an 'accruals' basis. This means that income and expenditure is recognised when it arises, or is incurred, rather than when it is received or paid.

For example, if you started renting out a property on 12ᵗʰ March 2015, at a monthly rent of £1,000, the income you need to recognise in your accounts for the year ending 5ᵗʰ April 2015 is:

$$£1,000 \times 12 \times 25/365 = £821.92$$

(You are renting it for 25 days in the 2014/15 tax year.)

Expenses should similarly be recognised as they are incurred (as explained in Section 3.8).

Concessionary Use of Cash Basis

By concession HM Revenue and Customs allows individual landlords with gross annual rental receipts not exceeding £15,000 to use a 'cash basis'. This means that income and expenditure may be recognised when received or paid. HM Revenue and Customs will only allow this method to be used if it is applied consistently and produces a reasonable result.

In most cases, since rent is usually received in advance and expenses are often paid in arrears, the cash basis will not be beneficial. Nevertheless, when you are starting out with a relatively modest level of rental income, it is an option to consider.

Landlords are **not** eligible for the other new 'cash basis' introduced from 2013/14 onwards which we will be examining in Section 5.11.

4.2 DEDUCTIBLE EXPENDITURE

The rules on what types of expenditure may be claimed as deductions in a property letting business are similar to, but not quite the same as, those for other types of business.

Some of the main deductions include:

- Interest and other finance costs
- Property maintenance and repair costs
- Heating and lighting costs, if borne by the landlord
- Insurance costs
- Letting agent's fees
- Advertising for tenants
- Accountancy fees
- Legal and professional fees
- The cost of cleaners, gardeners, etc, where relevant
- Ground rent, service charges, etc.
- Bad debts
- Pre-trading expenditure
- Landlord's administrative expenditure

If your tenant contributes part of the cost towards an otherwise allowable expense, you may claim only the net amount which you actually bear yourself.

In the next few sections, we will take a closer look at some of the more common areas of expenditure typically encountered in property letting businesses and examine what determines whether or not these expenses may be deducted for Income Tax purposes.

Please note, however, that this is not an exhaustive list and other types of expenditure which meet the general principles outlined in Section 3.8 will often also be allowable.

4.3 WHEN IS A PROPERTY A RENTAL PROPERTY?

Throughout this chapter, you will see me refer to 'rental property'. Whether a property is a 'rental property' at any given time is often crucial in determining whether, or how much of, a particular piece of expenditure is allowable.

Quite obviously, a property is a rental property whilst it is actually being rented out.

For most tax purposes, a property is usually also a 'rental property' when:

- It is available for letting but is currently vacant.
- It is being prepared for letting.
- It is being renovated between lettings, with the intention of letting it out again thereafter.

In each case, however, the property's 'rental property' status would be lost if it was actually used for something else (e.g. a family holiday for the investor's spouse and children). Nevertheless, merely sleeping there overnight, whilst redecorating the property for subsequent rental, should not usually harm the property's status.

Strictly, for Income Tax purposes, a vacant property ceases to be a rental property immediately once a decision is taken to sell it.

In practice, however, this rule will not usually be applied where the period between the decision and the sale is relatively brief.

HM Revenue and Customs generally regards the day on which your first rental property within each category (see Section 4.1) is let out for the first time as being the first day of your property letting business.

However, any eligible expenditure which is incurred within the seven year period before your first rental property in the category is first let should remain claimable as 'pre-trading expenditure' (see Section 3.8). This may sometimes mean that the expenditure has to be claimed in a later tax year.

Eligible expenses relating to your second, and subsequent, rental properties within each category may generally be claimed as incurred, even if the relevant property is not let by the end of that tax year.

Remember, however, that you have to treat each of the four categories described in Section 4.1 as separate businesses. Hence, a first overseas rental gets treated as a 'first property' even if you already have a portfolio of UK properties. The same goes for your first UK rental when you have a portfolio of overseas properties; your first furnished holiday let; etc.

4.4   INTEREST AND OTHER FINANCE COSTS

Interest is allowable and may be claimed against rental income if it is incurred for the purposes of the property business. There are two ways in which this can occur:

i) The interest arises on capital which has been introduced into the property business.

ii) The interest arises on other funds which have been utilised in the property business.

Until fairly recently, HM Revenue and Customs did not share the view that claims for interest relief under the first heading alone were valid. Thankfully, they now accept this view in principle, although differences of opinion over the precise interpretation of the rule sometimes still arise from time to time.

Leaving such difficulties to one side for the moment, the first heading above provides enormous scope for property investors to claim interest relief for Income Tax purposes.

When a property is rented out for the first time, the value of that property at that date represents capital introduced into the business.

Any other capital expenditure incurred on a rental property also represents capital introduced into the business, including Stamp Duty Land Tax and legal fees paid on the purchase and the cost of furnishing the property, where relevant. The fact that a deduction cannot generally be claimed for these expenses themselves does not prevent them from being capital introduced into the business.

Hence, subject to 'the catch' explained below, interest relief should always be available on any borrowings against a rental property up to its original value when first rented out PLUS all of the other capital expenditure incurred in purchasing it and preparing it for letting. *It does not matter what the borrowed funds are used for!*

You cannot double-count the same expenditure, however. For example, if you build an extension on a property before letting it out, its value when first rented out will be increased by this expenditure, so you cannot add it on again as further capital introduced.

For borrowings in excess of the capital introduced in respect of a property, we must rely on the second heading above. In other words, interest relief on these additional borrowings will only be available if the borrowed funds are used for business purposes.

Example 1

Matthew buys an investment property for £100,000 and immediately begins to rent it out unfurnished. He finances his original purchase with a buy-to-let mortgage of £75,000 and pays the remainder in cash. He also pays legal fees of £800. Naturally, he is able to claim relief for the interest on his buy-to-let mortgage against his rental income from the house.

A few years later, Matthew remortgages the property and borrows an additional £30,000 to bring his total borrowings up to £105,000. He spends the new funds on various personal items not related to his property business.

Despite having spent the new funds on personal items, Matthew remains entitled to interest relief against his rental income for the first £100,800 of his borrowings: i.e. an amount equal to the property's value when he first rented it out plus the legal fees he paid on the purchase. The last £4,200 of his borrowings are not eligible for relief, however, as these are in excess of the amount of 'capital' introduced into the business and have not been used for other business purposes either.

After a few more years, Matthew borrows a further £22,000 against the property. This time, he spends £12,000 by taking his partner on a luxury cruise but uses £10,000 to improve another rental property. Matthew cannot claim any interest relief on the £12,000 used personally as this does not represent 'capital' introduced into the business. However, he can claim interest relief on the £10,000 used to improve another rental property as this has been used for business purposes.

Matthew therefore now has a total of £110,800 of eligible borrowings for interest relief purposes out of his overall total of £127,000. (We will look at how investors should calculate their interest relief in this type of situation a little later.)

Another way to look at the position for interest relief is that:

i)   Borrowings against a rental property up to a sum equal to the original value of that property when first rented out PLUS any other capital expenditure relating to that property are generally allowable (subject to avoiding any 'double-counting' and also 'the catch' described below).

ii)   Other borrowings are allowable when the funds are used for business purposes.

Interest will therefore always be allowable if it arises on funds used to purchase or improve rental properties or otherwise expended for the purposes of the property business.

Example 2

Mark takes out a personal loan and spends the funds on making improvements to a flat which he subsequently lets out. The interest on his loan is deductible because it has been incurred for the purpose of his property business.

Example 3

Luke has a large property rental business and employs several staff to assist him. Whilst the business is generally buoyant, Luke runs into some cashflow *difficulties in January 2015 and has to borrow an extra £5,000 to pay his staff's wages.*

Luke's borrowings were used for business purposes and hence the interest he incurs will be an allowable deduction for tax purposes.

Example 4

John borrows an extra £50,000 by re-mortgaging his own home. He uses these funds as the deposit on two new properties which he then lets out.

John may claim the interest on his extra £50,000 of borrowing as it has been used for business purposes.

Practical Pointer

In a case like John's in our last example here, there will usually be the practical difficulty of establishing just how much interest should be claimed.

John will already have an outstanding balance on his mortgage so it would not be right for him to claim all of his interest as a business expense.

In practice, we have to do an apportionment.

Example 4 Resumed

Prior to re-mortgaging, John had a balance of £120,000 on the mortgage on his own home. The extra £50,000 of borrowings took that balance up to £170,000. John should therefore claim 50/170ths of his mortgage interest as a business expense.

Repayment Mortgages

Interest calculations are fairly straightforward in the case of an interest-only mortgage, but what about repayment mortgages?

The first and most important point to note is that you can only ever claim the interest element of your loan or mortgage payments as an expense. The capital repayment element may not be deducted. Your mortgage provider will usually send you an annual statement detailing the amount of interest actually charged.

Where you have a repayment mortgage which is only partly allowable for business purposes, an apportionment must be made, as outlined above.

However, as you repay capital, the total outstanding balance on the account will reduce, so how do you do your apportionment then? The usual approach is to stick with the apportionment ratio which you derived when you first did the re-mortgaging (e.g. 50/170ths in John's case above).

Some, more aggressive, accountants might suggest that all repayments should be treated as repaying the original 'non-business' element of the loan. This approach may, however, be subject to challenge by HM Revenue and Customs.

Tax Tip

To maximise the business element within your interest payments, arrange for the new funds obtained on re-mortgaging to be allocated to a separate mortgage loan account with the bank. Make the new account interest-only, whilst leaving the original mortgage account as a repayment account.

In this way, you can put beyond doubt the fact that the capital repayment element belongs exclusively to the 'non-business' part of your mortgage.

'The Catch': What Counts as 'Capital Introduced'?

Our last example raises another important point. John was able to claim interest relief for part of the mortgage on his own home because he had spent the funds for business purposes: as deposits on rental properties.

Those deposits, however, also count as part of the capital introduced into the business. In other words, this restricts the investor's ability to obtain any further relief for additional borrowings against the rental property.

Let's say that John used £25,000 from the mortgage on his own home as a deposit on a buy-to-let property purchased for £90,000 and that the other £65,000 was made up of £5,000 in cash and £60,000 from a buy-to-let mortgage. Let's also assume that John paid a further £1,200 in purchase costs (legal fees, etc).

Hence, at this stage, as far as this property is concerned, John has introduced 'capital' of £91,200 into his property business (i.e. the value of the rental property plus his purchase costs), but is already claiming interest relief on borrowings of £85,000 – i.e. the buy-to-let mortgage of £60,000 and £25,000 of the additional mortgage on his own home.

John can therefore only automatically claim interest relief on further borrowings against the rental property of just £6,200 – i.e. the same amount that he originally funded in cash (£5,000 + £1,200). Any further borrowings will only be eligible for interest relief if the funds are used for business purposes.

What John can do, however, is borrow further funds against his rental properties to repay some or all of the additional £50,000 mortgage on his own home. This would mean that he would be replacing one qualifying loan with another so he would continue to obtain interest relief on the new borrowings.

What Happens When Properties Are Sold Or Cease to Be Used In The Business?

An important point to note is that interest on borrowings used to finance the purchase or improvement of a property will generally cease to be allowable if that property ceases to be used in the rental business (e.g. if it is subsequently adopted as the owner's own residence).

However, the eligibility of the interest for tax relief will follow the use of the underlying funds. Consider this example:

Example 5

In 2014, Abel borrows £50,000 secured on his own home, Eden Cottage, and uses the money to buy a rental property, Babel Heights. At this stage, the interest on his £50,000 loan is clearly allowable.

A few years later, in 2017, Abel sells Babel Heights and uses the sale proceeds to buy a new rental property, Ark Villa. Abel's interest payments on the £50,000 loan continue to be allowable as the underlying funds have been reinvested in the business.

In 2019, Abel sells Eden Cottage and moves into a new house in Gomorrah. Abel's mortgage on the new Gomorrah property exceeds the balance on his Eden Cottage mortgage. The new mortgage therefore includes the original £50,000 borrowing used to acquire a business property and hence the appropriate proportion of Abel's interest payments should still be allowable.

In 2020, Abel sells Ark Villa in order to finance the costs of an extension he is building on his Gomorrah home. At this point, the interest on his £50,000 borrowings ceases to be allowable for Income Tax purposes.

Existing Property Introduced into the Business

The interest on any mortgage over a property which is newly introduced into the rental business becomes allowable from that point onwards. Hence, for example, the interest on the mortgage on your own former home may be claimed from the date on which you make it available for letting.

Furthermore, as the entire value of the house at that date represents capital which you have introduced into your business, you could also re-mortgage the property and the whole amount of any interest payable on loans secured on the property, up to its value on the first day you rent it out, will be deductible for tax purposes.

Example 5 Continued

By 2021, Abel's Gomorrah property is worth £500,000 and his outstanding mortgage is £300,000. Abel re-mortgages the Gomorrah property, realising an additional £150,000 which he uses to buy a new home in neighbouring Sodom.

Abel now starts to rent out his Gomorrah property.

The entire interest payable on the whole of Abel's £450,000 mortgage will now be allowable against his rental income.

Note that, where an existing property, such as a former home, is introduced into the rental business, the 'capital introduced' will be limited to its value when first rented out only. Previous capital expenditure on the property, such as legal fees paid on the purchase, cannot also be counted in this case. The current value of any contents rented out with the property (furniture, etc) can, however, be included.

Wealth Warning

It is in this sort of situation that HM Revenue and Customs has recently been putting a different interpretation on the 'capital introduced' principle. In some cases, they have argued that, for a person like Abel, the allowable interest should be restricted to the amount arising on funds actually expended on the property itself (e.g. £300,000 in our example above).

Whilst it remains reasonable to take the view that all of the interest on the entire outstanding mortgage should be allowable in a case like this (as, logically, it must all represent 'capital introduced'), there is unfortunately now a degree of doubt about the position.

Loans in Joint Names, etc.

Strictly, for interest to be claimed as a business expense, it must be a liability of the owner of the business. This generally means that the underlying loan must be in the name of the property investor themselves.

By concession, however, HM Revenue and Customs will allow qualifying interest paid by a property investor to still be claimed when the underlying loan is:

i)   In joint names with their spouse, or
ii)   In the sole name of their spouse.

Under scenario (ii), it is vital that the interest is actually paid by the property investor themselves, even though it is their spouse's liability.

Naturally, the interest is still only allowable if incurred for the purposes of the business, as detailed above.

Other Finance Costs

The treatment of other finance costs, such as loan arrangement fees, will generally follow the same principles as those applying to interest. In other words, these costs will generally be allowable where the borrowed funds either represent capital introduced into the business or are otherwise used for business purposes.

Difficulties may sometimes occur, however, over the timing of relief for such costs. Sometimes, general accounting principles may dictate that the cost should be spread over the life of the loan. In such cases, the tax treatment will follow the same principles.

Example

Eve has a large rental property portfolio and decides to consolidate her borrowings into one single 20-year loan.

The bank charges her an arrangement fee of £20,000 for this new finance. Eve should therefore claim £1,000 each year over the 20-year life of the loan.

After 15 years, however, she decides to re-finance her business again and terminates the 20-year loan agreement.

At this stage she may claim the remaining £5,000 of the original fee which she has not yet claimed for tax purposes.

HM Revenue and Customs usually regards early redemption fees as a personal cost rather than a business cost and does not generally consider them to be allowable for either Income Tax or Capital Gains Tax. An Income Tax claim might nevertheless still be justified where there is a good business reason for the early redemption.

As in Eve's case, any unclaimed portion of the original arrangement fees may usually be claimed in the event of a loan's early termination (as long as they qualified as a business expense in the first place of course).

The timing of relief for arrangement fees, etc, is unaffected by whether the investor pays them at the outset or adds them to the value of their loan. Furthermore, if fees incurred for business purposes are added to the value of a loan, there is no need to restrict the amount of relief claimed for subsequent interest charges.

4.5   LEGAL AND PROFESSIONAL FEES

Legal fees and other professional costs incurred for the purposes of the business may fall into one of three categories for tax purposes:

i)   Revenue expenditure
ii)   Capital expenditure
iii)   Abortive capital expenditure

See Section 3.8 for an explanation of the difference between revenue expenditure and capital expenditure.

Revenue Expenditure

Revenue expenditure may be claimed as a deduction against rental income.

These are the costs which are incurred year in, year out, in earning the rental profits. They will include items such as debt collection expenses, agent's fees and accountancy fees for the preparation of your annual accounts and the business part of your tax return.

Legal and professional costs relating to a tenants' lease of a year or less are also generally allowable (e.g. legal fees for preparing the lease).

However, HM Revenue and Customs regards any expenses connected with the first letting of a property for more than one year as a capital expense which cannot be claimed. Costs relating to subsequent long leases will generally be allowable provided that the new lease is on broadly similar terms and for a period of less than 50 years and the property has not been used for some other purpose in the interim.

Capital Expenses

Legal fees and other professional costs incurred on the purchase or sale of properties cannot be claimed for Income Tax purposes within a property letting or investment business.

As long as the purchase or sale in question goes through, however, all is not lost, as these items may then be claimed as allowable deductions for Capital Gains Tax purposes when the property is disposed of (see Chapter 6).

This category would include:

- Legal fees
- Estate agent's fees
- Stamp Duty Land Tax
- Survey fees
- Valuation fees
- Professional costs incurred on a successful application for planning permission

Note, however, that costs such as survey or valuation fees incurred when re-mortgaging a property (for business purposes) would be treated in the same way as loan arrangement fees, as detailed in the previous section.

Tax Tip

Part of the professional fees arising on the purchase of a property will often relate to the raising of finance – i.e. the mortgage.

It may therefore be worth arranging to have this element of the fees invoiced separately so that they can be claimed for Income Tax purposes, in the same way as loan arrangement fees, as detailed in the previous section.

This may not always be beneficial, however, as we shall discuss later in Section 8.25.

Abortive Capital Expenditure

As we all know, sometimes a purchase or sale will not go through. In these cases, the investor will often have incurred costs such as survey fees or legal fees. Unfortunately, when you have a property investment business, costs related to purchases or sales which do not proceed will not generally be allowable for Income Tax and neither will they be allowable for Capital Gains Tax purposes. These are what we sometimes call 'tax nothings'.

The same is true of professional costs incurred on an unsuccessful application for planning permission. (Although, if you can show that the same costs led to a later, successful, application they may still be regarded as part of the capital cost of the project for Capital Gains Tax purposes.)

This situation is a constant source of frustration to property investors and I would agree that it is very unfair.

Tax Tip

If you are incurring very significant costs of this nature, you might sometimes be better off being treated as a property trader. Whilst, as explained in Section 2.3, your tax status is not a matter of choice, if your situation is already pretty borderline, a small shift in your investment strategy may be enough to tip the balance.

Having said that, with effective tax rates on trading profits of up to 62%, the instances where investors will be better off as a property trader will be pretty rare!

'Pre-Decision' Expenditure

There is an argument that any costs incurred before making a decision to purchase or sell a property are part of the regular overhead costs of the property business and are therefore properly claimable as revenue expenditure of that business.

Example

Noah is considering buying an investment property in the Newcastle area. He spots a potential purchase in Gosforth and has a survey done on the property. However, he is unhappy with the results of this survey and decides not to pursue this purchase.

Noah may be able to claim that the cost of the Gosforth survey is an allowable business overhead expense.

Noah moves his attention to Durham and finds another potential investment property. He has a survey carried out and, happy with the results, this time he decides to proceed with the purchase. Things go well until the owner of the Durham property is made redundant and is forced to take it back off the market. By this time, Noah has incurred substantial legal fees.

Noah's legal fees were incurred after he decided to purchase the Durham property. These fees are therefore abortive capital expenditure which Noah is unable to claim. Noah may, however, still be able to claim the cost of the survey fees for the Durham property as, once again, these were incurred before he made a decision whether to proceed with a purchase of the property.

To assist any claims for 'pre-decision' expenditure of this nature, it is useful to retain documentary evidence which shows that the decision to purchase or sell had not yet been taken.

Whilst I believe that claims for abortive 'pre-decision' expenditure incurred for the purposes of a property business are perfectly valid, this is a view which HM Revenue and Customs may not necessarily share. Some dispute over claims of this nature may therefore arise.

4.6   REPAIRS AND MAINTENANCE

Nowhere in the field of taxation is the question of 'capital or revenue' more difficult than in the area of repairs and maintenance and/or capital improvements.

In this section, we will look at some of the general principles applying to this type of expenditure on all rental properties. Other aspects specific to commercial property and to furnished residential lettings are covered in more detail in Sections 4.8 and 4.9 respectively.

Fundamental Principles

There are two main fundamental principles which we must consider in order to determine whether any expenditure represents a repair (i.e. revenue expenditure) or a capital improvement (capital expenditure):

i)   When a property is first brought into the rental business, any expenditure which is necessary to make it fit for use in that business will be capital expenditure.

In most cases, a property will first be brought into use when it is purchased, but the same rule applies when the taxpayer's own former home becomes a rental property.

ii) Subject to (i) above, expenditure which merely restores the property to its previous condition (at a time earlier in the same ownership) will be a repair.

Conversely, any expenditure which enhances the property beyond its previous condition within the same ownership will be capital improvement expenditure.

The question of what constitutes an 'enhancement' to the property is determined as a question of fact, not opinion. Just because you think that a new extension on a building is hideous does not stop it from being classed as a capital improvement for tax purposes.

'Within the same ownership' may sometimes also apply to periods in a previous ownership, such as when a property has been transferred between spouses.

Repairs are deductible for Income Tax purposes (as long as the property is a rental property at the time) whereas capital improvements **may** be deductible for Capital Gains Tax purposes (see Chapter 6).

The treatment of any incidental expenditure incurred as part of a building project, such as skip hire for example, will follow the treatment of the project itself. This does not extend to interest and other finance costs, however, which continue to be treated as set out in Section 4.4.

Some Illustrative Examples

I could write an entirely separate book covering umpteen different examples of repairs or capital improvements. Here, however, I have tried to set out a few cases which will hopefully serve to illustrate how the principles outlined above apply in practice. Where a new principle emerges in the course of these examples, I have highlighted it for your attention as an 'Emerging Principle'.

Example 1

Melanie buys an old farmhouse intending to rent it out for furnished holiday lettings. However, when she buys the property, it has no mains electricity, no mains sewerage and a large hole in the roof. She spends £75,000 getting the property into a fit state to let it out, including £5,000 on redecoration.

The whole of Melanie's expenditure of £75,000 will be treated as capital expenditure and no Income Tax deduction will be available. The fact that part of the expenditure was for decorating is likely to be regarded as merely incidental to the overall capital nature of the work in this case.

Emerging Principle

Expenditure which might normally be regarded as revenue in nature will be treated as capital where it forms an incidental part of a predominantly capital project. (We will look at some planning issues revolving around this principle in a later example.)

Until 2001 HM Revenue and Customs was prepared to allow some deduction for the 'notional repair' element within capital improvements, but sadly this is no longer the case.

Example 2

Geri has a small townhouse in Kensington which she rents out. She decides to have a conservatory built on the back of the house at a cost of £40,000, including £2,000 to redecorate the room adjoining the new conservatory.

Geri's conservatory is a capital improvement and no Income Tax deduction will be available for this expenditure. Once again, the capital nature of this work also extends to the cost of redecorating the adjoining room, as this was necessitated by the major building work.

Example 3

Emma owns a row of shops which she has been renting to a number of sole traders. A massive storm severely damages the roofs of the shops and Emma has these repaired at a cost of £50,000. Emma's expenditure represents an allowable repair cost which she can claim against her rental income.

The same storm also damaged several windows in Emma's shops. The glazier advises her that it will actually be cheaper to replace the original wooden frames with new UPVC double glazing and she agrees to do this. This expenditure remains revenue expenditure despite the fact that the new windows represent an improvement on the old ones.

Emerging Principle

When, due to changes in fashion, or technological advances, it becomes cheaper or more efficient to replace something with the nearest modern equivalent, the fact that this represents an improvement may be disregarded and the expenditure may still be classed as a repair.

Replacing single-glazed windows with equivalent double-glazing has been specifically highlighted as meeting this criterion in HM Revenue and Customs' own publications.

Example 3 Continued

At the same time, Emma also decides to have bay windows fitted in two of the shops. This element of her expenditure is a capital improvement and will have to be added to the capital value of her shops rather than claimed as a repair.

Emerging Principle

Both capital improvements and repairs may sometimes be carried out simultaneously. In such cases, the expenditure must be apportioned between the two elements on a reasonable basis.

Readers may wonder why this apportionment is allowed here, when it was denied for both Melanie and Geri above. The key difference is that both Melanie and Geri **had to** do the redecoration at the same time as the other work, whereas Emma simply **chose** to install the bay windows. It is the element of choice which makes the difference.

Tax Tip

Where an apportionment of expenditure is necessary, it would be wise to obtain evidence of the allocation made in support of your claim. This can be achieved by asking the builder to separately itemise the repairs and capital improvement elements of the work on their invoices.

Example 4

Victoria has a flat which she has been renting to students for several years. She decides to upgrade the flat to make it more suitable for letting to the 'young professional' class (what we used to call 'yuppies'). She therefore incurs the following expenditure:

  i)   *£16,000 on a new kitchen, including £4,500 on new kitchen equipment*
  ii) *£7,000 redecorating the bathroom, including £2,000 to replace the existing fittings and £1,000 to install a shower (there was only a bath before)*
  iii) *£5,000 redecorating the rest of the flat*
  iv) *£3,000 on rewiring*

New Kitchen

The new kitchen expenditure needs to be examined on a detailed 'item by item' basis. The treatment of each item depends on whether the item concerned is:

  a) *An integral part of a fitted kitchen or a free-standing item, and*
  b) *A direct replacement or an improvement*

Any items which represent improvements cannot be claimed as repairs. Hence, for example, installing a new extractor fan within a fitted kitchen, where no such fan had existed before, would be a capital improvement. As the fan is an integral part of a fitted kitchen, this would represent an improvement to the property as a whole and could thus be added to the cost of the property for Capital Gains Tax purposes (subject to the points discussed in Section 6.10).

Similarly, buying a fridge-freezer to replace a fridge would also represent an improvement which could not be claimed as a repair. Where the new fridge-freezer is a free-standing item, it would represent a separate asset in its own right and so could not be added to the cost of the property for Capital Gains Tax purposes.

Fitted Kitchen Units and Integrated Equipment

A fitted kitchen is treated as part of the fabric of the building. The cost of a new fitted kitchen replacing a previous, broadly similar, set of units, work tops, sink, etc, would therefore be accepted as a repair expense.

This treatment extends to the replacement of any equipment which is an integral part of a fitted kitchen, such as an integrated cooker or fridge. It does not, however, extend to free-standing items (which are considered below).

Where the replacement of a fitted kitchen can be claimed as a repair, this treatment should also include the necessary additional costs of re-tiling, re-plastering, plumbing, etc.

The usual exemption for 'nearest modern equivalent' continues to apply when considering whether items have been improved or merely replaced.

If, however, Victoria's new fitted kitchen incorporates extra storage space or other extra features, then an appropriate proportion of the expenditure will need to be treated as a capital improvement. This would include any new integrated equipment which replaced an old free-standing item.

In an extreme case, where fairly standard units are replaced by expensive customised items using much higher quality materials, then the whole cost of the new kitchen will need to be regarded as a capital improvement.

Free-Standing Items

Free-standing, moveable items are not part of the fabric of the building for tax purposes. This generally includes most free-standing 'white goods' such as fridges, dishwashers, cookers, etc., as well as other moveable items such as tables, chairs, etc.

The treatment of these items depends on when the expenditure was incurred and on whether Victoria is claiming the 'wear and tear allowance' (see Section 4.9).

If Victoria is claiming the 'wear and tear allowance', she will not be able to claim anything in respect of her expenditure on new kitchen equipment of this nature.

If she is **not** claiming the 'wear and tear allowance' **and** the expenditure was incurred **before** 6· April 2013, she will be able to claim the cost of any equipment which is a direct replacement for the old equipment that she previously had in the flat, or its nearest modern equivalent.

If she is **not** claiming the 'wear and tear allowance' **but** the expenditure was incurred **after** 5· April 2013, the position is currently uncertain. We will examine this situation in more detail in Section 4.9.

Anything which is an entirely new item of equipment or a major improvement on the old equipment (i.e. not just the modern equivalent) will be capital expenditure and not allowable for Income Tax purposes; regardless of when the expenditure was incurred.

Hence, where a new fridge was purchased before 6· April 2013 to replace an old fridge of similar size this may have been allowable as a replacement (if the wear and tear allowance was not being claimed); but buying a fridge-freezer to replace a fridge would always have been a capital improvement and would probably never have been allowed for Income Tax purposes.

Bathroom Fittings

Replacing the existing bathroom fittings should usually be allowable repairs expenditure. Toilets, baths and washbasins are all regarded as part of the fabric of the building, so repairing or replacing them is generally allowable for Income Tax purposes.

Once again, however, replacing the existing fittings with expensive customised items using much higher quality materials would amount to a capital improvement.

Fitting the new shower will definitely be a capital improvement as this is an item of equipment which had not been present before.

The remaining bathroom redecoration costs will need to be apportioned between the repair element and capital improvement element. Any expense arising due to the installation of the new shower would have to be treated as part of the capital element.

Redecorating the Flat

Most of the redecoration work, in the absence of any building work in the rooms concerned, should be fairly straightforward repairs expenditure. As usual, we *need to be on the lookout for any improvement element, but a great deal of redecorating cost will always fall into the 'nearest modern equivalent' category.*

Carpets, curtains and other similar items need to be considered separately. These are classed as 'furnishings' and will be dealt with under the principles set out in Section 4.9.

In this context, it makes no difference if you are replacing carpets or curtains which you yourself fitted previously or which you acquired when you purchased the property.

Rewiring

The rewiring cost will be fully allowable if it is simply 'new for old'. If, on the other hand, Victoria took the opportunity to fit a few new sockets then there would be an improvement element and, as usual, an apportionment would be required. Such an apportionment would probably also necessitate an apportionment of the redecorating costs, as some of these would also be incurred due to the electrical improvements.

Emerging Principles

Moveable items, such as carpets, curtains and free-standing kitchen equipment, are not regarded as part of the fabric of the building and are therefore subject to different rules (see Section 4.9).

In complex cases, the question of 'repairs or capital improvements' will need to be examined room by room, or even item by item. The tax treatment of one item may have a knock-on effect on the tax treatment of another item.

Example 5

Mel buys a rather dilapidated house in Sunderland hoping to rent it out to a family or young couple. She gets the house at a very good price owing to its current state of repair but knows that safety regulations would bar her from letting it out to anyone in its current condition.

The house desperately needs rewiring and also some urgent plumbing work, which Mel carries out at a cost of £5,000. This expenditure will have to be treated as part of her capital cost.

At this point the house is basically habitable and will meet all necessary safety regulations, but it could really do with redecorating to make it attractive to the type of tenants that Mel is ideally looking for.

However, if Mel redecorates at this point then this expenditure too is also likely to be regarded as part of the capital cost of the property, especially since part of the redecorating will have been necessitated by the plumbing and rewiring work.

What Mel does instead, therefore, is to first let the house to a group of students for nine months.

After that, she is able to redecorate the property and to claim this as a revenue expense deductible for Income Tax purposes.

Tax Tip

Where there is a danger that repairs or maintenance expenditure might be regarded as an incidental part of a capital project, it will be beneficial to delay this element of the work, if possible, until after an intermediate period of letting.

In this way, the expenditure becomes an allowable revenue expense.

Naturally, any health and safety requirements will have to be observed before undertaking the initial letting period.

Example 6

Danni buys a flat from an elderly couple, intending to rent it out. The elderly couple lived in the flat right up to the date of completion. Although it was a bit 'run down' and the decoration was very old-fashioned, it was perfectly habitable and met all applicable safety requirements for a rental property.

Immediately after completion, Danni redecorates the flat in a modern style and then begins to rent it out. Danni's redecoration costs are an allowable maintenance cost for Income Tax purposes, even though she did the work straight away after buying the flat. The flat was already completely habitable and the redecoration work was purely a matter of choice or taste.

Emerging Principle

Normal routine repairs and redecoration work on newly acquired properties is usually considered allowable. Such expenditure will generally be regarded as 'normal' if the property could have been used without it and the price of the property was not significantly affected by its condition.

HM Revenue and Customs' View on Expenditure on Newly Acquired Rental Properties

HM Revenue and Customs' view is that expenditure to rectify 'normal wear and tear' on a newly acquired rental property remains allowable as a deduction from rental income for Income Tax purposes. They take the view that there is only 'normal' wear and tear if the property's condition does not significantly affect its purchase price.

HM Revenue and Customs' manuals also specifically state that any expenditure on a newly acquired rental property which is not allowed for Income Tax purposes on the grounds that it represents capital expenditure should then be allowed for Capital Gains Tax purposes on a disposal of that same property.

Accounting Treatment

Where there are no statutory rules to the contrary, HM Revenue and Customs will generally expect the tax treatment of an expense to mirror its treatment in the accounts.

Wealth Warning

It is important to ensure that valid repairs expenditure is not treated as a capital item in your accounts, as this could prevent you from claiming that expenditure for Income Tax purposes.

See Section 8.25 for further important tax planning implications regarding the last two points.

Repair Cost Provisions

In accounting terms, a 'provision' is a charge made in your accounts in respect of a future cost. Provisions for future costs are not generally allowable until the costs have actually been incurred.

There are a few exceptions to this rule, however, and a provision for repair costs may be allowed for tax purposes if:

i)   There is a legal or contractual obligation to incur the expenditure,

ii) There is a specific programme of repair work to be undertaken, and

iii) The accounting provision has been computed with a reasonable degree of accuracy.

Example 7

Kylie owns three flats in 'Donovan Towers', a tenement block in Glasgow. In February 2015, she receives a statutory notice from the council requiring her (and the other owners in the same block) to carry out some urgent roof repairs.

The 'Donovan Towers Owners and Residents Association' approaches Jason, a local builder, who provides them with a quotation for carrying out the necessary work.

On 4 April 2015, the Donovan Towers Owners and Residents Association formally approves the quotation. Kylie's share of the cost will be £10,000.

Under these circumstances, Kylie may quite properly make a provision for her £10,000 share of the repair cost in her accounts for the year ending 5 April 2015, even though the work has not even started yet.

4.7 TRAINING AND RESEARCH

Many property investors these days spend a good deal of money on training and research. The first thing to note is the fact that this expenditure is often incurred before the business starts is not, in itself, a barrier to claiming it as a business expense. (Unless it was incurred more than seven years before the business started!)

The cost of books, DVDs, magazines and other information purchased for business purposes is usually allowable. This covers not only industry-specific publications, like trade magazines, but also books and other publications you buy to help you meet your legal and taxation obligations.

Books like this one, and many of Taxcafe's other guides, which keep you updated with developments in the field of property taxation, will therefore generally be tax deductible.

The expenditure must be relevant to your business. If you are planning to invest in Spanish property, then the cost of an English-Spanish dictionary might be allowable. A self-help book on diet and yoga, however, would be pushing it too far, even if it does somehow make you a better landlord.

As far as seminars and courses are concerned, the rule is that expenses incurred in updating or expanding existing areas of knowledge may be claimed, but any costs relating to entirely new areas of knowledge are a personal capital expense.

This can be a difficult distinction to draw, especially in a field such as property investment, where a great deal of industry knowledge is simply a blend of common sense and experience. It's not like you're training to become a brain surgeon after all!

My personal view is that property investment is a field of knowledge which most adults already have (e.g. from buying their own home) and that any such expenses are really only updating or expanding that knowledge and are therefore allowable. However, this view is not shared by everyone, most especially HM Revenue and Customs, and hence such claims may well be challenged.

In the end, the decision over any expense claims in this area will inevitably require you to use your own judgement.

4.8 CAPITAL ALLOWANCES FOR LETTING BUSINESSES

As we have seen in the last few sections, the most significant amounts of disallowable expenditure in a property investment business derive from capital expenditure on property improvements and on furniture, fixtures and fittings.

As we saw in Section 3.10, however, some capital expenditure is eligible for capital allowances.

The rules for capital allowances depend on the type of property being rented.

There are no longer any capital allowances available on the basic structure of the property itself. Capital allowances are, however, available on fixtures, fittings, furniture, equipment, and 'integral features' (see below) within:

- Commercial property (shops, offices, restaurants, etc.)
- Qualifying furnished holiday lets (see Section 8.15)
- Communal areas in rented residential property not falling within any individual 'dwelling'

The third category would, for example, include equipment in a utility room shared by the occupants of several self-contained flats in a rented building. As this category is fairly rare, I will not repeat it every time we discuss capital allowances in the rest of this section, but it is worth bearing in mind that the rules applying to capital allowances in rented commercial property and furnished holiday lets apply equally to communal areas in residential property.

Subject to the exceptions discussed above, residential property does not usually attract any capital allowances at all. However, landlords may claim the 'wear and tear allowance' (see Section 4.9) on fully furnished lettings. Alternatively, the cost of replacement furniture, equipment, etc, could sometimes be claimed prior to 2013/14, as we saw in Section 4.6. (The position from 2013/14 onwards is currently unclear and is discussed further in Section 4.9.)

Plant & Machinery in Rental Property

As explained above, qualifying expenditure within commercial property or qualifying furnished holiday accommodation may be classed as 'plant and machinery' for capital allowances purposes.

Details of the capital allowances regime for 'plant and machinery' are given in Section 3.10. Note that, since property investors will generally be using a 5ᵃ April accounting year end date, the transitional rules applying to periods spanning 1ᵗ January 2013 and 1ᵗ January 2016 will usually apply (but those applying to periods spanning 6ᵃ April 2014 will not usually apply).

The annual investment allowance can be claimed on expenditure on qualifying plant and machinery within commercial rental property (subject to the 'wealth warning' below) or qualifying furnished holiday accommodation. This includes items classed as 'integral features' (see below).

Wealth Warning

Under certain circumstances, landlords providing fixtures and fittings within commercial property need to make a joint election with their tenants that the landlords will retain the right to capital allowances on that expenditure.

A landlord can, of course, only claim capital allowances on expenditure which they have incurred themselves and not on expenditure incurred by their tenants.

Nevertheless, property investors with commercial rental property or qualifying furnished holiday accommodation will be able to obtain immediate tax relief on up to the following amounts of qualifying expenditure on their rental properties each year:

2012/13:	£83,562
2013/14:	£250,000
2014/15:	£500,000
2015/16:	£375,409
2016/17 onwards:	£25,000

(Assuming a 5ᵃ April accounting date and subject to the further limitations discussed in Section 3.10.)

This will even include expenditure on so-called 'integral features' (see below).

Tax Tip

A couple holding investment property jointly (but not as a partnership) will each be entitled to their own annual investment allowance, meaning that up to twice as much relief will be available each year!

Qualifying Expenditure on Rental Property

Assets within commercial property and qualifying furnished holiday accommodation which qualify as plant and machinery for capital allowances purposes include the following:

- Integral features (see below)
- Manufacturing or processing equipment
- Furniture and furnishings, white goods, sinks, baths, showers and sanitary ware
- Sound insulation and gas or sewerage systems which are provided specifically to meet the particular requirements of a qualifying trading activity
- Storage or display equipment, counters and checkouts, cold stores, refrigeration and cooling equipment
- Computer, telecommunication and surveillance systems, including wiring and other links
- Fire and burglar alarm systems, sprinklers and other fire-fighting equipment
- Strong rooms and safes
- Moveable partitioning where intended to be moved in the course of a qualifying trading activity
- Decorative assets provided for public enjoyment in hotels, restaurants and similar trades
- Advertising hoardings, signs and displays

Expenditure on the alteration of a building for the specific purpose of installing qualifying plant and machinery also qualifies for plant and machinery allowances itself.

Qualifying assets within a commercial property or qualifying furnished holiday accommodation are eligible for the same rate of capital allowances whether they are purchased separately or as part of the purchase of the property.

Where a second-hand property is purchased, it therefore becomes vital to analyse the qualifying fixtures within the property in support of a capital allowances claim.

For property purchases taking place after 5ᵗʰ April 2012, the purchaser and seller now generally have to agree a value for the qualifying fixtures within the property and make a joint election to that effect (known as a 'Section 198 Election'), which the purchaser has to submit to HM Revenue and Customs within a fixed time period after the purchase in support of their claim.

For purchases taking place after 5ᵗʰ April 2014, the purchaser will not generally be able to claim capital allowances on any fixtures where the seller would have been entitled to make a capital allowances claim, but had failed to do so. Such failures to make legitimate claims are commonplace, so it is now vital to check the seller's capital allowances claims history.

Tax Tip

Sellers can still make retrospective capital allowances claims right up to the time they sell the property, so it will usually be possible to ensure that the purchaser's ability to claim capital allowances on fixtures is not diminished or lost – provided that appropriate action is taken prior to the date of purchase!

Practical Pointer

The new requirements for second-hand property applying to purchases taking place after 5ᵗʰ April 2012 and 5ᵗʰ April 2014 only apply where the property has been in 'qualifying use' at some time after 5ᵗʰ April 2012.

For commercial property this will generally be the case, but for purchases of residential property the new rules are only likely to apply where a previous owner has used the property as qualifying furnished holiday accommodation at some time since 5ᵗʰ April 2012, or where the property has been rented out since that date and has communal areas, as described above.

Integral Features

Expenditure on assets within a defined list of 'integral features' falls into the special rate pool, attracting writing down allowances at 8% instead of the usual 18% (10% instead of 20% before 6ᵗʰ April 2012).

However, as explained above, these assets remain eligible for the annual investment allowance, so substantial amounts of qualifying expenditure on assets in this category can still attract immediate 100% relief.

The following items are classed as integral features:

- Electrical lighting and power systems
- Cold water systems
- Space or water heating systems, air conditioning, ventilation and air purification systems and floors or ceilings comprised in such systems
- Lifts, escalators and moving walkways
- External solar shading

In a nutshell: All the wiring, lighting, plumbing, heating and air conditioning in any commercial property or qualifying furnished holiday accommodation qualifies for capital allowances, with immediate 100% relief for the first £500,000 spent on these items during 2014/15.

The integral features regime applies to all expenditure incurred after 5ᵗʰ April 2008, including qualifying items within second-hand buildings purchased after that date (subject to the requirements discussed above).

Any expenditure on integral features which is not covered by the annual investment allowance will fall into the special rate pool and attract writing down allowances at just 8%. This includes any items which might otherwise be regarded as falling under one of the other qualifying headings for plant and machinery within rental property given above.

The integral features regime does not apply to expenditure incurred before 6ᵗʰ April 2008 and much of this expenditure would not have qualified for capital allowances. The following items of expenditure incurred before 6ᵗʰ April 2008 would, however, qualify for capital allowances:

- Electrical or cold water systems provided specifically to meet the particular requirements of a qualifying trading activity.
- Heating, ventilation, air conditioning and air purification systems, including any floor or ceiling which is an integral part of the system.
- Lifts, escalators and moving walkways.

This remains relevant because it is always possible to claim writing down allowances on any qualifying expenditure incurred in earlier years, even if no allowances have been claimed previously, provided that the assets concerned are still in use in the business. (Subject to the rules outlined above for fixtures within second-hand properties purchased after 5ᵗʰ April 2012.)

Integral Features Benefits

Combining the integral features regime with the annual investment allowance, we can see that many property investors will be able to benefit quite significantly.

Example

In June 2014, Lulach buys an old property and converts it into office units to rent out. Although the office units are really just basic 'shells' with the absolute minimum of fixtures and fittings, Lulach's surveyors, Macbeth & Co., nevertheless calculate that he has spent £140,000 on 'integral features' and other fixtures qualifying as plant and machinery.

Lulach can therefore claim an annual investment allowance of £140,000 against his rental income in 2014/15.

Furthermore, as we shall see in Section 4.11, property investors may be able to claim any capital allowances in excess of their rental profits against their other income for the same tax year, or the next one (although this relief is now subject to certain limitations).

Remember also, that a couple buying property jointly (but not as a partnership) could claim annual investment allowances of up to £500,000 *each* in 2014/15. Such a couple could therefore potentially benefit from a total tax saving of up to £453,000 in 2014/15 simply by buying the right property!

(Based on income of £600,000 each before claiming annual investment allowances)

Thermal Insulation of Commercial Property

Expenditure on thermal insulation of an existing commercial building used in a qualifying business also falls into the special rate pool. The annual investment allowance is again available on this expenditure.

Landlord's Own Assets

As explained above, a landlord is unable to claim capital allowances on any assets, such as furniture and equipment, within his or her residential lettings (apart from assets in communal areas not within any individual 'dwelling').

Any landlord may however claim 'plant and machinery' allowances, as detailed in Section 3.10, on equipment purchased for their own business use, such as computers and office furniture.

Capital allowances are available on motor vehicles used in the business, again as detailed in Section 3.10.

Landlord's Energy Saving Allowance

Residential landlords may claim an Income Tax deduction for up to £1,500 of qualifying energy saving expenditure per property per year (up until 2014/15). Without this special relief, this expenditure would often be regarded as a capital item and hence disallowed.

The expenditure qualifying for this allowance comprises: new loft or cavity wall insulation, solid wall insulation, draught proofing, insulation for hot water systems and floor insulation.

Wealth Warning

2014/15 is the *last year* that this relief will be available. Landlords therefore have until 5ᵗʰ April 2015 to install qualifying insulation which will benefit from this allowance.

The landlord must already own the property at the time the relevant expenditure is incurred. Furthermore, the insulation must be installed in an existing building and not during construction of a new one.

The relief is not available if the property is treated as qualifying furnished holiday accommodation (see Section 8.15) or if rent-a-room relief is being claimed.

If the landlord has not yet commenced their letting business then, unlike most pre-trading expenditure, the insulation work must take place within a six-month period before commencement of the business.

The relief operates on a 'per property' basis, which is very useful for landlords owning flats, as it means that the full allowance may be claimed on each dwelling within the same building.

If the property is held jointly, however, the amount which may be claimed is limited to £1,500 per property in total (e.g. £750 each for two equal joint owners). Amounts allowed under this relief do not, unfortunately, count as capital allowances for the purposes of loss relief (see Section 4.11).

106

4.9 FURNISHED LETTINGS

Furnished residential lettings need to be divided into three categories for tax purposes:

- Fully furnished lettings
- Partly furnished lettings
- Furnished holiday lettings

In this section, I will look at the tax relief available in respect of furnishings within fully furnished lettings and partly furnished lettings. Furnished holiday lettings are subject to an entirely different regime which I will examine in Section 8.15 (the key difference being that qualifying items within furnished holiday lettings are eligible for capital allowances).

It should also be noted that any items within 'communal areas' lying outside any individual dwelling (e.g. the common parts of a house divided into self-contained flats) will also be subject to a different regime and may be eligible for capital allowances (see Section 4.8 for details).

Before we look at the tax relief available for furnishings, it is important to stress that nothing in this section affects the landlord's ability to claim repairs expenditure under the principles which we examined in Section 4.6.

In particular, remember that the cost of replacing fixtures and fittings can usually be claimed as repairs expenditure (subject to the principles discussed in Section 4.6).

What Are Furnishings?

The first, and most important, thing to understand is that fixtures, fittings, and anything else which is part of the fabric of the building, are not classed as furnishings for tax purposes.

Generally speaking, anything which is permanently fixed to the building is not classed as a 'furnishing' and replacing these items will often be claimable as a repair expense, as discussed in Section 4.6, regardless of how the furnishings in the property are being dealt with.

Hence, items which are classed as 'furnishings' for tax purposes include:

- Furniture
- Electrical equipment
- Free-standing 'white goods', such as fridges, dishwashers, etc.
- Carpets and other floor coverings

- Curtains, blinds, etc.
- 'Soft furnishings', such as cushions, lampshades, etc.
- Cutlery, crockery and cooking utensils
- Bed linen

Carpets often cause a lot of confusion as many people see them as a 'fitting' rather than a 'furnishing'. For tax purposes, however, they are classed as furnishings.

Items classed as fixtures and fittings for tax purposes include:

- Baths, toilets, sinks, showers, etc.
- Fitted kitchens, including fitted (not free-standing) equipment which is an integral part of a fitted kitchen
- Central heating equipment (boilers, radiators, etc.)
- Air conditioning
- Light fittings

Where these items are replaced, the expenditure will generally be dealt with as a repair – subject to the points outlined in Section 4.6.

The fitted equipment in a modern kitchen under the second heading above might include various items which would have been free-standing in a more traditional kitchen; including cookers, fridges, dishwashers and many other items. As long as both the old item and the new one are an integral part of a fitted kitchen, the cost of the replacement may be claimed as a repair expense (subject, as always, to the principles covered in Section 4.6).

Fully Furnished Lettings

From 2013/14 onwards, landlords with fully furnished lettings should generally claim the 'wear and tear allowance'. This allowance is examined in detail below.

For 2012/13 and earlier tax years, landlords with fully furnished lettings had the choice of claiming either the 'wear and tear allowance' or the cost of renewals and replacements, sometimes known as the 'replacements basis'. This alternative treatment is also examined below.

Whichever basis the landlord chose prior to 2013/14, they had to use it on all of their fully furnished lettings. Prior to 2011/12, this was a permanent choice which had to be followed every year; for 2011/12 and 2012/13, the choice could be made on a 'year by year' basis.

Technically, from 2013/14 onwards, claiming the wear and tear allowance continues to be a choice which landlords with fully furnished lettings are able to make on a 'year by year' basis. The choice is usually made simply by electing to claim the wear and tear allowance in your tax return.

Wealth Warning

Landlords must elect to claim the wear and tear allowance no later than the first anniversary of the normal filing date for the relevant tax year. For example, a landlord must elect to claim the wear and tear allowance for the year ending 5ᵗ April 2015 by 31ˢᵗ January 2017. If no such election has been made by that date, the landlord is technically ineligible to claim the allowance.

Tax Tip

Whilst the election to claim the wear and tear allowance is usually made simply by claiming the allowance in the tax return, there is no prescribed form for the election and a landlord could submit a 'wear and tear allowance election' by way of a letter sent to HM Revenue and Customs prior to the deadline described above.

This would be a useful solution in any case where a landlord knew they wished to claim the wear and tear allowance for a tax year, but was unable to submit a tax return by the first anniversary of the normal filing date. (Note, however, that there are significant penalties for the late filing of tax returns.)

Whilst claiming the wear and tear allowance continues to be a choice which landlords may make on a 'year by year' basis, the withdrawal of the 'replacements basis' for expenditure incurred after 5ᵗ April 2013 means that, in practice, it will generally make sense for all landlords with fully furnished lettings to claim the wear and tear allowance each year from 2013/14 onwards.

What Is a Fully Furnished Letting?

To be classed as a 'fully furnished letting', the landlord must provide sufficient furnishings so that the property is capable of 'normal residential use' without the tenant having to provide their own furnishings. Typically, this will include beds, chairs, tables, sofas, carpets or other floor coverings, curtains or blinds, and kitchen equipment.

The key phrase here is whether the property is capable of 'normal residential use' and the level of furnishings and equipment required must be considered in this context. In essence, the landlord must provide the tenant (or each tenant) with some privacy, somewhere to sit, somewhere to sleep, somewhere to eat, and the facilities required to feed themselves.

Partly Furnished Lettings

Where some furniture, equipment or other furnishings are provided, but not sufficient to enable the property to be classed as 'fully furnished' (as described above), the property will be regarded as a 'partly furnished letting'.

For 2012/13 and earlier tax years, landlords with partly furnished lettings were able to claim the cost of renewals and replacements under the concessionary 'replacements basis' (see below).

From 2013/14 onwards, the only relief available to these landlords for the cost of replacement items is the statutory 'renewals allowance', which may be considerably less generous in scope and is also examined below.

The Wear and Tear Allowance

A 'wear and tear allowance' of 10% of the relevant rental income may be claimed each year against the rental income from fully furnished residential lettings. This allowance is given instead of capital allowances, which are not usually available for residential property.

In calculating the allowance, we first need to establish the amount of 'relevant rental income' for the property in question. 'Relevant rental income' means the total rent receivable less any amounts borne by the landlord which would normally be a tenant's own responsibility (e.g. council tax, water rates or electricity charges).

Example

Cherie owns a large flat in central Bristol which she lets out for £2,500 per month (£30,000 per annum). Cherie pays the water rates for the property, which amount to £1,000 per year, but the tenant pays their own council tax.

Cherie is therefore able to claim a wear and tear allowance as follows:

Total Rent Received:	*£30,000*
Less:	
Water Rates	*£1,000*
Relevant Rental Income:	*£29,000*
Wear and Tear Allowance:	*£2,900 (10%)*

The Effect of a Wear and Tear Allowance Claim

When a landlord claims the wear and tear allowance for any tax year, it automatically applies to all fully furnished lettings made by that landlord for that tax year.

As a consequence, the landlord cannot also claim any of the following in relation to any of their fully furnished lettings during that tax year:

- The renewals allowance (see below)
- The replacements basis (see below; not applicable from 2013/14 onwards)
- Repairs to furniture

Note that it is only repairs to furniture which are excluded. It would appear that repairs to equipment (e.g. 'white goods' such as cookers or fridges) and other furnishings (e.g. carpets) could still be claimed.

The above costs are also only excluded when they are attributable to a period during which the property is subject to a fully furnished letting. However, it seems likely that furniture repairs which become necessary following a fully furnished letting period will usually be properly attributable to that period.

Despite the exclusions detailed above, the uncertainty surrounding the scope of the new 'renewals allowance' (see below) means that the vast majority of landlords with fully furnished lettings will be better off claiming the wear and tear allowance from 2013/14 onwards: including those who previously claimed under the 'replacements basis' (see below).

The 'Replacements Basis'

For 2012/13 and earlier years, landlords could claim the cost of replacing furniture and other furnishings. For landlords with fully furnished lettings, this was an alternative to claiming the wear and tear allowance; for landlords with partly furnished lettings it was the only option available to them.

It was not possible to claim the costs of the original furnishings when the property was first let out, nor the cost of improvements or additional items.

For example, replacing one bed with another would normally have been allowed under the replacements basis, but replacing an old single bed with a king-size four poster would not, as it would represent an improvement.

The 'Renewals Allowance'

From 2013/14 onwards, the concessionary 'replacements basis' described above is no longer available.

A statutory 'renewals allowance' continues to be available instead, however.

The new renewals allowance is based on a provision within existing tax legislation which allows all businesses to claim the cost of replacing 'tools' used in the business. The legislation goes on to define 'tools' as being any 'implement, utensil, or article'.

The definition of 'tools' within tax legislation could potentially be interpreted very broadly. As a result, some people have argued that the 'renewals allowance' should effectively be the same as the old 'replacements basis' described above.

Sadly, however, the latest HM Revenue and Customs guidance on this issue suggests that, in their view, the 'renewals allowance' has to be interpreted rather more narrowly and that the new allowance should only apply to smaller items, or items with only a short useful life.

The guidance specifically states that HM Revenue and Customs does not consider the renewals allowance to cover free standing 'white goods' such as cookers, fridges or dishwashers.

It also states that carpets would not normally be covered, although they do acknowledge that there may be some exceptions to this where the carpets have a very short useful life (e.g. a cheap hall carpet in a house let to students which is replaced annually).

It should be borne in mind here that HM Revenue and Customs' guidance is not the law and that there are alternative views regarding the scope of the 'renewals allowance'. Indeed, the allowance has been successfully used in the past (by different types of business) to claim the cost of replacing far larger items than fridges, cookers and carpets.

Hence, there is a case for arguing that it would not be unreasonable for landlords to place a broad interpretation on the scope of the 'renewals allowance' and to continue to make the same claims as would have been available under the old 'replacements basis'.

Whether such claims will ultimately be successful, however, is currently uncertain. Landlords who make claims beyond the scope of HM Revenue and Customs' guidance face the risk of penalties if those claims are ultimately found to be excessive: a highly unsatisfactory outcome given the background to this situation and the fact that many people still consider such claims to be perfectly legitimate!

Any landlord who is prepared to make a claim under the renewals allowance which is beyond the scope suggested by HM Revenue and Customs' guidance would be wise to include details of the items claimed in one of the 'additional information' boxes on their tax return.

An additional note explaining that the landlord considers these items to be within the scope of the renewals allowance on the basis of the relevant legislation (Section 68 ITTOIA 2005) and decided case law should also be included.

In this way, the stance taken will have been fully disclosed and justified and one would hope that this should prevent any penalties from arising.

The alternative, of course, is simply to allow HM Revenue and Customs' more restrictive interpretation to prevail instead of following the law as laid down by Parliament and interpreted by the Courts.

Renewals Allowance Summary

Not everyone will wish to take the risk of making claims beyond the scope of HM Revenue and Customs' guidance.

To assist readers in considering what items to claim under the renewals allowance, the current situation regarding the validity of claiming the cost of replacement items is summarised below.

Readers must bear in mind, however, that the position regarding all but the first batch of items below (i.e. those listed under 'Definitely Covered') remains uncertain.

Definitely Covered

The following items appear to fall within HM Revenue and Customs' guidance and are therefore definitely covered by the renewals allowance:

- Low cost 'soft furnishings', such as cushions, lampshades, etc.
- Cutlery, crockery and cooking utensils
- Bed linen
- Rugs

Probably Covered

The following items are not specifically mentioned within the HM Revenue and Customs guidance but would appear to fall within the spirit of the guidance and would therefore probably also be covered within HM Revenue and Customs' interpretation of the renewals allowance:

- Curtains, blinds, etc.
- Small items of equipment, such as lamps, kettles, toasters and microwave ovens

Sometimes Covered

The following items would not generally be covered within HM Revenue and Customs' interpretation of the renewals allowance but would be covered where they needed to be replaced on a regular basis, such as every two years, or more frequently. These items would always be covered under the broader interpretation of the 'renewals allowance' which some people support:

- Carpets and other floor coverings

Open to Interpretation

The following items are **not** covered within HM Revenue and Customs' interpretation of the renewals allowance, although they would continue to be covered under the broader interpretation which some people support:

- Furniture
- Larger items of electrical equipment, such as televisions, etc.
- Free-standing 'white goods', such as fridges, dishwashers, etc.

One thing which remains beyond doubt is that, as with the replacements basis, the renewals allowance does not cover the costs of the original furnishings when the property was first let out, or the cost of improvements or additional items.

Repairs to Furnishings

As explained above, when the wear and tear allowance is being claimed, the landlord cannot claim any furniture repair costs in the same tax year which are attributable to a fully furnished letting.

Apart from this exclusion, however, landlords may claim the cost of repairs to any items of equipment, furniture or furnishings in any rental properties. Such repair costs are claimable under general principles and are not dependent on the interpretation of the renewals allowance discussed above (the renewals allowance only applies to replacements, not repairs to existing items).

4.10 RENT-A-ROOM RELIEF

A special relief, called 'rent-a-room relief', applies to income from letting out a part of your own home. For this purpose, the property must be your main residence (see Section 6.13) for at least part of the same tax year. The letting itself must also at least partially coincide with a period when the property is your main residence.

The relief covers income from lodgers and even extends to the letting of a self-contained flat, provided that the division of the property is only temporary.

Complete exemption is automatically provided where the gross annual rent receivable from lettings in the property does not exceed £4,250. The gross rent receivable for this purpose must include any contributions towards household expenses which you receive from your tenants and any balancing charges arising (see Section 3.8).

The taxpayer may elect not to claim rent-a-room relief. They might do this, for example, if the letting is actually producing a loss which, otherwise, could not be claimed.

This election must be made within 12 months after the 31ˑ January following the tax year. (E.g. for the tax year 2014/15, the election would need to be made by 31ˑ January 2017.)

Where the gross rent receivable exceeds the rent-a-room limit, the taxpayer may nevertheless elect (within the same time limit as outlined above) for a form of partial exemption.

The partial exemption operates by allowing the taxpayer to be assessed only on the amount of gross rents receivable in excess of the rent-a-room limit instead of under the normal basis for rental income.

Example

Duncan rents out a room in his house for an annual rent of £5,000. His rental profit for 2014/15, calculated on the normal basis, is £1,800. He therefore elects to use the rent-a-room basis, thus reducing his assessable rental income to only £750.

Other Points on Rent-a-Room Relief

Where the letting income is being shared with another person, the rent-a-room limit must be halved. Where there is letting income from the same property during the same tax year which does not qualify for the relief, none of the income from the property that year may be exempted.

An election to claim rent-a-room relief is deemed to remain in place for future years unless withdrawn (the same time limit applies for a withdrawal).

Rent-a-room relief continues to apply to income from lodgers where additional services are provided, such as cooking, cleaning, etc. Income in excess of £4,250 per year may, however, be regarded as trading income rather than rental income in these circumstances.

Where you are claiming complete exemption under rent-a-room relief, you should put an 'X' in Box 4 on page UKP1 of your tax return.

4.11 RENTAL LOSSES ON UK PROPERTY

As explained in Section 4.1, all your UK property lettings, apart from any furnished holiday lettings which you have, are treated as a single UK property business. For loss relief purposes, however, it is necessary to separate UK rental property into three categories:

- Non-commercial lettings (see Section 4.15)
- Furnished holiday lettings (see Section 8.15)
- Other UK rental property (which I will refer to as 'normal' rental property for the sake of illustration)

Losses arising on furnished holiday lettings or non-commercial lettings are subject to special rules which we will look at in Sections 8.15 and 4.15 respectively.

Losses arising on 'normal' rental property are automatically set off against profits on other 'normal' UK rental property for the same period. Losses on 'normal' rental property may also be set off against profits on non-commercial lettings.

Any overall net losses from 'normal' rental property remaining after this may be carried forward and set off against future profits from 'normal' UK rental property.

Losses consisting of capital allowances may also be set off against the landlord's other income of the same tax year and the next one (subject to the tax relief 'cap' discussed in Section 3.11).

The treatment of losses from overseas lettings is covered in Section 4.14 below.

Example

In the tax year 2014/15, Owain has employment income of £70,000, from which he suffers deduction of tax under PAYE totalling £17,627.

He also has a portfolio of rented commercial property on which he has made an overall loss of £15,000, including £10,000 of capital allowances.

Owain can claim to set his capital allowances off against his employment income, which will produce a tax repayment of £4,000.

How Long Can Rental Losses Be Carried Forward?

Rental losses from 'normal' rental property may be carried forward for as long as you continue to have a 'normal' UK property rental business. There are two major pitfalls to watch out for here.

Firstly, rental losses are personal. They cannot be transferred to another person, not even your spouse, and they do not transfer with the properties. If you die with rental losses, they die with you.

Secondly, if your 'normal' UK property business ceases, you will lose your losses. It may therefore sometimes be vital to keep your 'normal' UK property business going. Remember that as long as you continue to have at least one 'normal' UK rental property, you still have a 'normal' UK property business.

Example

Fergus has a large UK property portfolio. Despite having made some good profits in the past, by 2014/15 he has rental losses of £1,000,000 carried forward.

Fergus decides he's had enough and begins to sell off his UK property empire. Before his rental income ceases, however, he buys one small lock-up garage in Argyllshire and starts to rent it out.

Fergus's lock-up garage is enough to ensure that he still has a UK property rental business. It doesn't matter that it is tiny by comparison with his previous ventures; this one small garage keeps his rental losses alive, with the possibility of saving him up to £450,000 one day (£1m at 45%).

The only absolutely safe way to ensure that you have a continuing 'normal' UK property rental business is to ensure that you always have at least one 'normal' UK rental property let out on a commercial basis.

However, HM Revenue and Customs will sometimes accept that a total cessation of all 'normal' rental income is not necessarily the same as a cessation of your 'normal' UK rental business, especially where the rental properties are still held.

They will usually accept that the rental business has not ceased:

- Where you can provide evidence that you have been attempting unsuccessfully to let out your property.

- Where rental has only ceased temporarily whilst repairs or alterations are carried out.

They will, however, generally regard the rental business as having ceased if there is a gap of more than three years between lettings and different properties are let before and after the gap.

They may sometimes accept a gap of less than three years as not being a cessation, but not if you have clearly employed all of your capital in some other type of business, or spent it for personal purposes, such as buying yourself a new home.

If in doubt though, rent out that garage!

Wealth Warning

Remember, an overseas property will not preserve your 'normal' UK property business. A furnished holiday letting or a non-commercial letting (e.g. to your aunt for £1 a year) will not do either.

Another Wealth Warning

On page UKP1 of the tax return, you are asked to put an 'X' in Box 2 if you do not expect to receive any rental income in the next tax year. Completing this box may be seen as a strong indication that your UK property business has ceased.

I would therefore recommend leaving this box blank where you have rental losses carried forward unless you are absolutely certain that you will not have any UK rental income in the future. (Assuming that you are completing your tax return by the normal due date, you cannot yet know that you will not have any rental income in the next tax year anyway.)

4.12   OTHER PROPERTY INVESTMENT INCOME

Most forms of income derived from investments in land and property will be subject to Income Tax under the regime outlined in this chapter.

This will include tenant's deposits retained at the end of a lease and usually also any dilapidation payments received.

Since 2007, landlords in England and Wales have been required to hold tenant's deposits in escrow. A similar law was introduced in Scotland in 2012.

Whatever the legal position, it is important to include deposits retained within your rental income at the end of the lease, but not before. Refunded deposits should never be included in rental income.

Dilapidation payments may sometimes be regarded as a capital receipt instead if the landlord does not rent the property out again (e.g. if the landlord sells it or adopts it as their own home).

Some items are specifically excluded from treatment as property income, including:

- Any amounts taxable as trading income
- Farming and market gardening
- Income from mineral extraction rights

Wayleave (right of access) payments are, however, sometimes included as property income.

In the next section we will look at another important source of property income: lease premiums.

4.13 LEASE PREMIUMS

Premiums received for the granting of short leases of no more than 50 years' duration are subject to Income Tax. The proportion of the premium subject to Income Tax is, however, reduced by 2% for each full year of the lease's duration in excess of one year.

The part of the premium not subject to Income Tax falls within the Capital Gains Tax regime (see Section 6.34) and will be treated as a part disposal of the relevant property.

Example

Alexander owns the freehold to a property and grants a 12-year lease to Kenneth for a premium of £50,000. The lease exceeds one year by eleven years and hence 22% of this sum falls within the Capital Gains Tax regime. Alexander is therefore subject to Income Tax on the sum of £39,000 (i.e. £50,000 less 22%).

4.14 OVERSEAS LETTINGS

All of a taxpayer's commercially let overseas properties (with the exception of any furnished holiday lettings within the European Economic Area) are treated as a single business in much the same way as, but separate from, a UK property business.

A UK resident and domiciled taxpayer (see Section 3.7) with overseas lettings is taxed on this income under exactly the same principles as for UK lettings except:

   i)   Separate accounts will be required for properties in each overseas territory where any double tax relief claims are to be made.

   ii) Overseas furnished holiday lettings outside the European Economic Area are not included within the special regime applying to qualifying furnished holiday accommodation (as detailed in Section 8.15).

Prior to April 2009, all overseas furnished holiday lettings were excluded from the special regime applying to qualifying furnished holiday accommodation in the UK. At that point, however, the regime was extended to all qualifying property within the European Economic Area (see Appendix D) with retrospective effect. See Section 8.15 for further details.

Travelling expenses may be claimed when incurred wholly and exclusively for the purposes of the overseas letting business.

The UK tax treatment of losses arising from an overseas letting business is exactly the same as for a UK property business except, of course, that this is treated as a separate business from any UK lettings which the taxpayer has. Hence, again, for loss relief purposes, overseas property must be separated into three categories, as follows:

- Non-commercial overseas lettings (see Section 4.15)
- Furnished holiday lettings within the European Economic Area (see Section 8.15)
- Other overseas rental property (which I will refer to as 'normal' overseas property for the sake of illustration)

As before, the special rules outlined in Sections 8.15 and 4.15 apply to qualifying furnished holiday lettings within the European Economic Area and non-commercial overseas lettings respectively.

Losses arising on 'normal' overseas property are automatically set off against profits derived from other 'normal' overseas lettings or non-commercial overseas lettings, with the excess carried forward for set off against future 'normal' overseas rental profits. The same rule as set out in Section 4.11 applies to any capital allowances.

Where there are substantial 'normal' overseas rental losses carried forward, it will be worthwhile ensuring that this business continues.

The same principles as set out in Section 4.11 will apply here, except that, to continue the business, it is necessary to continue to have 'normal' overseas rental property.

Whilst the property must be let on a commercial basis and must be outside the UK, it can be in any other part of the world and need not be in the same country as the property which gave rise to the original rental losses. A loss made in Albania might conceivably be set off against a profit in Zanzibar!

As before, it is essential to remember that a qualifying furnished holiday letting property within the European Economic Area will not suffice to preserve rental losses from 'normal' overseas property.

4.15 NON-COMMERCIAL LETTINGS

Where lettings are not on a commercial or 'arm's length' basis, they cannot be regarded as part of the same UK or overseas property business as any commercial lettings which the taxpayer has. Profits remain taxable, but any losses arising may only be carried forward for set off against future profits from the same letting (i.e. the same property let to the same tenant).

Typically, this type of letting involves the lease of a property to a relative or friend of the landlord at a nominal rent, considerably less than the full market rent which the property could demand on the open market.

Where the tenant of such a non-commercial letting is a previous owner of the property (e.g. a parent of the landlord), the 'Pre-Owned Assets' Income Tax benefit-in-kind charge may apply to the benefit so received by the tenant. In many cases this will result in the tenant being charged Income Tax on the difference between the nominal rent which they pay and the full market rent.

4.16 NATIONAL INSURANCE ON PROPERTY INCOME

For details of National Insurance rates, etc., see Section 5.5 and Appendix A.

Property income is not classed as 'earnings' and hence Class 4 National Insurance should never be due on it. Any incidental trading income arising as part of the same business may, however, be subject to Class 4 National Insurance.

The position regarding Class 2 National Insurance is less clear as this is payable by any taxpayer aged between 16 and state pension age (see Section 5.5) who is in receipt of business income in excess of the 'small earnings exception' (see Appendix A).

Nonetheless, property income should not generally be regarded as 'business income' for National Insurance purposes and the vast majority of landlords should not, therefore, be subject to Class 2 National Insurance. This was confirmed in the 2003 tax case of 'Rashid v Garcia'.

Despite this, some HM Revenue and Customs offices have recently been seeking to collect Class 2 National Insurance from landlords. Part of the reason for this relates to the way in which landlords have registered for self-assessment with HM Revenue and Customs.

When registering for self-assessment, it is important for landlords with property income (as described in this chapter) to register as an 'individual with property income' and not as 'self-employed' or as a 'business'.

Notwithstanding any of the above, landlords aged between 16 and state pension age who have incidental trading income in excess of the 'small earnings exception' may again be subject to Class 2 National Insurance.

Chapter 5

How to Save Tax on a Property Trade

5.1   THE TAXATION OF PROPERTY TRADING INCOME

Where your property business is deemed to be a trade, such as property development or property dealing, you will be taxed under a different set of principles to those outlined in the previous chapter.

In this section, we will take a brief look at the major differences which you need to be aware of before we proceed to look at these and other issues in more detail throughout the rest of the chapter.

In this section and most of the remainder of this chapter we will be concentrating mainly on the trades of property development and property dealing. Property management, which does not normally involve the ownership of any property, is treated slightly differently again and we will look at this briefly in Section 5.9.

The major points to note are:

    i)   Properties held for development or sale are treated as trading stock rather than capital assets.

    ii)   Taxpayers with property trades may choose any calendar date as their accounting year end.

    iii)   Profits on property disposals are subject to both Income Tax and Class 4 National Insurance. Property traders must also pay Class 2 National Insurance.

    iv)   Most 'abortive' legal and professional fees should be allowed as incurred, as an Income Tax deduction.

    v)   A broader range of administrative expenditure will be claimable.

    vi)   Capital allowances will usually only be available on your own business's long-term assets.

    vii)   Trading losses may be set off against all of your other income and capital gains for the same tax year and the previous one (subject to the restrictions explained in Sections 3.11 and 5.10).

    viii)   The same trade may involve both properties in the UK and properties overseas.

ix) Non-resident individuals are taxed on a trade if it is managed in the UK. (For a UK resident but non-domiciled individual, a foreign-based property trade may be taxed on the remittance basis, with the usual potential drawbacks – see Section 8.23.)

x) Individuals with small trading businesses may elect to use the new 'cash basis' outlined in Section 5.11 from 2013/14 onwards.

5.2   PROPERTIES AS TRADING STOCK

The properties which you hold in the business for development and/or sale are not regarded as long-term capital assets. They are, instead, regarded as trading stock.

For tax purposes, all of your expenditure in acquiring, furnishing, improving, repairing or converting the properties becomes part of the cost of that trading stock.

Many of the issues we examined in Chapter 4 regarding the question of whether expenditure is revenue or capital therefore become completely academic. Most professional fees and repairs or improvement expenditure are treated as part of the cost of the trading stock in a property trade.

(As explained in Section 3.8, 'revenue expenditure' means expenditure deductible from income; capital expenditure is subject to different rules.)

The way in which trading stock works for tax purposes can be illustrated by way of an example.

Example

In November 2014, Camilla buys a property in Windsor for £260,000. She pays Stamp Duty Land Tax of £7,800 and legal fees of £1,450. Previously, in October, she also paid a survey fee of £750.

Camilla is a property developer and draws up accounts to 31· December each year. In her accounts to 31· December 2014, the Windsor property will be included as trading stock with a value of £270,000, made up as follows:

	£
Property purchase	*260,000*
Stamp Duty Land Tax	*7,800*
Legal fees	*1,450*
Survey fee	*750*

	270,000
	======

Points to Note

The important point to note here is that, whilst all of Camilla's expenditure is regarded as revenue expenditure, because she is a property developer, she cannot yet claim any deduction for any of it, because she still holds the property.

Example Continued

Early in 2015, Camilla incurs further professional fees of £10,000 obtaining planning permission to divide the property into two separate residences. Permission is granted in July and by the end of the year, Camilla has spent a further £40,000 on conversion work. In her accounts to 31· December 2015 the property will still be shown in trading stock, as follows:

	£
Costs brought forward	*270,000*
Additional professional fees	*10,000*
Building work	*40,000*

	320,000
	======

Camilla still doesn't get any tax relief for any of this expenditure.

By March 2016, Camilla has spent another £5,000 on the property and is ready to sell the two new houses she has created. One sells quickly for £185,000. Camilla incurs a further £3,500 in estate agent's and legal fees in the process. Camilla's taxable profit on this sale is thus calculated as follows:

	£	£
Sale proceeds		*185,000*
Less Cost:		
Total cost brought forward:	*320,000*	
Additional building costs:	*5,000*	

Trading Stock prior to sale of		
first property	*325,000*	

Allocated to property sold (50%):	*162,500*	
Add additional costs:	*3,500*	

		166,000

Profit on sale		*19,000*
		======

This profit will form part of Camilla's trading profit for the year ending 31 December 2016.

Points to Note

The additional building spend of £5,000 was allocated to trading stock as this still related to the whole property.

The legal and estate agent's fees incurred on the sale, however, were specific to the part which was sold and may thus be deducted in full against those sale proceeds.

In the example I have split the cost of trading stock equally between the two new houses. If the two new houses are, indeed, identical then this will be correct. Otherwise, the costs should be split between the two properties on a reasonable basis – e.g. by total floor area, or in proportion to the market value of the finished properties.

The latter approach would be the required statutory basis if these were capital disposals. Although it is not mandatory here, it might still be a useful yardstick.

The most important point, however, is that, even if Camilla fails to sell the second new house before 31 December 2016, her profit on the first new house will still be taxable in full.

There is one exception to this, as we shall now examine.

Net Realisable Value

Trading stock is generally shown in the accounts at its cumulative cost to date.

On this basis, Camilla's second house, if still unsold at 31 December 2016, would have a carrying value of £162,500 in her accounts.

If, however, for whatever reason, the market value of the property is less than its cumulative cost then, as trading stock, its carrying value in the accounts may be reduced appropriately.

Furthermore, since the act of selling the property itself will lead to further expenses, these may also be deducted from the property's reduced value in this situation. This gives us a value known in accounting terminology as the property's 'net realisable value'.

Practical Pointer

Trading stock should always be shown in the accounts at the lower of cost or net realisable value.

Example

The second new house in Windsor doesn't sell so quickly, so, in September Camilla decides to take it back off the market and build an extension on the back to make it a more attractive proposition to potential buyers.

Unfortunately, however, there are some problems with the foundations for the extension and the costs are more than double what Camilla had expected.

By 31ˢᵗ December, Camilla has spent £27,500 on the extension work and it still isn't finished. Her total costs to date on the second new house are thus £190,000.

Camilla's builder estimates that there will be further costs of £12,000 before the extension is complete and the property is ready to sell.

The estate agent reckons that the completed property will sell for around £200,000. The agent's own fees will amount to £3,000 and there will also be legal costs of around £750.

The net realisable value of the property at 31ˢᵗ December 2016 is thus:

	£	£
Market value of completed property		*200,000*
Less:		
Costs to complete	*12,000*	
Professional costs to sell	*3,750*	

		15,750

Net Realisable Value at 31/12/2016		*184,250*
		======

Since this is less than Camilla's costs to date on the property, this is the value to be shown as trading stock in her 2016 accounts.

The result of this is that Camilla will show a loss of £5,750 (£190,000 less £184,250) on the second house in her 2016 accounts. This loss will automatically be set off against her £19,000 profit on the first house.

By March 2017, the second house is ready for sale. Fortunately, there is an upturn in the market later in the year and Camilla manages to sell the property for £215,000 in October 2017.

Her actual additional expenditure on the extension work amounted to £11,800 and the professional fees incurred on the sale were actually £3,900.

Camilla's taxable profit on this property in 2017 is thus:

	£	£
Sale proceeds		*215,000*
Less:		
Value of trading stock brought forward, as per accounts:	*184,250*	
Additional building cost	*11,800*	
Professional fees on sale	*3,900*	

		199,950

Taxable profit in year to 31/12/2017		*15,050*
		======

Points to Note

When Camilla calculates her profit for 2017, she uses actual figures for everything which took place after 31· December 2016, her last accounting date (i.e. the sale price, the final part of the building work and the professional fees on the sale).

However, the property's net realisable value in the accounts at 31· December 2016 is substituted for all of the costs which Camilla incurred up until that date.

Hence, the apparent loss which Camilla was able to claim in 2016 effectively reverses and becomes part of her profits in 2017.

In this example, some of the actual figures turned out to be different to the estimates previously available. Taxpayers would generally be expected to use the most accurate figures available at the time that they are preparing their accounts.

In the case of sale price, however, this should be taken to mean an accurate estimate of the completed property's market value at the accounting date (i.e. 31· December 2016 in this example), rather than its actual eventual sale price.

5.3   WORK-IN-PROGRESS & SALES CONTRACTS

Generally, for speculative property developers, their trading stock, as we have seen, is valued at the lower of its cumulative cost to date or its net realisable value. However, if a contract for the sale of the property exists, the developer has to follow a different set of rules.

This is a complex area of accounting but, broadly speaking, the developer is required to value properties under development, for which a sale contract already exists, at an appropriate percentage of their contractual sale value. This is done by treating the completed proportion of the property as if it had already been sold.

The same proportion of the expected final costs of the development can be deducted from this notional sale. Any remaining balance of development costs is included in the accounts as 'work-in-progress', which is simply a term for trading stock which is only partly completed.

Example

Aayan is building a new house on a plot of land and has already contracted to sell it for £500,000. Aayan draws up accounts to 31ᵗ March each year and, at 31ᵗ March 2015, the new house is 75% complete. Aayan's total costs to date are £320,000, but he expects to incur a further £80,000 in order to complete the house.

Aayan will need to show a sale of £375,000 (75% of £500,000) in his accounts to 31ᵗ March 2015. He will, however, be able to deduct costs of £300,000, which equates to 75% of his anticipated final total costs of £400,000 (£320,000 + £80,000).

In other words, Aayan will show a profit of £75,000 in his accounts to 31ᵗ March 2015, which is equal to 75% of his expected final profit of £100,000.

The remaining £20,000 of Aayan's costs to date will be shown in his accounts at 31ᵗ March 2015 as work-in-progress.

During the following year, Aayan completes the property at an actual cost of £77,000.

His accounts for the year ending 31ᵗ March 2016 will show a sale of £125,000, i.e. the remaining 25% of his total sale proceeds of £500,000. From this, Aayan can deduct total costs of £97,000, which is made up of his £20,000 of work-in-progress brought forward and his actual costs in the year of £77,000.

This gives Aayan a development profit of £28,000 for the year ending 31ᵗ March 2016.

As we can see from the example, the effect of this accounting treatment is to accelerate part of the profit on the development. As there is no specific rule to the contrary, the tax position will also follow the accounting treatment, so that the developer is taxed on part of their property sale in advance.

It follows that the whole profit on a property for which a sales contract exists will need to be included in the developer's accounts once the property is fully completed.

Where this accounting treatment applies, the developer may nevertheless claim deductions to reflect:

- Any doubt over the purchaser's ability, or willingness, to pay
- Rectification work which is still to be carried out
- Administration and other costs relating to completion of the sale

Tax Tip

Individuals with total income over £150,000 in a tax year are subject to 'super tax': currently at a rate of 45%. The rate was 50% from 2010/11 to 2012/13 and may return to that level again in the near future if Labour win the General Election in May 2015.

The fact that general accounting standards may require developers to account for part of the profit on their property sales in an earlier accounting period may not, therefore, be an entirely bad thing.

This is worth bearing in mind when calculating how much profit should be accounted for in each accounting period.

Whilst accounting standards must be adhered to in principle, there is often some leeway regarding the exact amounts to be taken into account in practice. The more profit that falls into an accounting period where the developer has total income of less than £150,000 and is thus being taxed at 40%, the less there will be to be taxed in a later period at 45% or more.

5.4   ACCOUNTING DATE

As a property developer or dealer, you may choose any accounting date you like and do not have to stick with a 5ᵗ April year end. This provides some useful tax-planning opportunities.

For example, if you feel that you are generally likely to make more sales in the late Spring and Summer, a 30ᵗʰ April accounting date may be very useful.

Profits made on sales in May or June 2014 would then form part of your accounting profit for the year ending 30ᵗʰ April 2015. For tax purposes, this accounting period falls into the 2015/16 tax year, as it is generally the accounts year end date which determines when profits are taxable.

Under self-assessment, the Income Tax and National Insurance due on these profits would not therefore be payable until 31ˢᵗ January 2017, almost ***three years*** after you made the sales!

Early Years

There are special rules which apply in the first two or three years of a trading business which would lead to a different effect: sometimes more beneficial and sometimes less so.

Generally, in these early years, if your profit is static, or increasing, you will benefit from an accounting date early in the tax year, such as 30ᵗʰ April.

This usually results in some of your early profits being taxed twice (in two different tax years), but the tax on your later profits is effectively deferred by a year. You will ultimately get a deduction, known as 'overlap relief', for the profits which have been taxed twice, when you cease trading, or sometimes earlier if you change your accounting date.

If, however, you are starting on high profits and expect them to fall thereafter, then a 31ˢᵗ March or 5ᵗʰ April accounting date will generally be preferable.

Accounting periods ending during your first three tax years of trading can generally be of almost any duration. Thereafter, you are generally expected to prepare accounts for twelve month periods, unless you change your accounting date, as explained below.

Change of Accounting Date

You can change your accounting date at any time, although, for the change to be recognised for tax purposes, you cannot generally make a second change within five tax years of a previous change.

5.5   NATIONAL INSURANCE

Unlike a property investment business, the profits of a property trade are regarded as 'earnings' for National Insurance purposes.

This means that property dealers or developers operating on their own as sole traders, jointly with one or more other people, or in a more formal partnership structure, will be liable for Class 2 and Class 4 National Insurance.

Class 2

Most self-employed traders will be liable to pay Class 2 National Insurance at the rate of £2.75 per week for 2014/15. In practice, it will usually be collected via monthly direct debits of either £11.00 or £13.75, depending on the number of Sundays in the month.

Property trades are no exception, but there are other exceptions. Taxpayers are exempt from Class 2 National Insurance if they:

i) Have reached state pension age (see below) on or before the first day of the tax year,
ii) Are aged under 16, or
iii) Have profits below the 'small earnings exception' limit (£5,885 for 2014/15). This exemption must be applied for.

Subject to these exceptions, your Class 2 liability as a property trader will amount to a mere £143 per year.

"Big deal", I hear you say. Well, yes, it's true that Class 2 National Insurance is not exactly the most important tax issue you're going to face.

In many cases, however, it is the first, and for this reason HM Revenue and Customs now uses it as a means to police new unincorporated trading businesses. Registering for Class 2 National Insurance gets you into the tax system and, from then onwards, HM Revenue and Customs becomes your silent partner every step of the way!

Hence, unless you fall within one of the first two exceptions described above, you will need to register for payment of Class 2 National Insurance within three months from the end of the calendar month in which you commence your property trade.

Wealth Warning

Failure to register for Class 2 National Insurance within three months of the commencement of trading is subject to a penalty of £100. A hefty penalty indeed for an annual tax bill of only £143 – equivalent to around 70%!

In the case of a partnership or joint owners, each individual must register for Class 2 National Insurance. However, if any person is already paying Class 2 contributions due to some other existing source of self-employment trading income, there is no need to register again.

Class 4

Class 4 National Insurance is payable on trading profits at the rates set out in Appendix A. The profits on which the National Insurance is based are exactly the same trading profits as those calculated for Income Tax purposes.

For profits falling to be taxed in the tax year 2014/15, this has the result of giving most property traders with no other sources of income the following overall effective tax rates, combining Income Tax and Class 4 National Insurance:

Profits up to £7,956:	Nil
Profits between £7,956 and £10,000:	9%
Profits between £10,000 and £41,865:	29%
Profits between £41,865 and £100,000:	42%
Profits between £100,000 and £120,000:	62%
Profits between £120,000 and £150,000:	42%
Profits over £150,000:	47%

However, like Class 2, taxpayers are also exempt from Class 4 National Insurance if they:

i)   Have reached state pension age (see below) on or before the first day of the relevant tax year, or

ii) Are aged under 16 on the last day of the tax year.

National Insurance for Property Traders in Practice

To see the impact of National Insurance on property traders in practice, let's revisit an earlier example.

Example

In Section 3.4, we saw that Meera was paying a total of £3,827 in Income Tax under self-assessment for 2014/15.

Let us now assume that Meera is, in fact, a property developer and her £10,000 of property income is actually a property trading profit. In addition to her Income Tax bill, therefore, Meera will also be liable for Class 4 National Insurance of £184 (9% of £10,000 less £7,956), bringing her total self-assessment tax liability up to £4,011.

In fact, adding in Meera's £143 of Class 2 National Insurance will give her a total tax bill on her property profits of £4,154.

Taxpayers like Meera with both employment and self-employed trading income may end up paying more in National Insurance than the law actually demands.

This can arise where there is more than one source of earned income and the total income from all such sources exceeds the sum of:

i)	The upper threshold for the main rate of National Insurance (currently £41,865), and
ii)	The National Insurance primary threshold (currently £7,956)

For the 2014/15 tax year, the relevant sum is £49,821.

In such cases, taxpayers may apply for a refund of the excess National Insurance paid or, if they are able to foresee in advance that this situation is likely to arise, apply for a deferment of their Class 2 or Class 4 contributions.

Tax Tip

If you are already in receipt of other earnings and anticipate that your property trading profits will result in your total earnings for the tax year exceeding £49,821 you may wish to consider applying for deferment of National Insurance.

Remember that 'earnings' is generally restricted to employment income and self-employed or partnership trading income. It does not include pensions, rental income or other investment income.

State Pension Age

Taxpayers over state pension age on the first day of the relevant tax year are exempt from both Class 2 and Class 4 National Insurance. This includes taxpayers reaching state pension age on 6ᵗʰ April.

The current state pension age is 65 for men and somewhere between 62 and 63 for women. Broadly speaking, women now reach state pension age two months after 6ᵗʰ March 2010 for every month, or part month, after 5ᵗʰ April 1950 that they were born.

The Government is proposing to further increase the state pension age for both genders in the near future.

5.6   TRADING DEDUCTIONS: GENERAL

From 2013/14 onwards, some individuals or partnerships with small property trades may be able to elect to use the new 'cash basis' which we will look at in Section 5.11.

Apart from that, the basic principles outlined in Sections 3.8 and 3.9 continue to apply to the deduction of business expenditure from trading profits. Many of the points discussed in Chapter 4 will also remain relevant.

On the other hand, however, the different treatment of the profits arising on property sales in a trading scenario naturally creates some differences too!

As we already know, under general principles, expenditure must usually be 'revenue expenditure' if it is to be claimed for Income Tax purposes. As we have seen, however, this rule operates quite differently in the context of a property trade.

Expenditure on long-term assets for use in the trade will nevertheless continue to be capital in nature. Such assets might include:

- Office premises from which to run the trade
- Motor vehicles for use in the trade
- Computers
- Building tools and equipment

Capital allowances will be available on much of this expenditure as we shall see in Section 5.8.

Expenses incurred which are ancillary to the purchase of capital assets continue to be treated as capital expenditure also. Hence, whilst the legal fees incurred on the purchase of trading stock are a revenue expense, similar fees incurred on the purchase of the business's own trading premises will be capital in nature.

5.7   TRADING DEDUCTIONS: SPECIFIC AREAS

Most forms of business expenditure which meet the criteria outlined in Section 3.8 should be allowable as deductions from trading income. These will include the items which we covered in Section 3.9.

There are a few exceptions which are specifically disallowed, such as business entertaining and gifts. (Even here there can be exceptions to the exceptions.)

In this section, we will quickly look at some of the other main trading deductions to be considered in the specific context of a property trade. As in Chapter 4, however, this is certainly not meant to be an exhaustive list of potential trading expenses.

Interest and Other Finance Costs

Interest is allowable if it is incurred on funds used for the purposes of the trade. The question of where the borrowings are secured is generally irrelevant (although borrowings secured on the business's own trading premises will follow the same principles as set out in Section 4.4).

The treatment of other finance costs, such as loan arrangement fees, will generally follow the same principles.

However, where accounting principles dictate that a cost should be spread over the life of the loan, the tax relief will have to be spread over the same period.

Legal and Professional Fees

Legal fees and other professional costs incurred on the successful purchase or sale of properties classed as trading stock will be allowed as part of the cost of those properties in the computation of the profits arising on sale.

As explained previously, however, costs relating to the purchase or sale of the business's long-term assets remain capital expenses.

Other professional costs incurred year in, year out, in earning trading profits may include items such as debt collection expenses and accountancy fees. These costs are deductible as general overheads of the business.

Abortive Expenditure

In a property development or dealing trade, abortive costs such as survey fees, advertising or legal fees relating to unsuccessful transactions should be allowed as a trading expense.

This should also extend to the costs of any unsuccessful planning applications attempted in the course of the trade.

Training

The rule here is that expenses incurred in updating or expanding existing areas of knowledge may be claimed, but any costs relating to entirely new areas of knowledge are a personal capital expense.

Hence, if you are already a competent plumber but go on a plumbing course to learn the latest techniques in the industry then the cost of this course should be allowable.

The cost of the same course would, however, not be allowable if you knew nothing about plumbing.

Health & Safety

Notwithstanding the general rules given in Section 3.8, any expenditure on safety boots, hard hats and other protective clothing or equipment will be allowable.

This may sometimes extend to 'all-weather' clothing if the taxpayer spends all or part of their working life outdoors and does not use that clothing for any non-business purposes.

5.8   CAPITAL ALLOWANCES FOR PROPERTY TRADES

The basic principles of capital allowances were explained in Section 3.10. Items typically qualifying as 'plant and machinery' include the following:

- Building equipment and tools
- Computers
- Office furniture, fixtures and fittings
- Vans

In general terms, property developers are likely to have greater scope for claiming capital allowances than those with residential property investment businesses but possibly less scope than those with commercial property investments.

Property dealers and those with property management businesses will not usually be able to claim quite as many allowances, although the same principles continue to apply.

Capital allowances cannot generally be claimed on any expenditure which is included within trading stock.

Capital allowances are available on motor cars used in a property trade, as again detailed in Section 3.10.

5.9 PROPERTY MANAGEMENT TRADES

Most of the principles outlined in this chapter apply equally to property management trades. The biggest difference is the fact that these trades are unlikely to hold properties as trading stock.

Other than their own office premises, any properties held are likely to be investment properties and dealt with in accordance with Chapter 4 for tax purposes.

Staff costs are often a significant issue in a property management trade. The National Insurance consequences are examined in Section 7.14.

5.10 TRADING LOSSES

As stated in Section 5.1, trading losses can be set off against your other income and capital gains for the same tax year and the previous one. The same loss can only ever be relieved once.

Where trading losses are being set off against income (not capital gains), the relief is subject to the tax relief 'cap' discussed in Section 3.11. This does not apply where the losses are being set off against earlier profits from the same trade, or to the extent that the losses include 'overlap relief' (see Section 5.4).

In addition, a 'non-active sole trader' may only claim tax relief against his or her other income and gains for a maximum of just £25,000 of trading losses each year.

Personally, I find the term 'non-active sole trader' to be as much of a contradiction in terms as an 'honest politician', but it is taken to mean someone who spends less than ten hours per week engaged in trading activities. Sadly, this restriction may hit many part-time property developers and other property traders. For those whose business activities average only just over the ten hours per week threshold, it will make sense to keep diaries or other time records to demonstrate the hours spent on the business.

Loss relief is also barred altogether for the trading losses of a 'non-active sole trader' as a result of arrangements made for tax avoidance purposes.

5.11 THE CASH BASIS

From 2013/14 onwards, individuals and partnerships with small trading businesses may elect to be taxed under a new 'cash basis'. The 'cash basis' will generally only be available where the annual turnover (i.e. sales) of the business does not exceed the VAT registration threshold (currently £81,000); although those already using the 'cash basis' may continue to do so provided their turnover does not exceed twice the VAT registration threshold (i.e. £162,000 at current rates).

Businesses electing to use the 'cash basis' will be taxed simply on the difference between business income received during the year and business expenses paid during the year, instead of under normal accounting principles (the 'accruals basis' – see Section 3.8).

Where the 'cash basis' is being used, there will be no distinction between 'revenue expenditure' and 'capital expenditure' (see Section 3.8) and capital expenditure may simply be claimed as it is paid, except that:

- Expenditure on the purchase of cars will not be allowed on a cash basis. Motor expenses must continue to be claimed under one of the two alternative methods described in Section 3.9.
- The cost of vans or motor cycles may be claimed on a cash basis, but if the purchase cost is claimed in this way, the mileage allowances described in Section 3.9 will not be available.
- Capital expenditure may only be claimed under the 'cash basis' where it would otherwise normally be eligible for capital allowances as 'plant and machinery' (see Section 5.8).

In addition to these restrictions, businesses using the 'cash basis' will be limited to a maximum claim of £500 per year in respect of interest on cash borrowings.

Losses arising under the 'cash basis' can only be carried forward for set off against future profits from the same trade and will not be eligible for the loss relief described in Section 5.10.

In view of these restrictions, and the turnover limits described above, it seems unlikely that the 'cash basis' will benefit many property developers or dealers. A few property management businesses might perhaps benefit but, again, the restrictions on loss relief and interest relief will often make the 'cash basis' unattractive.

Chapter 6

How to Save Capital Gains Tax

6.1 THE IMPORTANCE OF CAPITAL GAINS TAX

Although its impact is not as immediate as that of Income Tax, Capital Gains Tax is nevertheless perhaps the most significant tax from a property investor's perspective (though not those who are classed as property developers or property dealers, as we have already seen in Chapter 5).

Most property investments will eventually lead to a disposal and every property disposal presents the risk of a Capital Gains Tax liability arising and reducing the investor's after-tax return drastically. Paradoxically, however, Capital Gains Tax is also the tax which presents the greatest number and variety of tax-planning opportunities. We will be examining some of these further in Chapter 8.

Most readers will be aware that major changes to the Capital Gains Tax regime took place in June 2010, including the introduction of a new 'higher rate' of Capital Gains Tax at 28%. This followed hard on the heels of another set of major changes which took place in April 2008.

In this chapter, we will be examining the current Capital Gains Tax regime and taking a detailed look at how it affects property investors and other people disposing of property.

We will not be looking at the previous Capital Gains Tax regimes applying in earlier years. Any readers who still need to deal with Capital Gains Tax calculations relating to disposals in 2010/11 or earlier should refer to earlier editions of this guide.

Before we look at the current regime, it is worth recalling how Capital Gains Tax developed and looking at how it affects property investors today.

6.2 THE DEVELOPMENT OF CAPITAL GAINS TAX

Capital Gains Tax was introduced by Harold Wilson's first Labour Government in 1965 in order to combat a growing trend for avoiding Income Tax by realising capital gains, which at that time were mostly tax free.

The high inflation of the late 1970s and early 1980s brought about a significant change after 31· March 1982, with the introduction of indexation relief. This was designed to exempt gains which arose purely through the effects of inflation.

In 1987, Capital Gains Tax moved from a flat rate of 30% to a system which was to last for 21 years, where gains were taxed at the taxpayer's top rate of Income Tax. The next major change came in 1988 with so-called 're-basing' which exempted all pre-31· March 1982 gains.

The Conservative Governments of the late 1980s and early 1990s continued to introduce a number of Capital Gains Tax exemptions and reliefs, including some very generous holdover reliefs for reinvestment of gains, as well as substantial increases in the annual exemption.

By 1997, the Conservatives were set well on a path towards the abolition of Capital Gains Tax and a return to the pre-1965 situation. However, that year saw the election of Tony Blair's 'New Labour' Government and those with potential capital gains awaited the seemingly inevitable crackdown.

When it came down to it though, Blair's 'New Labour' seemed to recognise that the immense changes in British society over nearly two decades of Conservative Government meant that capital gains were no longer the perquisite of the privileged few, but were very much a part of life for a significant proportion of the population in the modern economy of investment and enterprise.

Over the next few years, Gordon Brown, as Chancellor, introduced, and then refined, his brainchild: taper relief. This was designed to reward long-term investment by progressively reducing the effective rate of Capital Gains Tax as investments were held over a longer period. Eventually, we reached the point where the effective Capital Gains Tax rate on most commercial property was just 10% after just two years of ownership.

Then, suddenly, the golden days were over and, in April 2008, new Chancellor Alistair Darling abolished both taper relief and indexation relief and, after 21 years, took us back to a flat rate system: this time at 18%. The 'inevitable crackdown' had finally arrived, ten years later than expected.

The General Election in May 2010 led to the UK's first Coalition Government since the Second World War. Almost immediately, the new Government announced that it would be significantly increasing the rate of Capital Gains Tax. So we awaited another 'inevitable crackdown'!

That 'crackdown' came in June 2010 when 'new kid on the block' George Osborne took us into a 'two tier' Capital Gains Tax system by introducing a 'higher rate' of 28%.

Finally then, now that every major political party has 'stuck their oar in', we find ourselves lumbered with a Capital Gains Tax system where there is no protection against the effects of inflation and no reward for long-term investment.

In fact, what the latest change actually means is that, when you do hold property as a long-term investment, inflation alone is likely to push you into a higher tax rate!

And this makes understanding the tax system, the reliefs available, and the planning opportunities they give rise to, more important than ever!

6.3   WHO PAYS CAPITAL GAINS TAX?

Capital Gains Tax is ***currently*** payable in the UK by:

i)   UK resident individuals
ii)   UK resident trusts
iii)   Non-resident persons trading in the UK through a branch, agency or other permanent establishment
iv)   Companies and other 'non-natural' persons owning residential dwellings worth more than £2m located in the UK

Apart from persons falling under (iii) or (iv) above, non-UK residents are currently usually exempt from UK Capital Gains Tax.

However, proposed changes which are currently expected to come into force from 6ᵗʰ April 2015 will mean that non-UK residents will be subject to UK Capital Gains Tax on gains arising on UK residential property from that date onwards. This will reduce, but not eliminate, the potential benefits of being, or becoming, non-UK resident and we will look at this subject in more detail in Sections 8.32 and 8.33.

The £2m limit under (iv) above is also to be reduced from 6ᵗʰ April 2015; and reduced again from 6ᵗʰ April 2016. We will look at this in more detail in Section 7.15.

In this chapter, however, we will be concentrating mainly on category (i) above: UK resident individuals investing in property.

Individuals who are UK resident and UK domiciled are liable for Capital Gains Tax on their worldwide capital gains. Individuals who are UK resident but not UK domiciled remain liable for Capital Gains Tax on capital gains arising from the disposal of UK property but may opt to only be liable for Capital Gains Tax on 'foreign' capital gains if and when they remit their disposal proceeds back to the UK (see Section 8.23 for further details).

The tax concepts of residence and domicile were examined in Section 3.7. We will also take a closer look at the rules on residence in Section 8.32.

6.4 CAPITAL GAINS TAX RATES

Capital Gains Tax is currently paid at three rates:

- 10% where entrepreneurs' relief is available
- 18% on other gains made by basic rate taxpayers
- 28% on other gains made by higher rate taxpayers

Entrepreneurs' relief is seldom available to property investors, except in the case of furnished holiday letting properties (see Section 8.15). The relief may, however, be highly valuable to property developers, property dealers and those with property management businesses and we will therefore look at it in detail in Section 6.28.

The 'Higher Rate' of Capital Gains Tax

The higher rate of 28% applies to capital gains made by an individual to the extent that:

i)   Their total taxable income for the tax year (after deducting their personal allowance and any other available deductions), plus

ii)   Their total taxable capital gains arising during the tax year,

exceeds the Income Tax basic rate band (£31,865 for 2014/15).

Individuals who have sufficient income to fully utilise their basic rate band therefore now pay Capital Gains Tax at 28% on all their capital gains.

Basic rate taxpayer individuals pay Capital Gains Tax at 18% on the first part of their capital gains until their basic rate band is exhausted. Thereafter, any further gains are taxed at 28%.

In all cases, the rate applying is reduced to 10% where entrepreneurs' relief is available (see Section 6.28).

Tax Tip

The rate of Capital Gains Tax you pay is linked to the amount of income you have in the tax year.

This means that you may be able to reduce your Capital Gains Tax bill by ensuring that your gains fall into a tax year in which you have a lower level of income.

We will take a closer look at the potential savings arising in Section 8.30.

Example

Boudicca is a property investor with several 'buy-to-let' investments. In December 2014, she sells a property and realises a gain of £49,000.

Boudicca's taxable income for 2014/15 is £26,865, meaning that £15,000 of her basic rate band remains available (£41,865 - £26,865).

Boudicca deducts her annual exemption of £11,000 (see Section 6.29) from the £49,000 gain, leaving a taxable gain of £38,000. The first £15,000 is taxed at 18% and the remainder at 28%, giving her a Capital Gains Tax bill of:

£15,000 x 18% =	*£2,700*
£23,000 x 28% =	*£6,440*
Total	*£9,140*

Allocating the Annual Exemption and Capital Losses

Taxpayers are free to allocate their annual exemption (see Section 6.29) and any capital losses which they have available (see Section 6.33) in the most beneficial manner.

This facility has little impact, except in the case of someone with both gains which are eligible for entrepreneurs' relief and gains which are not. In these circumstances, it will make sense to allocate the annual exemption and any available capital losses to the gains which are **not** eligible for entrepreneurs' relief.

Effective Capital Gains Tax Rates

The Capital Gains Tax rates described above apply to the taxable capital gain, not the total gain. The **effective** rates of Capital Gains Tax can vary tremendously, depending on the circumstances.

6.5   WHAT IS A CAPITAL GAIN?

A capital gain is the profit arising on the disposal, in whole or in part, of an asset, or an interest in an asset.

Put simply, the gain is the excess obtained on the sale of the asset over the price paid to buy it. (However, as we will see in the sections that follow, matters rarely remain that simple.)

Sometimes, however, assets are held in such a way that their disposal gives rise to an Income Tax charge instead. The same amount of gain cannot be subject to both Income Tax and Capital Gains Tax.

Where both taxes might apply, Income Tax takes precedence, so that no Capital Gains Tax arises. (There is little comfort in this, as Income Tax will generally be charged at a higher rate than Capital Gains Tax and is not subject to any of the various Capital Gains Tax reliefs.)

The most common type of asset sale which gives rise to an Income Tax charge, rather than Capital Gains Tax, is, of course, a sale in the course of a trade. In other words, where the asset is, or is deemed to be, trading stock.

If a person buys sweets to sell in their sweet shop, those sweets are quite clearly trading stock and the profits on their sale must be subject to Income Tax and not Capital Gains Tax. This is pretty obvious because there are usually only two things you can do with sweets: eat them or sell them.

Properties, however, have a number of possible uses. A property purchaser may intend one or more of several objectives:

a) To keep the property for personal use, either as a main residence or otherwise.
b) To provide a home for the use of family or friends.
c) To use the property in a business.
d) To let the property out for profit.
e) To hold the property as an investment.
f) To develop the property for profit.
g) To sell the property on at a profit.

Where objectives (f) and/or (g) are the sole purpose behind the purchase of the property, this will render the ultimate gain on the property's sale a trading profit subject to Income Tax as explained in Chapter 5.

All of the other objectives listed above make the property a capital investment subject only to Capital Gains Tax.

This is simple enough where the objectives described in (f) and (g) above are either completely absent or the sole purpose of the purchase.

Naturally though, in the majority of cases, objective (g) is present to some degree. This does not necessarily render the gain on the property's sale a trading profit subject to Income Tax. This would only be the case where (g) is the sole or overwhelmingly dominant objective behind the purchase.

In practice, there is often more than one objective present when a property is purchased and objectives (f) and (g) may exist to a lesser or greater extent. In many cases, the correct position is obvious but, in borderline situations, each case has to be decided on its own merits.

Some of the key factors to consider are described in Section 2.9. Here though, it is perhaps worth looking at a few more detailed examples.

Example 1

James bought a house in 1990 which he used as his main residence throughout his ownership. In 2005 he built an extension, which substantially increased the value of the house. He continued to live in the house until eventually selling it in 2014.

This is clearly a capital gain because James carried on using the house as his private residence for several years after building the extension. Furthermore, the house will be exempt from Capital Gains Tax, as it was James' main residence throughout his ownership.

Example 2

Charles bought a house in 1990 and used it as his main residence for five years. In 1995, he moved into a new house and converted the first one into a number of flats. Following the conversion, Charles let the flats out until he eventually sold the whole property in 2014.

Charles has also realised a capital gain as the conversion work was clearly intended as a long-term investment. (Charles would have a partial exemption under the main residence rules.)

Example 3

William, a wealthy man with three other properties, bought a derelict barn in 2013. He developed it into a luxury home. Immediately after the development work was complete, he put the property on the market and sold it in 2015.

This would appear to be a trading profit subject to Income Tax. William simply developed the property for profit and never put it to any other use. (But see Section 2.9 regarding the importance of the investor's original intentions.)

Example 4

Anne bought an old farmhouse in 2014. She lived in the property for three months and then moved out while substantial renovation work took place. After the work was completed, she let it out for six months.

Halfway through the period of the lease she put the property on the market and sold it with completion taking place the day the lease expired.

This is what one would call 'borderline'. Anne has had some personal use of the property, and has let it out, but she has also developed it and sold it after only a short period of ownership. This case would warrant a much closer look at all of the circumstances. It should be decided on the basis of Anne's intentions but who, apart from Anne herself, would ever know what these truly were?

Such a case could go either way. The more Anne can do to demonstrate that her intention had been to hold the property as a long-term investment, the better her chances of success will be. Her personal and financial circumstances will be crucial. For example, if she had got married around the time of the sale, or had got into unexpected financial difficulties, which had forced her to make the sale, then she might successfully argue for Capital Gains Tax treatment.

Note that, just because the profit arising on the sale of an asset is a capital gain, this does not necessarily mean that it is subject to Capital Gains Tax.

A number of assets may be exempt from Capital Gains Tax, including motor cars, medals and Government securities.

Most importantly for property investors, the taxpayer's only or main residence is also exempt and we will return to this in Section 6.13.

The bad news is that no relief is allowed for capital losses derived from exempt assets.

6.6   WHEN DOES A CAPITAL GAIN ARISE?

For Capital Gains Tax purposes, a disposal is treated as taking place as soon as there is an unconditional contract for the sale of an asset.

The effective disposal date may therefore often be somewhat earlier than the date of completion of the sale.

This is an absolutely vital point to remember when undertaking any Capital Gains Tax planning.

Example

Aidan completes the sale of an investment property on 8 April 2015. However, the unconditional sale contract was signed on 1 April 2015.

Aidan's sale therefore falls into the tax year ending on 5 April 2015 and any Capital Gains Tax due will be payable by 31 January 2016.

The effective acceleration of Aidan's Capital Gains Tax bill is bad enough, but what if he had also emigrated on 3 April 2015?

Where the contract remains conditional on some event beyond the control of the parties to it, then the sale is not yet deemed to have taken place for Capital Gains Tax purposes. The most common scenarios here are for the sale to be conditional on:

- The granting of planning permission
- Completion of a satisfactory survey
- Approval of finance arrangements

Many English investors who have travelled north of the border get caught out by the Scottish system where the conclusion of missives generally creates an unconditional binding contract.

6.7 SPOUSES AND CIVIL PARTNERS

There are a number of cases where, although an asset is held as a capital investment, there is deemed to be no gain and no loss arising on a disposal.

The most important instance of this is that of transfers between spouses or registered civil partners. The effect of this is that these transfers are **totally exempt** from Capital Gains Tax.

The exemption comes into force on the date of marriage or registration and thereafter continues to apply for the whole of any tax year during any part of which the couple are living together as spouses or civil partners.

Separated couples remain 'connected persons' (see Section 6.9) even after the exemption has been lost. Divorced couples only become unconnected persons for tax purposes once more following the grant of a decree absolute.

Wealth Warning

If the couple separate, the exemption ceases to apply at the end of the tax year of separation.

6.8 THE AMOUNT OF THE GAIN

Having established that a gain is subject to Capital Gains Tax, we now need to work out how much the gain is.

As stated in Section 6.5 above, the essence of this is that the gain should be the excess obtained on the sale of the asset over the price paid to buy it. However, in practice, thanks to the many complexities introduced by tax legislation over almost 50 years, there are a large number of other factors to be taken into account.

Hence, one has to slightly amend the definition of a capital gain to the following:

'A capital gain is the excess of the actual or deemed proceeds arising on the disposal of an asset over that same asset's base cost.'

A shorter version of this is: Gain = Proceeds Less Base Cost

The derivation of 'Proceeds' is examined in Section 6.9 below. 'Base Cost' is covered in Sections 6.10 and 6.11.

6.9 PROCEEDS

In most cases, the amount of 'Proceeds' to be used in the calculation of a capital gain will be the actual sum received on the disposal of the asset. However, from this, the taxpayer may deduct incidental disposal costs in order to arrive at 'net proceeds', which is the relevant sum for the purposes of calculating the capital gain.

Incidental disposal costs which may be deducted from sales proceeds include any expenditure incurred wholly and exclusively for the purpose of making the sale, such as legal fees, estate agents' commission, advertising costs and the cost of producing a 'Seller's Pack'.

Professional fees incurred for the preparation of valuations required for Capital Gains Tax purposes may also be included in disposal costs.

Example

In July 2014, George sells a house for £375,000. In order to make this sale, he spent £1,500 advertising the property, paid £3,750 in estate agents' fees and paid £800 in legal fees. His net proceeds are therefore £368,950 (£375,000 LESS £1,500, £3,750 and £800).

Now this sounds very simple, but it is not always this easy.

Exceptions

There are a number of cases where the proceeds we must use in the calculation of a capital gain are not simply the actual cash sum received. Three of the most common exceptions are set out below.

Exception 1 – Connected persons

Where the person disposing of the asset is 'connected' with the person acquiring it, the open market value of the asset at the time of the transfer must be used in place of the actual price paid (if any). Connected persons include:

- Husband, wife or registered civil partner (but note that no gain usually arises in such transfers)
- Mother, father or remoter ancestor
- Son, daughter or remoter descendant
- Brother or sister
- Mother-in-law, father-in-law, son-in-law, daughter-in-law, brother-in-law or sister-in-law
- Business partners
- Companies under the control of the other party to the transaction or of any of his/her relatives as above
- A trust where the other party to the transaction, or any of his/her relatives as above, is a beneficiary

Example

Mary sells a property to her son Philip for £500,000, at a time when its market value is £800,000. She pays legal fees of £475.

Mary will be deemed to have received net sale proceeds of £800,000 (the market value). The legal fees she has borne are irrelevant, as this was not an 'arm's-length' transaction.

Exception 2 – Transactions not at 'arms-length'

Where a transaction takes place between 'connected persons' as above, there is an automatic assumption that the transaction is not at 'arm's-length' and market value must be substituted for the actual proceeds.

There are, however, other instances where the transaction may not be at 'arm's-length', such as:

- The transfer of an asset from one partner in an unmarried couple to the other
- A sale of an asset to an employee
- A transaction which is part of a larger transaction
- A transaction which is part of a series of transactions

The effect of these is much the same as before – the asset's market value must be used in place of the actual proceeds, if any.

The key difference from Exception 1 is that it's the circumstances involved in the transaction which determine whether or not it's at 'arm's-length', rather than there being an automatic assumption that it is not at 'arm's-length' simply because of the relationship between the parties.

Example

John has a house worth £200,000. If he sold it for this amount, he would have a capital gain of £80,000.

Not wishing to incur a Capital Gains Tax liability, John decides instead to sell the house to his friend Richard for £120,000. However, John only does this on condition that Richard also gives him an interest-free loan of £80,000 for an indefinite period.

The condition imposed by John means that this transaction is not at 'arm's-length'. The correct position is therefore that John should be deemed to have sold the house for £200,000 and still have a capital gain of £80,000.

Wealth Warning

Where a person has disposed of an asset at less than an 'arm's length' value, whether to a connected person or not, there is a danger of Income Tax charges arising if the original owner later makes any use of, or derives any benefit from, the transferred asset.

Inheritance Tax charges may also arise if the original owner dies within seven years of making the transfer.

Exception 3 – Non-cash proceeds

Sometimes all or part of the sale consideration will take a form other than cash. The sale proceeds to be taken into account in these cases will be the market value of the assets or rights received in exchange for the asset sold.

Example

Matilda is an elderly widow with a large house. She no longer needs such a large house, so she offers it to Stephen, who lives nearby with his wife and young children. Rather than pay the whole amount in cash, Stephen offers £150,000 plus his own much smaller house, which is worth £200,000.

Matilda incurs legal fees of £2,400 on the transaction and also pays Stamp Duty Land Tax of £2,000 to acquire Stephen's house. 75% of the legal fees are for the sale of her old house and the rest for the purchase of Stephen's house.

Matilda's total sale proceeds are £350,000. This is made up of the cash received plus the market value of the non-cash consideration received, i.e. Stephen's house. Matilda may deduct her incidental costs of disposal from her proceeds in her Capital Gains Tax calculation. This is unaltered by the existence of non-cash consideration: the transaction has still taken place on 'arm's-length' terms.

However, as far as her legal fees are concerned, it is only the element which relates to the disposal of her old house (£1,800) which may be deducted.

The element relating to the purchase of Stephen's house will be treated as an acquisition cost of that house, as will the Stamp Duty Land Tax Matilda paid.

Hence, the net sale proceeds to be used in Matilda's Capital Gains Tax calculation are £348,200 (£350,000 LESS £1,800).

6.10 BASE COST

The 'Base Cost' is the amount which may be deducted in the Capital Gains Tax calculation in respect of the cost of the asset being disposed of. The higher the base cost, the less Capital Gains Tax payable!

In most cases, the basic starting point will be the actual amount paid. To this may be added:

- Incidental costs of acquisition (e.g. legal fees, Stamp Duty Land Tax, etc)
- Enhancement expenditure (e.g. the cost of building an extension to a property)
- Expenditure incurred in establishing, preserving or defending title to, or rights over, the asset (e.g. legal fees incurred as a result of a boundary dispute)

Interest payable and any other costs associated with raising finance, i.e. mortgaging or re-mortgaging the property, cannot be included in the base cost. For a rental property, these are dealt with as described in Section 4.4.

Survey fees will often be part of the cost of raising finance, especially if the survey was only carried out at the lender's request. However, a survey carried out at the purchaser's own instigation prior to their making, or finalising, any offer for the property may be claimed as an acquisition cost for Capital Gains Tax purposes.

Any costs claimed for Income Tax purposes cannot also be claimed for Capital Gains Tax purposes. As explained in Section 4.6 however, any expenditure on newly acquired rental properties which is not allowed for Income Tax purposes on the grounds that it is capital in nature should be allowed for Capital Gains Tax purposes on the disposal of that property.

Example

George (remember him from Section 6.9?) bought a house in July 1984 for £60,000. He paid Stamp Duty of £600, legal fees of £400 and removal expenses of £800.

Shortly after moving into the house, George spent £3,000 on redecorating it. £1,800 of this related to one of the bedrooms, which was in such a bad state of repair that it was unusable. The remainder of the redecorating expenditure merely covered repainting and wallpapering the other rooms in the house.

In March 1985, George's neighbour erected a new fence a foot inside George's back garden, claiming this was the correct boundary. George had to take legal advice to resolve this problem, which cost him £250, but managed eventually to get the fence moved back to its original position.

In October 1987, the house's roof was badly damaged by hurricane-force winds. The repairs cost £20,000, which, unfortunately, George's insurance company refused to pay, claiming he was not covered for an 'Act of God'.

In May 1995, George did a loft conversion at a cost of £15,000, putting in new windows and creating an extra bedroom. Unfortunately, however, he had not obtained planning permission and, when his neighbour filed a complaint with the council, George was forced to restore the loft to its original condition at a further cost of £8,000.

In August 1998, George had the property extended at a cost of £80,000. He also incurred professional fees of £2,000 obtaining planning permission, etc.

When George eventually sold the property in July 2014 for £375,000, his base cost for the house for Capital Gains Tax purposes was made up as follows:

- Original cost - £60,000
- Incidental costs of acquisition - £1,000 (legal fees and Stamp Duty, but not the removal expenses, which were a personal cost and not part of the capital cost of the property)
- Enhancement expenditure - £1,800 (restoration of the 'unusable' bedroom; the remaining redecoration costs are not allowable, however, as the other rooms were already in a fit state for habitation and George's expenditure was merely due to personal taste, rather than being a capital improvement)
- Expenditure incurred in defending title to the property - £250 (the legal fees relating to his neighbour's new fence)
- Further enhancement expenditure - £82,000 (the cost of the new extension, including the professional fees incurred to obtain planning permission)

Total base cost: £145,050

Notes to the Example

i. If the house were George's only or main residence throughout his ownership, his gain would, in any case, be exempt from Capital Gains Tax. However, we are assuming that this is not the case here for the purposes of illustration.

ii. The cost of George's roof repairs do not form part of his base cost. This is not a capital improvement, but repairs and maintenance expenditure of a revenue nature.

iii. Neither the cost of George's loft conversion, nor the cost of returning the loft to its original condition, form part of his base cost. This is because enhancement or improvement expenditure can only be allowed in the capital gains calculation if the relevant 'improvements' are reflected in the state of the property at the time of the sale.

iv. Based on net proceeds of £368,950 (Section 6.9), George has a capital gain of £223,900 (£368,950 - £145,050) before any applicable reliefs.

Wealth Warning

An additional point to note under (iii) above is that enhancement or improvement expenditure is only deductible if still reflected in the state of the property at the date of <u>completion</u> of the sale.

6.11 BASE COST – SPECIAL SITUATIONS

As with 'Proceeds', there are a number of special situations where base cost is determined by reference to something other than the amount paid for the asset. The major exceptions fall into two main categories:

- The asset was not acquired by way of a 'bargain at arm's length'.
- The asset was acquired before 1· April 1982.

Inherited Assets

All assets are 'rebased' for Capital Gains Tax purposes on death. Hence, the base cost of any inherited asset is determined by reference to its market value at the date of the previous owner's death.

Note that, whilst transfers on death are exempt from Capital Gains Tax, they are, of course, subject to Inheritance Tax. See the Taxcafe.co.uk guide *'How to Save Inheritance Tax'* for further details.

Example 1

Albert died on 20· January 2001, leaving his holiday home, a cottage on the Isle of Wight, to his son Edward. The property was valued at £150,000 for probate purposes. In August 2002, Edward had a swimming pool built at the cottage at a cost of £40,000. He sold the cottage for £287,000 in March 2015.

Edward's base cost is £190,000. His own improvement expenditure (£40,000) is added to the market value of the property when he inherited it. Any expenditure incurred by Albert is, however, completely irrelevant.

Assets acquired from spouses

As explained in Section 6.7, when an asset is transferred between spouses, that transfer is treated as taking place on a no gain/no loss basis. In the case of a subsequent disposal, the transferee spouse effectively takes over the transferor spouse's base cost.

Example 2

Henry bought a house for £350,000 in 1999. He spent £100,000 on capital improvements and then gave the house to his wife Katherine in 2001. Katherine had the house extended in 2003 at a cost of £115,000 and eventually sold it in 2014 for £750,000.

Katherine's base cost for the house is £565,000. This includes both her own expenditure and her husband's.

The 'no gain/no loss' rule does not apply in the case of a transfer on death, when the inheritance rules explained above take precedence.

Note that, where the transferor spouse originally acquired the property before April 1998 and transferred it to the transferee spouse before 6 April 2008 (but not on death), the indexation relief which the transferor would have been entitled to at that time (if they had actually sold the property) is added to the transferee spouse's base cost.

Example 3

Andrew bought a house for £100,000 in March 1985. In March 2008, he transferred the house to his wife Sarah. If Andrew had actually sold his house before 6 April 2008, he would have been entitled to indexation relief at 75.2% (see Appendix B), i.e. £75,200. Sarah's base cost for the house is therefore £175,200.

Details of indexation relief rates which apply to a transfer between spouses which took place any time between 1 April 1998 and 5 April 2008 (inclusive) are given in Appendix B.

Where a part share in a property has been transferred between spouses, the same principles continue to apply to the part which was transferred.

Assets acquired from connected persons or by way of a transaction not at 'arm's length'

As explained in Section 6.9 above, the transfer of an asset to a connected person is deemed to take place at market value. The market value rule also applies in other circumstances where an asset has not been acquired by way of a transaction at 'arm's length'. ('Exception 2' in Section 6.9 above provides further guidance on circumstances where this might arise.)

In both cases, for the person acquiring an asset by way of such a transfer, the market value at that date becomes their base cost.

Assets with 'held-over gains'

From 6 April 1980 to 13 March 1989, it was possible to elect to hold over the gain arising on the transfer of any asset by way of gift.

Since then, it has only been possible to hold over gains arising on transfers by way of gift which are:

- Transfers of business assets, or
- Chargeable transfers for Inheritance Tax purposes.

Even in these cases, the ability to hold over a gain was blocked for transfers into a 'settlor-interested trust' after 9ᵗ December 2003.

A 'settlor-interested trust' means a trust which includes the transferor, their spouse or, from 6ᵗ April 2006, a dependent minor child of the transferor, as one of its beneficiaries.

The base cost of an asset which was subject to a hold-over election when it was acquired is reduced by the amount of the held over gain.

Example 4

In January 1989, Arthur gave Camelot to his son Lancelot. Camelot's market value at that date was £100,000 and Arthur and Lancelot jointly elected to hold over Arthur's gain of £70,000. In 1990 Lancelot had the property extended at a cost of £55,000.

Lancelot's base cost for Camelot is £85,000 (£100,000 LESS £70,000 PLUS £55,000 – his own enhancement expenditure is still added on, as normal).

Where the held over gain arose before 6ᵗ April 2008, the amount held over will be the gain arising after any indexation relief.

Hence, as with transfers between spouses (see above), where the transferor originally acquired the property before April 1998, the transferee's base cost will effectively include the indexation relief which the transferor would have been entitled to if they had actually sold the property.

Note that, whilst gains held over before 6ᵗ April 2008 were calculated after indexation relief, any taper relief which the transferor would have been entitled to is simply ignored.

In other words, a held over gain preserved the transferor's indexation relief but their taper relief was lost.

Assets acquired for non-cash consideration

Where an asset was acquired for non-cash consideration, its base cost will be determined by reference to the market value of the consideration given.

Example 5

Julius bought a house in Chester from his friend Brutus. Instead of paying Brutus in cash, Julius gave him his ancient sword collection, which he had recently had valued at £125,000. Julius's base cost in the Chester house will therefore be £125,000.

Assets acquired before 1 April 1982

Where an asset was acquired before 1 April 1982, its market value at 31 March 1982 must be substituted for its original cost.

Example 6

Alfred bought a house for £20,000 in December 1981. He also incurred legal fees and other incidental costs of £1,000. The house's market value on 31 March 1982 was £19,750.

Alfred's base cost in the house is therefore £19,750. His original purchase cost and all other costs incurred prior to 1 April 1982 are ignored.

Where a property was originally acquired before 1 April 1982, any enhancement or improvement expenditure may only be included where it was incurred after 31 March 1982.

6.12 CAPITAL GAINS TAX RELIEFS

It is at this point in the Capital Gains Tax calculation, after deducting the base cost, that most reliefs and exemptions may be claimed, where appropriate. These include:

- Principal private residence relief (for taxpayers selling their current or former only or main residence). This is covered in detail from Section 6.13 onwards.
- Private letting relief (where a property which is eligible for principal private residence relief has also been let out as private residential accommodation). This is covered in detail in Section 6.14.
- Relief for reinvestment of gains in Enterprise Investment Scheme shares or Seed Enterprise Investment Scheme shares (see Sections 8.19 and 8.21 for further details).
- Holdover relief on gifts of business assets.
- Holdover relief in respect of chargeable transfers for Inheritance Tax purposes.
- Holdover relief on transfer of a business to a limited company.
- Rollover relief on replacement of business assets (see Section 8.28).

All these reliefs are claimed before entrepreneurs' relief, capital losses and the annual exemption. We shall look at these last three items later, but first we must look at the most important relief for the residential property investor: principal private residence relief.

6.13   THE PRINCIPAL PRIVATE RESIDENCE EXEMPTION

Most people are well aware that the sale of their own home is exempt from Capital Gains Tax. In technical terms, this is known as the 'Principal Private Residence' exemption. What is less well known is just how far principal private residence relief can extend, especially when combined with other available exemptions and reliefs.

Each unmarried individual, and each legally married couple, is entitled to the principal private residence exemption in respect of their only or main residence. The principal private residence exemption covers the period during which the property was their main residence PLUS their last eighteen months of ownership.

Example

Elizabeth bought a flat for £180,000 in January 2007. In January 2013, she married Philip and moved out of her flat. In July 2014, she receives an offer to sell the flat for £220,000, but is concerned about her potential tax liability.

Elizabeth needn't worry. If she makes this sale, her gain on the flat will be exempt under principal private residence relief. The first six years of her ownership are exempt because it was then her main residence and the last eighteen months because it was a former main residence.

Disposals Prior to 6th April 2014

For disposals which took place prior to 6ᵗʰ April 2014, the additional final period of ownership which gains automatic exemption was three years instead of eighteen months.

This longer exemption period will apply to any disposals which are deemed to have taken place before 6ᵗʰ April 2014. As explained in Section 6.6, it is the date of unconditional contract which is regarded as the disposal date for Capital Gains Tax purposes. Hence, a property sale which was completed at a later date would still be eligible for the longer exemption period if there was an unconditional contract prior to 6ᵗʰ April 2014.

But what if the property has been let out?

Because the principal private residence exemption always extends to the final eighteen months of ownership of a former main residence, letting the property out for up to eighteen months after you have moved out of it will make no difference to your Capital Gains Tax position if you then go ahead and sell the property. (Income Tax is, of course, due on the rental profits.)

If you retain the property for more than eighteen months after it ceased to be your main residence, you will no longer be fully covered by the principal private residence exemption alone. However, at this point, as long as the property is being let out as private residential accommodation, another relief will come into play: private letting relief. We will examine this further in the next section.

Does The Property Have to Become Your Main Residence Immediately on Purchase to Qualify?

To be *fully* exempt from Capital Gains Tax under the principal private residence exemption alone, the property will generally need to become your only or main residence immediately on purchase; or perhaps shortly afterwards, under the circumstances outlined in Section 6.17.

Practical Pointer

Technically, a property which was your only or main residence at some point and which you then sold no more than eighteen months after purchase should also be fully covered by principal private residence relief. However, such a short period of ownership could lead to doubts over whether the property was genuinely purchased as a capital asset (see Sections 2.9 and 6.5 for further details).

Similarly, a very short period of occupation of the property can lead to doubts over whether it is genuinely a private residence (see Section 8.9).

Nonetheless, where there are good reasons for the short period of ownership and residential occupation, full relief may remain available.

If you don't fit one of the situations above, you won't be fully covered by principal private residence relief alone.

However, you will still get a proportional relief based on your period of occupation of the property as your main residence, plus last eighteen months of ownership.

When combined with other reliefs, this will often be enough to prevent any Capital Gains Tax from arising, although you may have to report the gain on your tax return.

Example

Alexander buys a house in June 2008 as an investment and lets it out for two years. In June 2010, he sells his own home and moves into the new house. Alexander then sells the new house in June 2014.

Alexander has used the house as his own main residence for four years out of six and hence he will be exempt on four sixths of his capital gain by virtue of principal private residence relief.

Alexander cannot benefit from the additional 'last eighteen months of ownership' rule because he was living in the house at the time anyway. The extra eighteen month period is not given in addition to an exemption for actual occupation during the same period. (He will, however, still be eligible for some private letting relief, as we shall see in the next section.)

This is why when people ask me "do you need to live in the house at the beginning to get principal private residence relief?" I always answer "no, but it works best that way".

Tax Tip

Occupying a property as your only or main residence will produce the best result if this is not within the last eighteen months of your ownership.

What If Part Of The Property Is Unused?

The principal private residence exemption is not restricted merely because part of the house is left vacant and unused. Restrictions will apply, however, where part of the house is used for some purpose other than the owner's own private residential occupation.

6.14   PRIVATE LETTING RELIEF

In the previous section, we saw how the principal private residence exemption often extends to cover the capital gain on a former only or main residence for a further eighteen months after it ceases to be your own home.

Additionally, however, any property which qualifies as your only or main residence at any time during your period of ownership, and which you have, at some time, let out as private residential accommodation, will also qualify for private letting relief.

Private letting relief will also apply where you let out a part of your home.

Private letting relief is given as the lowest of:

i) The amount of gain already exempted under principal private residence relief,
ii) The gain arising as a consequence of the letting, and
iii) £40,000.

Usually, it is the lower of (i) and (iii), especially if the property has been let out ever since the owner ceased to reside in it.

Example

Since marrying Philip in January 2013, Elizabeth has been renting her flat out. She turned down the July 2014 offer, but in January 2022 she receives an offer of £260,000. Again, she is concerned about her potential tax liability.

Elizabeth still has nothing to worry about. As before, a total of seven and a half years of her ownership is exempt under principal private residence relief. Her total gain over 15 years is £80,000. Half of this (7½ out of 15) is covered by principal private residence relief, leaving £40,000, which is covered by private letting relief.

Hence, Elizabeth still has no Capital Gains Tax liability on her flat!

Bayley's Principal Private Residence Relief Law

The general rule here is that a gain of up to £80,000 is covered until at least 2N + 3 years after you first bought the property. 'N' is the number of years that it was your own main residence, not counting the last eighteen months of ownership.

In Elizabeth's case 'N' was 6, so 2N + 3 is 2 x 6 + 3 = 15 years of exemption!

Multiple Sales of Former Homes

The £40,000 private letting relief limit described above applies to every property which has been your only or main residence at any time during your ownership. Hence, even if you were to sell two or more former homes during the same tax year, you would still be entitled to up to £40,000 of private letting relief on each property.

What if the property was let out <u>before</u> it became your main residence?

Any property which qualifies for partial exemption under principal private residence relief, and which has also been let out as private residential accommodation at <u>any time</u> during the taxpayer's ownership, is also eligible for private letting relief.

Hence, although in our example we have been looking at a <u>former</u> main residence, which is subsequently let out, private letting relief will apply equally in a case where a property is let out first and then subsequently becomes the owner's main residence.

If, in the latest example, Elizabeth had instead rented her flat out from 2007 to 2009, then lived in it as her main residence for six years before continuing to rent it out again, the result would have been exactly the same.

(Note that Elizabeth's flat would have had to be Philip's main residence too after they got married, as a married couple are only allowed one main residence for principal private residence relief purposes.)

As we have already seen though, there is no additional benefit to be derived from the extension to the principal private residence exemption for a former main residence's last eighteen months of ownership if, in fact, it is still your main residence throughout that time in any case.

We left Alexander in just this sort of situation in Section 6.13. How will private letting relief operate in his case?

Example

Alexander, as we know, had a rented property from 2008 to 2010 which he then lived in as his own main residence from 2010 to 2014.

His total capital gain was £180,000 and four sixths of this was covered by the principal private residence exemption.

This leaves him with a gain of £60,000. He will be able to claim private letting relief of £40,000, leaving a taxable gain of just £20,000.

Even this may not be the end of the story for Alexander, as he will probably still have his annual exemption to reduce his taxable gain still further (see Section 6.29). This would reduce his taxable gain to just £9,000 (£20,000 - £11,000), giving him a Capital Gains Tax bill somewhere between £1,620 (18%) and £2,520 (28%). Even at the most, this is still just 1.4% of his total gain of £180,000.

6.15 PLANNING WITH PRINCIPAL PRIVATE RESIDENCE RELIEF

In our first example in Section 6.14, Elizabeth managed to make a tax-free capital gain of £80,000 despite living in her flat for only six years out of a total of fifteen and she didn't even need to use her annual exemption. This remarkable result arose due to the powerful combination of reliefs available for a former main residence.

These reliefs are invaluable to both those with a former home they now wish to sell and those who wish to plan for future tax-free capital growth.

Things were not quite so rosy for Alexander and he did end up with a tax bill after only six years of ownership, despite living in the property for four years.

To some extent, this shows how much better the principal private residence exemption works if you move into the property as your main residence immediately on purchase.

However, Alexander's effective tax rate of just 1.4% on his £180,000 gain still shows how the combination of reliefs available on a property occupied as your main residence at any time during your ownership frequently operates to eliminate most, if not all, of any taxable capital gain.

Planning Ahead

The examples in the previous two sections demonstrate how the principal private residence exemption and its associated reliefs can be used to great effect to allow a taxpayer to invest in property with little or no exposure to Capital Gains Tax. This subject is covered in depth in Chapter 8 later in the guide.

6.16 GARDENS AND GROUNDS

There have been a large number of cases before the Courts over the question of whether the 'grounds' of a house, including some of the subsidiary outbuildings, are covered by the principal private residence exemption.

In the usual situation, where a house has a reasonably normal sized garden and perhaps a shed, a garage or other small outbuildings, there is no doubt that the entire property is covered by the principal private residence exemption.

Naturally, we are talking here only of the situation where there is no use of any of the property other than private residential occupation.

Where the whole property is let out at some point, so that private letting relief also applies, the garden and 'modest' grounds continue to be covered by the relevant reliefs in the same way as already outlined in the previous sections.

The general rule for grounds is that these are deemed to form a normal part of the property where they do not exceed half a hectare (1.235 acres) in area (including the area on which the house itself stands). Beyond this, it is necessary to argue that the additional space is required 'for the reasonable enjoyment of the dwelling-house as a residence'.

What does this mean? Well, unfortunately, this is one of those rather enigmatic answers which judges love to give and which can only be decided on an individual case-by-case basis.

The whole situation changes once any part of the property is used for any other purpose. Here the position differs for buildings or gardens and grounds.

For gardens and grounds, they will obtain the same exemptions that are due on the house itself as long as they are part of the 'private residence' at the time of sale.

For subsidiary buildings, it becomes necessary to apportion any gain arising between the periods of residential occupation and the periods of non-residential use.

Example

Lady Jane has a large house with grounds totalling half a hectare in area. For several years, she leased half her grounds to a neighbouring amusement park for use as a car park.

Within the half of her grounds let to the amusement park there is a small outbuilding. Whilst she was letting the space to the amusement park, this outbuilding was used as the parking attendant's hut.

In 2006, the amusement park gave up its lease over Lady Jane's grounds and she hired a landscape gardener to restore them. The outbuilding reverted to its previous use as a storage shed for garden equipment.

In 2014, Lady Jane sold the entire property. Apart from the lease of the car park, the whole property had been used as her main residence throughout her ownership.

Lady Jane's main house and her entire grounds will be fully covered by the principal private residence exemption. However, the element of her gain relating to the outbuilding must be apportioned between the periods of private use and the period of non-residential use. The non-residential element of the gain will be chargeable to Capital Gains Tax.

Tax Tip

Lady Jane may have been better off demolishing the outbuilding prior to the sale of her house. No part of her gain would then have related to this building and her entire gain would have been covered by the principal private residence exemption. Naturally, it is only worth doing this if demolishing the building does not impact on the whole property's sale price by more than the amount of the potential tax saving.

Wealth Warning

Unlike the house itself, the principal private residence exemption does not extend to unused outbuildings or gardens and grounds and <u>actual use</u> for private residential purposes is required.

6.17   DELAYS IN OCCUPYING A NEW HOME

Many people buy a 'run-down' property and then embark on substantial renovation works before occupying it as their own main residence. In other circumstances, a planned move may be held up by unforeseen delays in selling the existing home.

The tax rules cater for this and the principal private residence exemption specifically extends to cover any period of up to one year in which the taxpayer cannot occupy a newly acquired property due to either:

i)   An unavoidable delay in selling their old property, or
ii) The need to await the finalisation of renovation or construction work on the new property.

During this period, it is possible for both the old and new properties to simultaneously be covered by the principal private residence exemption. Of course, the scope for claiming this exemption is lost if the new property is being used for some other purpose between purchase and initial occupation as the taxpayer's main residence. (Although private letting relief could apply to this period in appropriate circumstances.)

Under exceptional circumstances, HM Revenue and Customs may allow this initial period to be extended to up to two years. This extension is not granted lightly and is reserved for genuine cases of delay caused by factors beyond the taxpayer's control. You would also be expected to have done everything in your power to facilitate the property being ready for your occupation within the original one year period.

If the delay in occupation extends beyond the first year or beyond any additional period which HM Revenue and Customs permit, then the principal private residence exemption is lost for the whole of the period prior to occupation of the property.

The initial period allowed for the renovation of property also applies to a new property which you have built on a vacant plot of land.

In both cases the property or land must be bought with the intention of adopting it as your main residence and must not be used for any other purpose prior to occupation.

6.18   TEMPORARY ABSENCES

The principal private residence exemption remains available in full for certain temporary periods of absence, as follows:

i)   Any single period of up to three years, or shorter periods totalling no more than three years, regardless of the reason,

ii)   A period of up to four years when the taxpayer or their spouse is required to work elsewhere by reason of their employment or their place of work, and

iii)   A period of any length when the taxpayer or their spouse is working in an office or employment whose duties are all performed outside the UK.

These temporary absences are only covered by the principal private residence exemption if:

a)   Neither the taxpayer nor their spouse have any interest in any other property capable of being treated as their main residence under the principal private residence exemption (this restriction is broader than it may seem – see Section 6.21),

b)   The taxpayer occupies the property as their main residence for a period before the absence period, and

c)   Either:
   • The taxpayer occupies the property as their main residence for a period after the absence period, or
   • In the case of absences under (ii) or (iii) above, the taxpayer or their spouse is prevented from resuming occupation of the property following their absence by reason of their place of work or a condition imposed by their contract of employment which requires them to reside elsewhere.

A condition imposed on an employee under (c) above needs to be a reasonable condition required to secure the effective performance of the employee's duties.

6.19   DEPENDENT RELATIVES

A property occupied before 6ᵗ April 1988 by a 'dependent relative', as their main residence, may be covered by the principal private residence exemption. For this purpose, a 'dependent relative' must be either

a) The taxpayer's widowed, separated or divorced mother or mother-in-law, or
b) Another relative who is either elderly or dependent on them by reason of ill-health or disability. HM Revenue and Customs classes anyone over the current male state pension age of 65 as 'elderly'.

Where the qualifying 'dependent relative' commenced occupation of the property as their main residence prior to 6ᵗ April 1988, their entire period of continuous occupation provides principal private residence relief in exactly the same way as if it had been the taxpayer's main residence for that same period. This includes relief for the last eighteen months of ownership (or three years in the case of a disposal which took place before 6ᵗ April 2014).

If the dependent relative moves out of the property after 5ᵗ April 1988, however, any subsequent re-occupation of the property will not be counted.

Properties qualifying for principal private residence relief due to the occupation of the property by a dependent relative as explained above will also qualify for private letting relief under the same principles as set out in Section 6.14.

This provides opportunities for further tax-free capital growth if the property is retained as a rental property after the dependent relative ceases occupation.

6.20   PROPERTIES HELD IN TRUST

A trust is a separate legal entity in its own right for tax purposes and here the principal private residence exemption is no exception. The exemption extends to a property held by a trust when the property is the only or main residence of one or more of the trust's beneficiaries.

However, from 10 December 2003, the principal private residence exemption is not available on a property held by a trust if a hold-over relief claim was made on the transfer of that property into the trust.

In some cases this may lead to a difficult decision:

- Decline to make a hold-over relief claim at the outset and pay some Capital Gains Tax immediately, or

- Make the hold-over relief claim and risk paying a great deal more Capital Gains Tax on the eventual sale of the property.

In essence, one has to weigh up the prospective current tax bill against the ultimate tax potentially arising in the future.

Properties with held over gains which were already held in trust before 10 December 2003 are still eligible for principal private residence relief in respect of any periods of occupation by a beneficiary as their only or main residence prior to that date. The additional eighteen month period of relief at the end of the trust's ownership does not, however, apply in these circumstances.

Similar restrictions apply where a hold over relief claim has been made when a property was transferred out of a trust.

Once again, principal private residence relief cannot be claimed on a subsequent disposal of that property by the transferee.

Despite these restrictions, trusts can still be used as a useful mechanism to obtain principal private residence relief on properties occupied by adult children or other friends and relatives. We will return to this subject later, in Section 8.13.

Trusts also have their own annual exemption. This is generally half the amount of an individual's annual exemption (see Section 6.29), but must be further reduced where the same person has transferred assets into more than one trust.

Subject to any available reliefs (including entrepreneurs' relief), trusts pay Capital Gains Tax at the single flat rate of 28%.

6.21   WHAT IS A RESIDENCE?

Before we go any further, it is worth pausing to consider what we mean when we refer to a property as a taxpayer's residence.

As we will see in the next section, we are sometimes concerned with situations where a taxpayer has more than one residence.

One of these will be their main residence and will qualify for principal private residence relief.

But no property can be a **_main_** residence until it is **_a_** private residence of that individual taxpayer or married couple.

A residence is a dwelling in which the owner habitually lives. Whilst it needs to be habitual, however, their occupation of the property might still be occasional and short.

Example

Constantine owns a small cottage in Pembrokeshire but lives and works in London. Constantine bought the Pembrokeshire cottage as a holiday home, but he only manages to visit it about two or three times each year, when he will typically stay for the weekend. Despite the rarity of Constantine's visits to his cottage, it nevertheless qualifies as his private residence.

Some actual physical occupation of the property (including overnight stays) is necessary before it can be a residence. Constantine's situation is probably just about the minimum level of occupation which will qualify.

'Dwelling' means a property suitable for occupation as your home and can include a caravan or a houseboat. It will not, however, include a plainly unsuitable property such as an office, a shop or a factory. (Although there are flats over shops and offices which are dwellings!)

To 'live' in a property means to adopt it as the place where you are based and where you sleep, shelter and have your home. For these purposes, the Capital Gains Tax regime does not make any distinction between property in the UK and property overseas, so a foreign property may also be classed as the owner's residence where appropriate.

Some other use of a property at other times, when not occupied as the taxpayer's private residence, does not necessarily prevent it from qualifying as a residence. If such a property were to be treated as your main residence though, there would be a proportionate reduction in the amount of principal private residence relief available.

Example

On 1∙ April 2005, Bonnie bought a small cottage on Skye for £100,000. For the next ten years, she rented the cottage out as furnished holiday accommodation for 48 weeks each year and occupied it herself for the remaining four weeks.

Bonnie's regular occupation of the cottage is enough to make it a residence. In this example we are also going to assume that it is her main residence throughout her ownership.

On 1· April 2015, Bonnie sells the cottage for £204,000, realising a total capital gain of £104,000. For the eight and a half year period from 1· April 2005 to 1· October 2013, Bonnie is only entitled to principal private residence relief on 4/52nds of her capital gain, reflecting her own private use of the property. However, as usual, Bonnie is entitled to full relief for the last eighteen months of her ownership.

Bonnie's capital gain amounts to £10,400 per year (£104,000/10), so her total principal private residence relief is therefore as follows:

£10,400 x 8½ x 4/52 =	*£6,800*
£10,400 x 1½ =	*£15,600*

Total relief:	*£22,400*
	======

In addition to this, Bonnie will also be entitled to private letting relief of £22,400 and possibly also her annual exemption of £11,000. Assuming that the latter exemption is available in full, her taxable capital gain would thus be reduced to £48,200.

(Bonnie might also be entitled to several other reliefs and we will therefore return to this example in Section 8.15.)

In this example, Bonnie is still able to treat the cottage as her private residence, even though she is renting it out as holiday accommodation. However, where a property is rented out for longer periods under a lease, it cannot be regarded as the owner's residence during the period of the let.

A residence for Capital Gains Tax purposes must also be a property in which the taxpayer has a legal or equitable interest. A legal interest in a property means any form of ownership, sole or joint, including freehold, leasehold, commonhold, or the tenancy of a property rented under a lease.

An equitable interest in a property is less easy to define. Generally it must mean some sort of right over the property itself and not merely an ability to reside in it. Hence, for example, if an individual stays rent free with family or friends, they are occupying the property under a gratuitous licence and they clearly have no equitable interest.

Occupation of property may also be under contractual licence, such as staying in a hotel, hostel, guest house or private club. This also does not give the guest any equitable interest in the property.

An unmarried partner in a co-habiting couple may perhaps have an 'equitable interest' in the couple's home when it is owned wholly by the other partner, although this particular point has not yet been tested in the courts in connection with Capital Gains Tax.

For married couples, all of the principles regarding residences and main residences must be applied to the couple as a single unit.

Hence, for example, if William owns a property in Brixham which he has never visited, but his wife Mary stays there regularly, then that property must be counted as a private residence of the couple.

If an individual or married couple has only one property which qualifies as a private residence, then that property must be their main residence for Capital Gains Tax purposes. Indeed, HM Revenue and Customs' own Capital Gains manual sets out the principle that where an individual's main home is occupied under licence, but they also own another residence, the residence which that individual owns must be regarded as their main residence for Capital Gains Tax purposes.

However, once an individual or married couple has more than one eligible private residence, we will need to work out which one is their main residence.

6.22 SECOND HOMES

As already stated, each unmarried individual and each legally married couple can generally only have one main residence covered by the principal private residence exemption at any given time. Many people, however, have more than one private residence.

When someone acquires a second (or subsequent) private residence they may, at any time within two years of the date that they first occupy the new property as a residence, elect which of their properties is to be regarded as their main residence for the purpose of the principal private residence exemption (but see the 'Major Wealth Warning' at the end of this section regarding the potential withdrawal of this facility in the near future).

The election must be made in writing, addressed to 'Her Majesty's Inspector of Taxes' and sent to the taxpayer's tax office (see Section 1.6). An unmarried individual must sign the election personally in order for it to be effective. A married couple must both sign the election.

There is no particular prescribed form for the election, although the following example wording would be suitable for inclusion:

'In accordance with section 222(5) Taxation of Chargeable Gains Act 1992, [I/We] hereby nominate [Property] as [my/our] main residence with effect from [Date*].'

* - The first such election which an individual or a married couple makes in respect of any new combination of residences will automatically be treated as coming into effect from the beginning of the period to which it relates – i.e. from the date on which they first occupied that new combination of residences. It is this first election for the new combination of residences to which the two-year time limit applies.

However, once an election is in place, it may subsequently be changed, by a further written notice given to the Inspector under the same procedure, at any time. Such a new election may be given retrospective effect, if desired, by up to two years. We will take a closer look at the possible benefits of this in Chapter 8.

Example

Alfred lives in a small flat in Southampton where he works. In September 2009 he also bought a house on the Isle of Wight and started spending his weekends there. In August 2011, Alfred realised that his island house had appreciated in value significantly since he bought it. His small mainland flat had not increased in value quite so significantly. He therefore elected, before the expiry of the two-year time limit, that his island house was his main residence.

In 2014 Alfred sells the Isle of Wight house at a substantial gain, which is fully exempted by principal private residence relief. Alfred's flat will not be counted as his main residence from September 2009 until the time of sale of his island house. However, should he sell the flat, his final eighteen months of ownership will be covered by the principal private residence exemption.

Tax Tip

As soon as Alfred sold his Isle of Wight house, he should have submitted a new main residence election nominating the Southampton flat as his main residence once more, with effect from a date eighteen months previously. This would give an extra eighteen months of principal private residence exemption on the flat, whilst leaving the Isle of Wight house fully exempt.

In fact, where the annual exemption or other reliefs are available, it might be worth backdating the new main residence election a little further (up to two years).

Regardless of any election, however, a property may only be a main residence for principal private residence relief purposes if it is, in fact, the taxpayer's own private residence. Hence, a property being let out cannot be covered by the principal private residence exemption whilst it is being let. (It could nevertheless still attract private letting relief if it were the taxpayer's main residence at some other time.)

Furthermore, if one of a taxpayer's residences ceases to be occupied by them as a private residence (e.g. because it is let out or sold), any main residence election which has been made will cease to apply, even an election in favour of a different property!

Wealth Warning

A new election is required every time the taxpayer, or married couple, has a new combination of two or more private residences. Where a third residence is acquired, for example, a new election must be made. Remember that a property may qualify as a residence whenever the taxpayer or their spouse has *any* legal or equitable interest in it, no matter how small.

Where, however, the number of private residences reduces to one, no election is required as the sole remaining residence must now be the main residence.

In the absence of a valid election, the question of which property is the taxpayer's main residence has to be determined on the facts of the case. Often the answer to this will be obvious but, in borderline cases, HM Revenue and Customs may determine the position to the taxpayer's detriment. Clearly then, it is always wise to make the election!

The factors to be considered when determining which property was a taxpayer's main residence for any given period not covered by an election, include:

- The address given on the taxpayer's tax return.
- The address shown on other correspondence, utility bills, bank statements, etc.
- Where a mortgage was obtained over a property before 6· April 2000, whether mortgage interest relief (MIRAS) was claimed.
- Whether the mortgage over a property was obtained on the basis that it was the taxpayer's main home.
- The security of tenure (leasehold, freehold, etc) held over each residence.
- How each residence is furnished.
- Where the taxpayer's family spend the majority of their time.
- Where the taxpayer is registered to vote.
- The location of the taxpayer's place of work.

As always, a married couple have to be considered as a single unit for this purpose.

Each factor above is not conclusive in its own right but will contribute to the overall picture of which property may properly be regarded as the main residence.

In the previous section we considered the issue of whether a property was occupied under licence or whether an equitable interest existed. Where a taxpayer has only one residence in which they have a legal or equitable interest, a main residence election will not be valid. (Although, in certain limited circumstances HM Revenue and Customs may still honour such an election made before 16 October 1994.)

My advice, however, is that whenever there is any possibility that a taxpayer may have two or more eligible private residences they should make a main residence election.

If this election proves to be invalid, no harm is done and the property in which the taxpayer has a legal or equitable interest will automatically be treated as their main residence.

Major Wealth Warning!

Current Government proposals suggest that the facility to make main residence elections may be withdrawn from 6 April 2015 onwards.

Where possible, anyone with a second home should consider making a suitable election while they still can. The property must have been in use as the owner's private residence during the period covered by the election.

Tax Tip

If the two year period for making an election has expired, a new one can be opened up in a number of ways, such as:

- Acquiring an additional private residence
- Selling the main home and moving elsewhere
- Renting out one of the properties for a short period and then re-occupying it as a private residence thereafter

6.23   HOMES ABROAD

The principal private residence exemption applies in exactly the same way when the taxpayer or their spouse has a private residence overseas. The exemption applies to the taxpayer's main residence, not, as some people have mistakenly thought to their cost, their main UK residence.

Any new private residence acquired overseas will have exactly the same implications for any main residence elections as detailed in the previous section.

6.24   JOB-RELATED ACCOMMODATION

In many occupations, it is sometimes necessary, or desirable, for the taxpayer to live in accommodation specifically provided for the purpose. Examples include:

- Caretakers
- Police officers (in some rural areas)
- Pub landlords
- Members of the clergy
- Members of the armed services
- Teachers at boarding schools
- The Prime Minister and the Chancellor of the Exchequer

For people in this type of situation, the principal private residence exemption may be extended to a property which they own and which they eventually intend to adopt as their main residence.

In these circumstances, the principal private residence exemption will thus cover their own property during the period that they are living in 'job-related accommodation', despite the fact that their own property is not their residence at that time and even whilst they are letting out that property.

This provides an exception to the general rule that there must be some actual physical occupation of a property for it to be eligible for principal private residence relief.

This treatment can also be extended to a property owned by the spouse of a person living in job-related accommodation, which the couple eventually intend to adopt as their main residence.

If a taxpayer in job-related accommodation has a property which might qualify as a main residence under these rules but also has another residence, such as a holiday home, for example, they can use a main residence election to determine which property is given the principal private residence exemption.

The election will also be appropriate where the taxpayer has some legal or equitable interest in the job-related accommodation itself.

6.25 WHAT IF PART OF YOUR HOME IS NOT PRIVATE?

Whenever any part of your home is put to some use other than your own private residential occupation, you are inevitably putting your principal private residence exemption at risk. In the next two sections, we will look at the most common types of 'other use' and their tax implications.

One fundamental principle to note, however, is that if any part of your home is used exclusively for purposes other than your own private residential occupation throughout the period when that property qualifies as your main residence, then that part will not be eligible for any principal private residence relief at all.

Private letting relief does extend to a part of a main residence which has never been used privately by the owner, where appropriate; although there is sometimes some resistance on this point from HM Revenue and Customs.

Hence, to maximise your principal private residence relief claim and to avoid any potential dispute over private letting relief, I would always recommend making some private use of every part of the property at some time whilst it is your main residence.

6.26 LETTING OUT PART OF YOUR HOME

Taking a Lodger

HM Revenue and Customs generally accepts that taking in one individual lodger does not necessitate any restriction to the principal private residence exemption. In this context, a 'lodger' is someone who, whilst having their own bedroom, will otherwise live as a member of the taxpayer's household.

As a general rule, where 'rent-a-room' relief is available for Income Tax purposes, or would be if the rent were lower (see Section 4.10), the principal private residence exemption is unlikely to be affected.

Other lettings within the same 'dwelling'

Where a part of the house is let out under other circumstances, the principal private residence exemption will be restricted. However, private letting relief is available to cover this restriction in very much the same way as it applies to the letting out of the whole property (subject to the points raised in the previous section).

Example

Robert, a higher rate taxpayer, bought his five-storey house for £200,000 in 1998. From March 2008 to March 2014 he let the top two floors out as a flat. He then resumed occupation of the whole house, before selling it in September 2014 for £650,000.

Robert's total gain of £450,000 is covered by the principal private residence exemption as follows:

Lower three floors: The gain of £270,000 (three fifths of the total) is fully covered by the principal private residence exemption.

Upper two floors: The gain of £180,000 is covered by the principal private residence exemption from 1998 to 2008 AND for the last eighteen months of Robert's ownership, a total of 11½ years out of 16. Hence, £129,375 of this gain is exempt, leaving £50,625 chargeable.

Robert can then claim private letting relief equal to the lowest of:

> *i)   The amount of principal private residence exemption on the <u>whole</u> property: £399,375 (i.e. £270,000 PLUS £129,375),*
> *ii) The gain arising by reason of the letting: £50,625, or*
> *iii) £40,000*

The relief is thus £40,000, leaving Robert with a gain of only £10,625. Assuming he has not used his 2014/15 annual exemption of £11,000 elsewhere, this will exempt the remaining part of his gain, leaving him with no Capital Gains Tax to pay at all!

Now, all that Robert probably did was to fit a few locks in order to separate the flat from his own home. As a result, re-occupying the whole property was a simple matter and when he came to sell it, it remained a single 'dwelling' for tax purposes.

The situation would have been quite different, however, if he had carried out extensive conversion work in order to create a number of separate dwellings and we will examine the position arising in those circumstances in Section 8.11.

Adult Placement Carers

Any occupation of part of your home by another person under an adult placement scheme is disregarded for principal private residence relief purposes.

6.27 USING PART OF YOUR HOME FOR BUSINESS PURPOSES

Where any part of the property is used **exclusively** for business purposes, the principal private residence exemption is not available for that part of the property for the relevant period.

Where the exclusive business use covers the entire period that the property is the taxpayer's main residence, the exemption for the final eighteen months of ownership will also be withdrawn for this part of the property.

The effect on the principal private residence exemption is the same whether part of the property is being used exclusively in the taxpayer's own business or is being rented out for use in someone else's. However, where it is the taxpayer's own trading business which is concerned, then this part of the property becomes 'business property' for the purposes of a number of tax reliefs, including entrepreneurs' relief (see Section 6.28), rollover relief and holdover relief for gifts.

Where the 'business use' of part of the property requires extensive conversion work, that part will no longer be part of the original 'dwelling' and hence the principal private residence exemption will not be available for the last eighteen months of ownership.

Non-Exclusive Business Use (The 'Home Office')

Where part of the home is used non-exclusively for business purposes, there is currently no restriction on the principal private residence exemption. This is a fairly common situation amongst self-employed people who work from an office or study within their home.

To safeguard the principal private residence exemption, it is wise to restrict your Income Tax claim in respect of the office's running costs to, say, 99%, in order to reflect the room's occasional private use. Hence, for example, if the office is one of four rooms in the house (excluding hallways, kitchen and bathrooms), one would claim 99% of one quarter of the household running costs.

Just about any kind of private use will suffice, such as:

- A guest bedroom
- Additional storage space for personal belongings
- A music room
- A library

Naturally, it makes sense to adopt some form of private use which will only lead to a small reduction in the Income Tax claim.

Tax Tip

Whilst restricting one room to, say, 99% business use, you may also be able to argue for 1% business use in another room, thus effectively reversing the effect of the restriction without affecting your Capital Gains Tax position on the house.

Section 3.9 provides further details of how to claim an expense deduction for Income Tax purposes when using part of your home as an office from which to run your business. Claiming the new flat rate allowances available from 2013/14 onwards should not affect your home's Capital Gains Tax exemption, although it remains important to avoid exclusive business use of any part of the property.

6.28 ENTREPRENEURS' RELIEF

Entrepreneurs' relief currently operates by simply applying a reduced Capital Gains Tax rate of 10%.

Gains on which entrepreneurs' relief is claimed are taken to use up the individual's basic rate tax band first, in priority to any other gains.

Sadly, entrepreneurs' relief is not generally available to property investors, except in the case of qualifying furnished holiday accommodation (see Section 8.15). Unlike taper relief, entrepreneurs' relief is not generally available to landlords renting commercial property to qualifying businesses.

Nevertheless, entrepreneurs' relief will sometimes be available to property developers and other taxpayers with property trades (see Chapter 2) on the disposal of their own trading premises and other business assets.

Broadly speaking, entrepreneurs' relief is available on the disposal of:

i) The whole or part of a qualifying business
ii) Assets previously used in a qualifying business which has ceased
iii) Shares or securities in a 'personal company'

A qualifying business for this purpose is generally a trade, although, as already stated, furnished holiday letting businesses also qualify. We will return to look in more detail at the application of entrepreneurs' relief to qualifying furnished holiday accommodation in Section 8.15.

A 'part' of a business can only be counted for these purposes if it is capable of operating as a going concern in its own right, but an 'interest' in a business, such as a partnership share, may qualify.

A disposal of assets previously used in a qualifying business must take place within three years after the business ceases.

The individual making the disposal must have owned the qualifying business for at least a year prior to its disposal, or cessation, as the case may be.

Entrepreneurs' relief may sometimes also extend to property owned personally but used in the trade of a 'personal company', or a partnership in which the owner is a partner. A number of restrictions apply, however.

The relief is generally only available where the owner is also disposing of their shares in the company, or interest in the partnership, and is also restricted where any payment has been received for the use of the property after 5 April 2008.

Where the property was acquired after 5 April 2008 and a full market rent was received throughout the period of its use in the company or partnership's trade, no entrepreneurs' relief will be available. Where the property was acquired earlier, or rent was charged at a lower rate, there will be a partial restriction in entrepreneurs' relief.

The definition of a 'personal company' for the purposes of entrepreneurs' relief is broadly as follows:

i)   The individual holds at least 5% of the ordinary share capital
ii) The holding under (i) provides at least 5% of the voting rights
iii) The company is a trading company
iv) The individual is an officer or employee of the company (an 'officer' includes a non-executive director or company secretary)

Each of these rules must be satisfied for the period of at least one year prior to the disposal in question or, where the company has ceased trading, for at least one year prior to the cessation. In the latter case, the disposal must again take place within three years after cessation.

A disposal of property or other assets used in a trade carried on by the owner's 'personal company', or a partnership in which the owner is a partner, is referred to as an 'associated disposal'. The entrepreneurs' relief available on an associated disposal is also restricted to reflect any periods when the asset was not being used in a qualifying business carried on by the company or partnership.

There is no similar restriction on other entrepreneurs' relief claims and a property used in the owner's own qualifying business will be eligible for full relief as long as it was used in that business immediately prior to the disposal or cessation of the business.

Each individual may only claim entrepreneurs' relief on a maximum cumulative lifetime total of £10m of capital gains. This maximum applies to all claims made on gains arising after 5* April 2008. Thereafter, the Capital Gains Tax rate on all further business asset disposals will revert to 18% or 28%, as appropriate (see Section 6.4).

Example

Arkwright began trading as a property developer in the late 1980s. After over 25 years he decides to retire, ceasing trading in September 2014. For just over a year before cessation, Arkwright ran the business from an office building called Granville House which he purchased as an investment property in March 1989 for £5m and rented out for over 20 years.

In July 2013, Arkwright adopted Granville House as his trading premises and there he remained until he ceased trading in September 2014.

After his property development business ceased, Arkwright put Granville House up for sale and eventually sold it for £15.1m in March 2015, realising a capital gain of £10.1m.

As Arkwright owned his business for more than a year and sold Granville House within three years of cessation, he's eligible for entrepreneurs' relief on this gain. The fact that Granville House was an investment property for 24 years out of Arkwright's total ownership period of 26 years makes absolutely no difference!

His £10.1m gain does exceed the £10m lifetime limit, however, so Arkwright's Capital Gains Tax bill is calculated as follows:

	£
Total gain	*10,100,000*
Less:	
Annual exemption	*(11,000)*
Taxable gain	*10,089,000*
Capital Gains Tax due:	
£10m @ 10%	*1,000,000*
£89,000 @ 28%	*24,920*
Total	*1,024,920*

If Arkwright had not adopted Granville House as his trading premises, his Capital Gains Tax bill (assuming he is a higher rate taxpayer) would have been £2,824,920. That's £1.8m more!

As we can see from the example, adopting an investment property as your own trading premises prior to sale could save you up to £1.8m.

Not everyone already has a handy trading business like Arkwright, but we will look at how other property investors might benefit from entrepreneurs' relief in Section 8.18.

Note that entrepreneurs' relief is not mandatory and taxpayers may choose whether to claim it. This avoids the need to waste any of the cumulative lifetime maximum on claims which would be wholly or mainly covered by the annual exemption or by capital losses (see Section 6.33).

Wealth Warning

To qualify for entrepreneurs' relief, the individual making the disposal must have owned the qualifying business for at least a year prior to cessation. A pre-sale transfer of property to a spouse might therefore result in the loss of entrepreneurs' relief if the spouse did not also own a share of the business for at least a year prior to cessation.

Tax Tip

On the other hand, it is also worth noting that the £10m cumulative lifetime maximum applies on a 'per person' basis. Hence, if a share in the business were transferred to a spouse for at least a year prior to cessation, entrepreneurs' relief would then be available on total gains of up to £20m.

Another Tax Tip

It will also almost always be worth transferring a property to a spouse when they are using it in their own trading business. In addition to the possibility of obtaining entrepreneurs' relief on the property, the spouse using the asset in their trade would be eligible for several other reliefs, including rollover relief on replacement of business assets (see Section 8.28).

The asset would also generally be exempt from Inheritance Tax if held by the partner using it in their own trade.

6.29 THE ANNUAL EXEMPTION

Each individual taxpayer is entitled to an annual exemption for every tax year.

The annual exemption is available to exempt from Capital Gains Tax an amount of capital gains after all other reliefs have been claimed, including the compulsory set-off of capital losses arising in the same tax year.

Where capital losses are brought forward from a previous tax year, however, the set-off is limited to an amount which reduces the taxpayer's capital gains in the current year to the level of the annual exemption.

As explained in Section 6.4, individual taxpayers with more than one capital gain arising in the same tax year may allocate their annual exemption in the most beneficial way.

Any unused annual exemption is simply lost; it cannot be carried forward.

Tax Tip

To make the most of your available annual exemptions, try to time your capital gains so that each disposal falls into a different tax year whenever possible.

The current annual exemption, for capital gains arising during the year ending 5ᵗʰ April 2015, is £11,000.

Example

Harry has a capital gain of £12,000 in 2014/15, after claiming all relevant reliefs. After setting off his annual exemption of £11,000, he will be left with a taxable gain of just £1,000.

Note: in this example, as well as many others in this guide, we have assumed that the annual exemption is fully available.

This will not always be the case and it should be remembered that only one annual exemption is available each tax year.

6.30 WHEN IS CAPITAL GAINS TAX PAYABLE?

The total amount of Capital Gains Tax payable for each tax year is due and payable by 31ˢᵗ January following the end of the tax year. Hence, for example, any Capital Gains Tax liability for 2014/15 is due by 31 January 2016.

Capital Gains Tax liabilities are excluded from the instalment system applying to Income Tax liabilities under self assessment (see Section 3.4).

6.31 WHAT MUST I REPORT TO HM REVENUE AND CUSTOMS?

The general rule is that any disposals giving rise to proceeds exceeding four times the annual exemption, or which give rise to an actual Capital Gains Tax liability, will need to be reported.

Disposals which are fully covered by principal private residence relief and private letting relief are exempted from any reporting requirements. This does not include cases where the taxpayer is additionally relying on the annual exemption or any other relief to ensure full relief from Capital Gains Tax.

The return is due for submission by 31 January following the end of the relevant tax year if filed online (i.e. by the same date that any Capital Gains Tax liability is due), or by 31 October if a paper return is used.

If you have a reportable property disposal, you will need to complete a tax return, including the capital gains supplement, and attach a copy of your capital gains computation.

If you are not yet in the self-assessment system, it is sensible to advise HM Revenue and Customs that you have a reportable capital gain as soon as possible after the end of the relevant tax year and definitely by the 5 October following the tax year.

This is so that HM Revenue and Customs will be able to issue you with a Unique Taxpayer Reference ('UTR') to enable you to submit your tax return on time.

It is now almost impossible to submit a tax return without a UTR and, if you have not advised HM Revenue and Customs that you need to do so by the 5 October after the end of the tax year, the fact that you do not receive it in time will not be a valid excuse for filing late.

6.32 JOINTLY HELD ASSETS

Where two or more taxpayers hold assets jointly, they must each calculate their own Capital Gains Tax based on their own share of the net proceeds received less their own base cost.

Example

George and Charlotte are equal joint owners of a buy-to-let property which they bought together for £100,000. In November 2014 they sell the property for £200,000. Each person's taxable capital gain is calculated as follows:

	£
Net proceeds (£200,000 x ½)	*100,000*
Less:	
Base cost (£100,000 x ½)	*(50,000)*
	50,000
Less:	
Annual exemption	*(11,000)*
Taxable capital gain	*39,000*

George is a higher rate taxpayer, so his Capital Gains Tax bill, at 28%, amounts to £10,920.

Charlotte's total income for 2014/15 is less than her personal allowance (£10,000), so she pays Capital Gains Tax at 18% on the first £31,865 of her gain (the basic rate band) and 28% on the remainder:

£31,865 @ 18% =	*£5,736*
£7,135 @ 28% =	*£1,998*
Total	*£7,734*

The couple's total Capital Gains Tax bill therefore amounts to £18,654 (£10,920 + £7,734).

Had the property been owned by George alone, his Capital Gains Tax liability would have been £24,920 (£100,000 - £11,000 = £89,000 x 28%). The couple have therefore saved £6,266 (£24,920 - £18,654) by owning the property jointly. This is the value of an additional annual exemption (£11,000 x 28%) plus the saving generated by using Charlotte's basic rate band (£31,865 x 10%: the difference between 18% and 28%).

Hence, it can readily be seen that there will often be significant Capital Gains Tax savings to be had by owning investment property jointly.

There may also be other good reasons for holding property jointly, including significant Income Tax savings, as we shall see in Section 8.2.

Furthermore, another important point to note when looking at jointly held property is that the £40,000 limit for private letting relief (see Section 6.14) applies to each individual. Hence, a total of up to £80,000 can be exempted by that relief when a property is held jointly. We will examine the potential effect of this in more detail in Chapter 8.

6.33   CAPITAL LOSSES

Generally speaking, capital losses are computed in the same way as capital gains.

In the first instance, capital losses are automatically set off against any capital gains arising in the same tax year.

Where a taxpayer has an overall net capital loss for the year, it is carried forward and set off against gains in later years BUT only to the extent necessary to reduce future gains down to the annual exemption applying for that later year.

As explained in Section 6.4, individual taxpayers with more than one capital gain arising in the same tax year may generally allocate any available capital losses in the most beneficial way.

Where a taxpayer is claiming entrepreneurs' relief on the disposal of business assets, however, any capital losses arising on those disposals must be set off against capital gains on assets which were used in the same business. Entrepreneurs' relief is then claimed on the overall net gain.

Any other capital losses set off against gains subject to entrepreneurs' relief are set off after entrepreneurs' relief has been claimed, meaning that the relief for those losses is given at an effective rate of only 10% and more of the taxpayer's lifetime maximum will have been used up.

Capital losses arising on any transactions with 'connected persons' (see Section 6.9) may only be set off against gains arising on transactions between the same parties.

Furthermore, relief is denied for 'artificial' capital losses arising as a result of transactions which were carried out with a main purpose of creating a tax advantage.

6.34   LEASES

Granting a long lease of more than 50 years' duration

This is a capital disposal, fully chargeable to Capital Gains Tax (subject to applicable reliefs). The base cost to be used has to be restricted under the 'part disposal' rules. In essence, what this means is that the base cost is divided between the part disposed of (i.e. the lease) and the part retained (the 'reversionary interest') in proportion to their relative values.

Example

Llewellyn owns the freehold of a commercial property in Cardiff. He grants a 60-year lease to Brian, a businessman from Belfast moving into the area. Brian pays a premium of £90,000 for the lease. The value of Llewellyn's reversionary interest is established as £10,000. The base cost to be used in calculating Llewellyn's capital gain on the grant of the lease is therefore 90% of his base cost for the property as a whole.

Granting a short lease of no more than 50 years' duration

As we saw in Section 4.13, part of any lease premium obtained will be taxable as income. The rest is a capital disposal and is dealt with in the same way as the grant of a long lease, as outlined above.

Assigning a lease

This is treated entirely as a capital disposal and any applicable reliefs may be claimed in the usual way.

However, leases with less than 50 years remaining at the time of disposal are treated as 'wasting assets'. The taxpayer is therefore required to reduce their base cost in accordance with the schedule set out in Appendix C.

For example, for a lease with 20 years remaining, and which had more than 50 years remaining when first acquired, the base cost must be reduced to 72.77% of the original amount.

Where the lease had less than 50 years remaining when originally acquired, the necessary reduction in base cost is achieved by multiplying the original cost by the factor applying at the time of sale and dividing by the factor applying at the time of purchase.

Example

John takes out a ten year lease over a building and pays a premium of £10,000. Five years later, John assigns his lease to Roy at a premium of £6,000.

When calculating his capital gain, the amount which John may claim as his base cost is £10,000 x 26.722/46.695 = £5,723.

Note that any part of a lease premium which was treated as income in the hands of the grantor under the rules outlined in Section 4.13 will not form part of the grantee's base cost for the lease. The grantee may, instead, be able to claim an Income Tax deduction for this part of the premium, spread over the period of the lease (if the grantee is using the property for business purposes).

In the example above, I have assumed for the sake of illustration that this did not apply in John's case.

Chapter 7

Other Taxes to Watch Out For

7.1 STAMP DUTY – INTRODUCTION

Stamp Duty is the oldest tax on the statute books. It was several centuries old already when Pitt the Younger introduced Income Tax in 1799. Even today, we are still governed to a limited extent by the Stamp Act 1891. Since 2003, however, for transfers of real property (i.e. land and buildings, or any form of legal interest in them), Stamp Duty has been replaced by Stamp Duty Land Tax.

7.2 STAMP DUTY LAND TAX

The rates of Stamp Duty Land Tax applying to transfers of property are generally the same regardless of what type of property business the purchaser has. The rates are also mostly unaffected by whether the purchaser is an individual, a trust, a partnership or a company – with a few exceptions!

More significant differences arise in the rates applying to residential property and non-residential property.

The current rates of Stamp Duty Land Tax are as follows:

Residential Property – General Rates

Up to £125,000	Zero
Over £125,000, but not over £250,000	1%
Over £250,000, but not over £500,000	3%
Over £500,000, but not over £1m	4%
Over £1m, but not over £2m	5%
Over £2m	7%

Residential Property – Corporate Rate (See Below)

Over £500,000	15%

Non-Residential Property

Up to £150,000	Zero
Over £150,000, but not over £250,000	1%
Over £250,000, but not over £500,000	3%
Over £500,000	4%

For all types of property, the purchaser will generally be required to certify that the rate of Stamp Duty Land Tax which has been applied is correct.

Like Stamp Duty, the Stamp Duty Land Tax payable should always be rounded up to the nearest £5.

The thresholds given in the above tables generally refer to the actual consideration paid for the purchase, whether in cash or by any other means (but see Section 7.4 for potential exceptions).

It is important to understand that, whatever rate of Stamp Duty Land Tax applies to a property purchase, it applies to the **whole** of the purchase price.

It can therefore readily be seen from the above tables that a small alteration in the purchase price of a property can sometimes make an enormous difference to the amount of Stamp Duty Land Tax payable.

Example

Ian is just about to make an offer of £250,001 for a house in Carlisle when he realises that the Stamp Duty Land Tax payable on this purchase, at 3%, would be £7,505. Horrified at this prospect, he amends the offer to £250,000, thus reducing the potential Stamp Duty Land Tax payable to £2,500 (1%).

This sort of change is, of course, perfectly acceptable, because the whole situation is taking place at 'arm's-length'.

However, in more complex situations, where there are other elements to the transaction, such as a side agreement to acquire the moveable fittings in the property, for example, HM Revenue and Customs' Stamp Office is likely to scrutinise very closely any transactions where the consideration is equal to, or only just under, one of the limits set out above.

Nevertheless, a separate purchase of the moveable fittings in the property can still be a useful way to reduce the Stamp Duty Land Tax cost and we will look at this in a little more detail in Section 7.7.

Residential Property Purchases in Excess of £500,000 by 'Non-Natural' Persons

The 'corporate rate' of 15% applies to purchases of residential properties in excess of £500,000 by companies and other 'non-natural' persons, such as collective investment schemes, unit trusts and partnerships in which any 'non-natural' person is a partner.

The rate only applies where a single dwelling is purchased for a price in excess of £500,000, or where one or more separate dwellings included within the purchase of a larger portfolio are worth more than £500,000 each.

Properties are exempt from the 'corporate rate' when acquired for use in a business. This exemption covers both trading businesses and property investment businesses, so property investment companies should not generally have to pay the corporate rate. This issue is examined further in Section 7.15.

The 'corporate rate' should not generally apply to purchases by individuals. It will also not generally apply to purchases by most trusts or partnerships as, from a technical standpoint, the purchase is still being made by one or more individuals. In case of doubt, however, legal advice is essential!

Application to all UK Property

Stamp Duty Land Tax is currently payable on all transfers of UK property; regardless of where the vendor and purchaser are resident, and regardless of where the transfer documentation is drawn up.

Stamp Duty Land Tax will, however, cease to apply to property located in Scotland from April 2015 onwards. See Section 7.16 for further details.

Substantial Completion

The liability for Stamp Duty Land Tax is triggered when a purchase is 'substantially completed'. Generally, this occurs on the earlier of:

a)   Completion of the purchase contract, or
b)   Payment of 80% of the purchase price

7.3   WHO PAYS STAMP DUTY LAND TAX?

The liability for Stamp Duty Land Tax is the legal responsibility of the purchaser or transferee, although the vendor or transferor will sometimes arrange to pay it.

Property developers will sometimes advertise properties as 'Stamp Duty Free' or 'Stamp Duty Paid'. This does not usually mean that no Stamp Duty Land Tax is payable, it simply means that the developer is undertaking to pay the tax on behalf of the purchaser.

It is worth bearing in mind that this simply amounts to nothing more than a discount of between 1% and 7% (depending on the value of the property).

Tax Tip for Developers and Investors Selling Property

People hate paying tax. They particularly hate capital taxes (i.e. taxes on the capital value of things).

Offering to pay the Stamp Duty Land Tax on their purchase is therefore a powerful marketing incentive and tends to have a far greater effect than an equivalent discount on the price.

Illogical as it may seem, paying their 3% Stamp Duty Land Tax bill for them may appeal to buyers more than a 5% discount on the price!

For second-hand property sales, a 'Stamp Duty Free' offer will also incentivise the buyers to offer more. Hence, although you will foot the bill in the end, you will often recoup this through your sale price.

Wealth Warning for Investors Selling Property

A 'Stamp Duty Free' offer could backfire, however, where buyers make offers only slightly over one of the Stamp Duty Land Tax thresholds, so it may not be wise to use this strategy where your property is worth somewhere around one of the thresholds detailed in Section 7.2.

(You could adapt your offer to something like '1% Stamp Duty Free', however.)

Wealth Warning for Investors Buying Property

Don't be taken in by these 'Stamp Duty Free' offers. They are sometimes just an excuse for the seller to increase the price.

For example, it is better to pay £180,000 plus Stamp Duty Land Tax (total cost £181,800) than to pay £185,000 'Stamp Duty Free'.

7.4 MARKET VALUE AND MORTGAGES

Generally speaking, there is no 'market value' rule for Stamp Duty Land Tax and the tax is only payable on actual consideration.

Where property is transferred to a connected company, however, Stamp Duty Land Tax is payable on the market value of that property.

There is no Stamp Duty Land Tax exemption for transfers between spouses or civil partners, although many of these are, of course, gifts with no consideration.

Note, however, that where property is transferred subject to a mortgage, the balance outstanding on that mortgage will be treated as consideration for Stamp Duty Land Tax purposes.

Hence, for example, if a man transfers a house to his wife subject to an outstanding mortgage of £200,000, she will have a Stamp Duty Land Tax liability of £2,000 (£200,000 x 1%).

If the mortgage had been £255,000, the wife's Stamp Duty Land Tax cost would have been £7,650 (£255,000 x 3%).

Clearly, in such a case, it would be advisable to repay £5,000 of the mortgage prior to the transfer, thus reducing the outstanding balance to £250,000 and reducing the Stamp Duty Land Tax to £2,500 (£250,000 x 1%).

7.5 LINKED TRANSACTIONS

The rate of Stamp Duty Land Tax to be applied is determined after taking account of any 'linked transactions'.

'Linked transactions' can arise in a number of ways, including a simultaneous purchase of several properties from the same vendor.

The effect of the 'linked transactions' depends on whether 'averaging relief' is claimed. This relief is only available for multiple purchases of residential property.

First, however, let's look at the basic rule applying to linked transactions where averaging relief is not available.

Basic Rule without Averaging Relief

The basic rule which applies where averaging relief is not claimed is that the 'linked transactions' are treated as if they were a single purchase for Stamp Duty Land Tax purposes.

In practice, this will mainly apply to multiple purchases of non-residential property, although it will also apply to any other 'linked transactions' where averaging relief is not available.

For example, if a property investor were to buy three commercial properties from the same developer at the same time for £250,000 each, this would be treated for Stamp Duty Land Tax purposes as if it were one single purchase for £750,000. The rate of Stamp Duty Land Tax applying would therefore be 4% instead of the 1% which would have applied to a single purchase for £250,000.

Averaging Relief

Averaging relief is available where multiple **residential** properties are purchased from the same vendor at the same time.

Where averaging relief is claimed, the rate of Stamp Duty Land Tax is based on the **average** consideration paid for each 'dwelling': but with an overall minimum rate of 1%. The relief is not automatic and must be claimed by the purchaser.

This much fairer and more sensible approach can cut the rate of Stamp Duty Land Tax on some large property purchases down to 1%.

Example 1

Jat buys five houses from a developer for a total consideration of £1.2m. Without averaging relief, Stamp Duty Land Tax would be charged at 5%: £60,000.

However, as the average price for each property is £240,000, Jat claims averaging relief, thus reducing his Stamp Duty Land Tax rate to just 1% and giving him a total charge of only £12,000.

In a case like Jat's, the charge with averaging relief is clearly much fairer. The relief goes even further, however, and could actually be used to reduce the Stamp Duty Land Tax charge on a single large property.

Example 2

Pippa is planning to buy a new house in Middleton at a cost of £550,000. Stamp Duty Land Tax will be payable at 4% and will amount to £22,000.

In order to reduce her Stamp Duty Land Tax cost, however, Pippa arranges to buy two small flats from the same developer at the same time as her new house. The flats cost £70,000 each, bringing her total consideration to £690,000, but the average consideration is now just £230,000. Pippa can therefore claim averaging relief to give her a reduction in her Stamp Duty Land Tax charge to just £6,900 (1%).

Hence, by buying the flats at the same time as the house, Pippa has saved £15,100. That's equivalent to getting a discount of almost 11% on the flats!

A Major Benefit for Property Investors

Self-contained flats within a single property each constitute a separate 'dwelling' for the purposes of averaging relief. This provides a major benefit for property investors buying larger properties.

For example, if an investor buys a property which has been divided into four flats, this would constitute four dwellings, so that averaging relief can be claimed and potentially reduce the Stamp Duty Land Tax to 1%.

Mixed Purchases

Averaging relief does not apply to non-residential property, even when it forms part of a larger 'mixed' purchase.

Example 3

Rhys buys a development which consists of four houses and a shop for a total price of £625,000. The shop alone is worth £145,000.

Excluding the shop, the average price of the houses is £120,000. A claim under averaging relief will therefore reduce the rate of Stamp Duty Land Tax on the houses to 1%: the minimum rate permitted under the relief.

The relief is not available on the shop, however. As the aggregate consideration for the whole transaction is £625,000, the rate of Stamp Duty Land Tax applying to the shop is 4%, giving rise to a charge of £5,800.

So Rhys will pay Stamp Duty Land Tax of £4,800 on four houses worth a total of £480,000, but will also pay £5,800 on one shop worth just £145,000. This from a Government which claims to be determined to make tax simpler and fairer!

Alternative Treatment

A simultaneous purchase of six or more residential dwellings (from the same vendor) can alternatively be treated as a non-residential property purchase for Stamp Duty Land Tax purposes. This will seldom produce a better outcome than claiming averaging relief, however.

The Corporate Rate

Where the 'corporate rate' applies (see Section 7.2), this takes precedence over any of the rules outlined in this section. Hence, neither averaging relief nor the alternative treatment described above would be available.

7.6   STAMP DUTY LAND TAX ON LEASES

On the granting of a lease, Stamp Duty Land Tax is payable based on the 'Net Present Value' of all the rent payable under the lease over its entire term.

Where the net present value does not exceed £125,000 (for residential property), or £150,000 (for non-residential property), no Stamp Duty Land Tax will be payable.

For new leases with a net present value exceeding these limits, Stamp Duty Land Tax is payable at a rate of 1% on the excess.

VAT is excluded from the rent payable under the lease for the purposes of Stamp Duty Land Tax calculations <u>unless</u> the landlord has already exercised the option to tax (this applies to commercial property only).

Example

In January 2015, Clive takes on a ten year lease over a house in Kent at an annual rent of £18,000.

The Stamp Duty Land Tax legislation provides that the net present value of a sum of money due within the next 12 months is equal to the sum due divided by a 'discount factor'. The applicable discount factor is currently 103.5%.

Hence, the 'Present Value' of Clive's first year's rent of £18,000 is £17,391 (i.e. £18,000 divided by 103.5%).

Similarly, the second year's rent, which is due a further 12 months later, must be 'discounted' again by the same amount, i.e. £17,391/103.5% = £16,803.

This process is continued for the entire ten year life of the lease and the net present values of all of the rental payments are then added together to give the total net present value for the whole lease. In this case, this works out at £149,699.

The Stamp Duty Land Tax payable by Clive is therefore just £250 (1% of £149,699 less £125,000, £24,699, rounded up to the nearest £5).

Note that it does not matter for the purposes of this calculation whether the rent is payable monthly, quarterly or annually, or whether it is payable in advance or in arrears. Net present value is, in each case, always calculated by reference to the total annual rental payable for each year of the lease.

The current 'discount factor' (103.5%) may be changed in the future, depending on a number of factors, including the prevailing rates of inflation and interest.

Lease Premiums

Lease **premiums** also attract Stamp Duty Land Tax, usually at the same rates as shown in Section 7.2 for outright purchases.

However, where the lease of a commercial property is also subject to an annual rent of more than £1,000, the exemption for consideration not exceeding £150,000 does not apply and Stamp Duty Land Tax is payable at the rate of 1% on **any** premium up to £250,000.

The restriction of this rule to commercial property only means that it is sometimes possible to grant a lease over a residential property with a premium of up to £125,000 **and** annual rental with a net present value of up to £125,000 with no Stamp Duty Land Tax cost whatsoever.

7.7   FIXTURES AND FITTINGS

There is a great deal of misunderstanding over the issue of Stamp Duty Land Tax on fixtures and fittings.

Firstly, it must be understood that 'fixtures' are part of the fabric of the building and are therefore subject to Stamp Duty Land Tax. This includes items such as fitted kitchens, baths, toilets, sinks, etc, and is unaffected by whether these items qualify for capital allowances (see Section 4.8).

Moveable fittings, however, are **not** part of the fabric of the building and therefore not subject to Stamp Duty Land Tax.

This includes furniture, carpets, curtains and free-standing 'white goods' such as fridges, freezers and washing machines.

It is therefore often possible to allocate a small part of a property's purchase price to the moveable fittings in the property and thus reduce the Stamp Duty Land Tax cost.

For purchases over £250,000, this will save at least 3% of the amount allocated to the fittings and will therefore often be worthwhile.

For purchases at a price of £250,000 or less, however, the savings involved will not usually be significant enough to warrant much attention.

As we saw in Section 7.2, however, a small alteration in the purchase price of a property can sometimes make an enormous difference to the amount of Stamp Duty Land Tax payable when it reduces the price below one of the key Stamp Duty Land Tax thresholds.

This often leads purchasers to make an allocation of part of the purchase price to moveable fittings in order to reduce the consideration for the property itself below one of the thresholds.

This is fine as long as the allocation is reasonable and is supported by the circumstances of the case.

Remember, however, that it is only the moveable fittings which escape Stamp Duty Land Tax. There is a limit to how much can be allocated to carpets and curtains and, as I said in Section 7.2, you can expect HM Revenue and Customs to be vigilant.

Generally, it is sensible to purchase moveable fittings by way of a side agreement (which may be no more than a handshake). The informality of such an agreement does not, however, prevent it from having to be included as part of the property's purchase price if the price allocated to the fittings is excessive.

In summary, a small allocation of the purchase price to moveable fittings is a sensible way to reduce your Stamp Duty Land Tax bill; but be reasonable!

7.8   STAMP DUTY ON SHARES

Before we leave the subject of Stamp Taxes, it is just worth briefly mentioning that the rate of Stamp Duty on purchases of shares and securities in excess of £1,000 is just 0.5%.

Purchases not exceeding £1,000 are exempt (although where quoted shares are purchased through a broker, they will usually pass on the Stamp Duty which arises owing to the fact that they have purchased a larger block of shares in a single transaction).

This lower rate of Duty has led to many tax planning strategies, designed to avoid the excessive rates applied to property transactions by making use of this more palatable rate. However, anti-avoidance legislation introduced over the last few years has effectively blocked most of the more popular methods.

Nevertheless, for those investing in property through a company, there remains the possibility of selling shares in that company at a much lower rate of Duty than would apply to the sale of individual properties within the company. (But see Sections 7.2 and 7.15 regarding additional or higher tax charges on companies owning any individual residential property worth over £500,000 which is not being used for business purposes.)

7.9   VAT – INTRODUCTION

VAT, or Value Added Tax, to give it its proper name, is the 'new kid on the block' in UK taxation, having arrived on our shores from Europe in 1973.

Despite its comparative youth, VAT is one of the UK's most hated taxes and there are some nasty pitfalls awaiting the unwary property investor.

VAT is currently charged at three different rates in the UK: a standard rate of 20%, a reduced rate of 5% and a zero rate. All of these rates may be encountered by property businesses.

You may recall me stating in Section 2.2 that the type of property held by a business did not generally affect how that business was treated for Income Tax and Capital Gains Tax purposes.

For VAT, however, it does become important to distinguish between residential property and commercial property.

For VAT purposes, a sale of a property is a supply of 'goods' and rent on a property is a supply of 'services'.

Not all supplies of 'goods and services' are subject to VAT, some are exempt.

The VAT treatment of 'goods and services' in a property business depends on a number of things, including the type of property concerned.

Where a supply of 'goods or services' is subject to VAT at any of the three rates given above (including the 'zero rate') it is referred to as a 'taxable supply'.

Goods and services subject to VAT at the standard rate of 20% are often referred to as 'standard-rated'.

VAT Registration

VAT is charged by VAT registered businesses. Sadly, they do not keep it, but must pay it over to the Government. They are, however, able to claim back the VAT on their purchases of the goods and services used to make their own taxable supplies.

Where a business is making annual taxable supplies of goods or services in excess of the VAT registration threshold, it is compulsorily required to register for VAT.

The VAT registration threshold is currently £81,000. The threshold applying for the period from 1· April 2013 to 31· March 2014 was £79,000. (As explained in Sections 3.5 and 5.11, the VAT registration threshold is also relevant for certain other tax purposes.)

Businesses making taxable supplies of goods or services but whose annual sales are less than the VAT registration threshold may register for VAT voluntarily. This is particularly beneficial for those making 'zero rated' supplies, as we shall see later.

7.10   VAT ON RESIDENTIAL PROPERTY

Residential Property Letting

Generally speaking, a property investment business engaged primarily in residential property letting does not need to be registered for VAT. This is because the letting of residential property is an exempt supply for VAT purposes.

VAT is therefore not chargeable on rent, although, of course, VAT cannot be recovered on expenses and the landlord should therefore claim VAT-inclusive costs for Income Tax and Capital Gains Tax purposes.

The letting of holiday accommodation is, however, standard-rated for VAT purposes, whether or not it qualifies for the special treatment outlined in Section 8.15.

Beware also that the provision of ancillary services (e.g. cleaning or gardening) may sometimes be standard-rated, and hence subject to VAT at 20%, if the value of annual supplies of these services exceeds the VAT registration threshold.

Some landlords making ancillary supplies of this nature prefer to register for VAT, even if they have not reached the registration threshold, as this means that they are able to recover some of the VAT on their expenses.

Residential Property Development

Sales of newly constructed residential property are zero-rated for VAT purposes. This means that the developer can recover all of the VAT on their construction costs without having to charge VAT on the sale of the property. (In theory, VAT is charged, but at a rate of zero.)

This treatment is extended to the sale of a property which has just been converted from a non-residential property into a residential property (*e.g. converting a barn into a house*).

It is also extended to 'substantially reconstructed protected buildings'. In essence, this means the sale of a listed building following the carrying out of major alterations. Such alterations do, of course, require approval from the authorities.

Property developers carrying out construction work under any of these headings are therefore able to register for VAT and then recover the VAT on the vast majority of their business expenses.

Other Residential Property Sales

Other sales of residential property are generally an exempt supply meaning, once again, that the taxpayer making the sale is unable to recover any of the VAT on his or her expenses.

This means that VAT cannot be recovered by most residential property investors and most residential property dealers.

Furthermore, property developers who merely renovate or alter existing residential property prior to onward sale are also generally unable to recover VAT on their costs. Where, however, the work qualifies as a 'conversion', as described below, they may at least be able to reduce the amount of VAT payable.

Conversions

A reduced VAT rate of 5% is available in respect of any building work carried out on a residential property where the work results in a change to the number of dwellings in the property.

For example, this would apply to the conversion of:

- One house into several flats
- Two or more flats into a single house
- Two semi-detached houses into a single detached house

The reduced rate also applies to conversions of commercial property into residential use.

Property investors or developers carrying out projects of this nature should try to ensure that they only pay the lower VAT rate from the outset, as it is difficult to recover any excess paid in error.

Renovations of Vacant Property

The reduced rate of 5% also applies to renovation work on residential property which had been vacant for two years or more before the work commenced.

7.11   VAT ON COMMERCIAL PROPERTY

Commercial Property Letting

For commercial property, there is an 'option to tax'. In other words, the landlord may choose, for each property and on a property-by-property basis, whether or not the rent should be an exempt supply for VAT purposes.

If the 'option to tax' is exercised, the rent on the property becomes standard-rated for VAT purposes. The landlord may then recover VAT on all of the expenses relating to that property. Ancillary services are again likely to be standard-rated, regardless of whether you have opted to tax the rent itself.

Charging VAT on your commercial property rent is usually known as 'exercising the option to tax', although, technically, the proper term, as sometimes used by HM Revenue and Customs, is 'exercising the option to waive exemption from the requirement to charge tax'. Either way, it means the same thing.

Tax Tip

If the potential tenants of a commercial property are all, or mostly, likely to be VAT-registered businesses themselves, it will generally make sense to exercise the 'option to tax' on the property in order to recover the VAT on expenses incurred.

If your tenants themselves have a VAT-registered and fully taxable business (for VAT purposes), then everyone's happy. The problem comes when your tenants cannot recover some or all of the VAT which you are charging them. And remember that (after a short 'cooling off' period) you cannot change your option on a property for a minimum of 20 years once it has been exercised. Hence, if you opt to charge VAT to a fully taxable tenant, you will probably still need to charge VAT to the next tenant in the same property, even if they cannot recover it.

Sometimes, though, with non-taxable (for VAT) tenants, where you have not yet exercised your option to tax, you can refrain from doing so and negotiate a higher rent to compensate you for your loss of VAT recovery on your own costs.

Example

Norman owns an office building and hasn't yet opted to tax the rents. By early 2015, he has monthly costs of £500 plus VAT (i.e. £600 gross) and expects a monthly rent of £2,500. If Norman opts to tax he will recover £100 a month from HM Revenue and Customs and make a monthly profit of £2,000.

However, Lenny, the prospective tenant, is not registered for VAT. If Norman opts to tax the property, Lenny's rent will effectively be 20% higher, i.e. £3,000 per month.

So, as a better alternative, Norman and Lenny agree that Norman will not opt to tax the building but will, instead, charge Lenny £2,700 a month rent. Now Norman is making a monthly profit of £2,100 (£2,700 minus £600) and Lenny's rent is effectively £300 less than it would have been. Norman and Lenny both win and HM Revenue and Customs loses.

Commercial Property Sales & Purchases

Where the 'option to tax' has been exercised by the owner of a commercial property, their sale of that property will be standard-rated and this has major implications for such transactions.

Sales of new commercial property are also standard-rated for VAT purposes.

Wealth Warning

Where VAT must be charged on a commercial property sale, the Stamp Duty Land Tax arising must be calculated on the basis of the gross, VAT-inclusive price.

This can lead to effective combined VAT and Stamp Duty Land Tax rates of up to 24.8%!

This represents a pretty hefty cost if the purchaser is not VAT registered, possibly enough to prevent the sale from taking place in some cases. Imagine a large insurance company buying a new office block in central London – the combined VAT and Stamp Duty Land Tax cost would be astronomical!

Furthermore, even when the purchaser is able to recover the VAT on their purchase, the extra Stamp Duty Land Tax paid on that VAT cannot be recovered.

Where a property investor incurs VAT on the purchase of a commercial property, the only way to recover that VAT will be for the investor to exercise the 'option to tax' on the property. In this way, the Government generally forces everyone to maintain the taxable status of the building.

If a VAT registered property developer incurs VAT on the purchase of a commercial property, they can recover the VAT in the same way as on any other purchase of goods or services for use in the business. This initial recovery is not dependent on exercising the 'option to tax', as the developer has a taxable business for VAT purposes, but ...

Wealth Warning

If VAT has been recovered on the purchase of a commercial property, a sale of that property without first exercising the option to tax would be an exempt supply.

If that property were trading stock, this would result in the loss of all the VAT initially reclaimed on its purchase and on any development, renovation or conversion work carried out on it. Some of the VAT recovered on general overhead costs would probably also become repayable.

Furthermore, when more than £250,000 has been spent on the purchase or improvement of a property for use as the business's own trading premises, a sale of that property within ten years without first exercising the option to tax would also trigger a VAT liability.

7.12   VAT ON PROPERTY MANAGEMENT

Property management services are standard-rated for VAT and hence a property management business will need to be registered for VAT if its annual turnover exceeds the £81,000 registration threshold. The taxpayer may still register voluntarily even if the level of sales is below the threshold.

Whether the properties under management are residential or commercial makes no difference for this purpose.

Naturally, a property management business which is registered for VAT can recover the VAT on most of its business expenses. There are, however, a few exceptions where VAT cannot be wholly recovered, as we shall see in the next section.

7.13   INTERACTION OF VAT WITH OTHER TAXES

Any business which is registered for VAT should generally include only the net (excluding VAT) amounts of income and expenditure in its accounts for Income Tax purposes. Where VAT recovery is barred or restricted, however, the additional cost arising should be treated as part of the relevant expense.

Expenses subject to restrictions on the recovery of VAT include:

- Business entertaining
- Purchases of motor cars
- Provision of private fuel for proprietors or staff

As you can see, many of the expenses subject to a VAT recovery restriction are also subject to some form of restriction for Income Tax purposes.

A non-registered business should always include the VAT in its business expenditure for Income Tax purposes. Similar principles apply for Capital Gains Tax and Corporation Tax purposes.

7.14   NATIONAL INSURANCE

See Sections 4.16 and 5.5 for the National Insurance treatment of property rental income and property trading income respectively.

In addition to the points made in Section 4.16, individual taxpayers with income from furnished holiday lettings have, in a few instances, been charged for Class 2 National Insurance. The Class 2 rate is, however, only £2.75 per week for 2014/15.

206

Non-trading taxpayers can pay voluntary Class 3 National Insurance in order to secure state retirement benefits, etc, if they so wish. The rate of Class 3 contributions is, however, currently £13.90 per week, having been increased by almost 72% since 2009.

Naturally, if you should employ anyone to help you in your property business, then their salary will be subject to both employee's and employer's Class 1 National Insurance (at 12% and 13.8% respectively).

From April 2014 each employer is eligible to claim exemption from the first £2,000 of employer's National Insurance arising in the year. From 2015/16 employers will no longer be required to pay employer's National Insurance on earnings paid up to the upper earnings limit to any employee under the age of 21.

If you provide an employee with any taxable benefits-in-kind, you will additionally be liable for Class 1A National Insurance (again at 13.8%).

Capital Gains

National Insurance is never payable on capital gains.

Remember, however, that if you are classed as a property developer or a property trader, your profit on property sales will be taxed as trading income and hence will be subject to National Insurance.

7.15 MANSION TAXES

In 2012, the Government began to introduce a series of additional tax charges aimed at UK residential property owned by 'non-natural persons'. The definition of 'non-natural persons' includes companies, partnerships where a company is a partner, and collective investment schemes. Most commonly, the charges apply to companies. They do not apply to property investors operating purely as individuals.

Three charges are involved:

- The 15% 'corporate rate' of Stamp Duty Land Tax (see Section 7.2)
- The Annual Tax on Enveloped Dwellings
- Capital Gains Tax at 28% on the disposal of the property

These charges are often collectively known as 'mansion taxes' and they apply regardless of where the 'non-natural person' is resident for tax purposes.

However, the charges only apply to single dwellings worth in excess of the specified threshold. They do not only apply by reference to the total value of the property portfolio.

Business Exemption

The good news for most property investors operating through a company (or any other 'non-natural person') is that properties are exempt from these charges if they are being used in a business: including a property rental business. Hence, in most cases, property investment companies should be exempt from the three 'mansion taxes'; although it will be essential to ensure that properties are being acquired for use in the business, and continue to be held for business purposes thereafter.

The bad news, however, is that any company or other 'non-natural person' which is eligible for this exemption will need to claim it – whenever they buy property worth more than £500,000 for SDLT purposes; and on an annual basis when they own property worth more than the specified threshold for the purposes of the Annual Tax on Enveloped Dwellings.

Hence, even if there is no extra tax, there will still be plenty of extra administration to deal with!

Falling Thresholds

Prior to 20ᵗ March 2014, the three 'mansion taxes' only applied to property worth in excess of £2m. However, the 2014 Budget included the announcement that the scope of these charges will be substantially increased over the next couple of years, so that they will eventually apply to property worth in excess of just £500,000.

The 15% SDLT charge was applied to purchases of relevant property for a price in excess of £500,000 with effect from 20ᵗ March 2014.

The thresholds for the Annual Tax on Enveloped Dwellings and Capital Gains Tax charges are to be reduced progressively over the next couple of years.

The Annual Tax on Enveloped Dwellings

The Annual Tax on Enveloped Dwellings has applied to property worth in excess of £2m since 1ˢ April 2013. The rates applying for 2014/15 are:

Property Value	Charge
Over £2m, but not more than £5m	£15,400
Over £5m, but not more than £10m	£35,900
Over £10m, but not more than £20m	£71,850
Over £20m	£143,750

The Annual Tax on Enveloped Dwellings will apply to property worth over £1m, but no more than £2m, from 1· April 2015 and will initially be charged at £7,000 per annum on these properties. It will apply to property worth over £500,000, but no more than £1m, from 1· April 2016 and will initially be charged at £3,500 per annum on these properties.

All of the Annual Tax on Enveloped Dwellings charges will be increased annually in line with the Consumer Prices Index.

Capital Gains Tax Charges

The 28% Capital Gains Tax charge applies to gains on properties worth over £2m accruing after 5· April 2013.

It will apply to gains on properties worth over £1m, but no more than £2m, accruing after 5· April 2015 and to gains on properties worth over £500,000, but no more than £1m, accruing after 5· April 2016.

In each case, the Capital Gains Tax charge only applies to the increase in the property's value between the specified date and the date of disposal.

A UK company that is caught by this charge would also pay Corporation Tax in the usual way on the gain arising up to the specified date.

Other entities will be subject to tax on the gain arising up to the specified date according to whichever rules would normally apply in the absence of the Capital Gains Tax charge. Most non-resident entities would currently be exempt from any UK tax on capital gains accruing prior to the specified date, although the Government is proposing to introduce new rules to ensure that all gains accruing on UK residential property after 5· April 2015 will be subject to some form of UK tax charge.

Example

On 30· April 2014, Halfmill Investments Ltd bought two properties for £600,000 each: numbers 10 and 11 Wonding Street.

No. 10 Wonding Street is used as a rental property and is rented out to unconnected tenants.

No. 11 Wonding Street is used as a private residence by Mr Born-Oz, the company's owner.

Both properties are sold on 30 June 2017 at a price of £800,000 each.

The SDLT arising on the purchase of No. 10 (the rental property) will be at the normal rate of 4%: i.e. £24,000. As Halfmill Investments Ltd is a UK company, it will be subject to Corporation Tax on the gain arising on the sale of this property, which is £176,000 (£800,000 - £600,000 - £24,000). The company may, however, claim indexation relief based on the amount of inflation (measured by the Retail Prices Index) over the period of its ownership of the property. Let's say this amounts to 9%, giving relief of £56,160 (£624,000 x 9%).

The company thus pays Corporation Tax at 20% on £119,840 (£176,000 - £56,160), which is just £23,968.

This property will be exempt from the Annual Tax on Enveloped Dwellings, but the company will have to claim exemption from the charge on annual returns for 2016/17 and 2017/18.

The SDLT arising on the purchase of No. 11 (the private residence) will be at 15%: i.e. £90,000. The company will also be subject to the Annual Tax on Enveloped Dwellings at £3,500 for both 2016/17 and 2017/18 (although part of the later year's charge may subsequently be recoverable after the property has been sold).

When the company sells the property, it will be subject to Corporation Tax in the usual way on the part of the gain arising up to 5 April 2016. Let's say the property was worth £720,000 at that date, so this part of the gain amounts to £30,000 (£720,000 - £600,000 - £90,000).

Let's also say that the indexation relief for this period amounts to 5%, giving relief of £34,500 (£690,000 x 5%). This exceeds the amount of the gain, so no Corporation Tax is due. This may sound like a good outcome, but it only happens because of the huge amount of SDLT paid on the purchase of the property. Furthermore, the company is unable to claim any loss in respect of the excess indexation relief.

The remaining £80,000 of the gain on this property (i.e. the part of the gain arising between 6 April 2016 and 30 June 2017) is subject to Capital Gains Tax at a flat rate of 28%, i.e. £22,400.

In total, the tax paid on the private residence amounts to £119,400 (£90,000 + £3,500 x 2 + £22,400), compared with just £47,968 (£24,000 + £23,968) on the rental property. Mr Born-Oz might also be subject to Income Tax charges in respect of his private use of No. 11. If so, the company would be subject to Class 1A National Insurance on this too.

In short, holding private residences through a company is about to become a very expensive business!

7.16 SCOTTISH TAXES

Scotland is to hold an independence referendum on 18ᵗʰ September 2014. In the event of a 'Yes' vote, it is anticipated that Scotland will leave the UK and become an independent country on 24ᵗʰ March 2016.

Naturally, this will have far-reaching consequences for individuals, businesses and property in Scotland.

However, it is understood that no significant changes will be made to the tax system in Scotland as a consequence of independence until at least April 2017. Hence, in the event of Scottish independence, it is expected that all of the advice given in this guide will remain relevant to Scottish taxpayers and Scottish property until at least that time: subject to the further points below.

The Land and Buildings Transaction Tax

Regardless of the outcome of the independence referendum, Stamp Duty Land Tax will be abolished for all property located in Scotland from 1ˢᵗ April 2015 onwards. It will be replaced by a new Land and Buildings Transaction Tax.

There are no firm proposals regarding the rates of Land and Buildings Transaction Tax yet, but early indications suggest that it may work something along these lines:

Residential Property

- Exemption for the first £180,000 of purchase consideration
- A rate of 7.5% on any excess, up to total consideration of £1.5m
- A rate of 10% on any consideration in excess of £1.5m

Example

In May 2015 Isla buys a house in Aberdeen for £270,000. She pays Land and Buildings Transaction Tax at 7.5% on £90,000 (£270,000 - £180,000), which amounts to £6,750.

It is worth noting that Isla would have paid Stamp Duty Land Tax of £8,100 (£270,000 x 3%) if she had purchased a house South of the border at the same price.

Early indications suggest that the switch to Land and Buildings Transaction Tax will yield savings for those buying residential property in Scotland from April 2015 onwards with a purchase consideration of less than £207,700, or between £250,001 and £299,999. None of this is certain yet, however.

For non-residential property, the early indications are that Land and Buildings Transaction Tax will work on a similar basis along these lines:

Non-residential Property

- Exemption for the first £150,000 of purchase consideration
- A rate of 3% on consideration between £150,000 and £250,000
- A rate of 4.4% on any consideration in excess of £250,000

Example

In July 2015 Alex buys an office building in Glasgow for £325,000. The Land and Buildings Transaction Tax payable is as follows:

£150,000 @ 0% =	*£0*
£100,000 @ 3% =	*£3,000*
£75,000 @ 4.4% =	*£3,300*
Total:	*£6,300*

The Scottish Rate of Income Tax

If Scotland remains in the UK, Scottish taxpayers will be subject to the new Scottish Rate of Income Tax from 2016/17 onwards.

The Scottish Rate of Income Tax will operate by replacing 10p in the pound of UK Income Tax with the new Scottish Rate.

For example, if the Scottish Rate of Income Tax were set at 9%, Scottish taxpayers would be subject to the following overall Income Tax rates:

Basic rate:	19% (10% UK + 9% Scottish)
Higher rate:	39% (30% UK + 9% Scottish)
'Super tax':	44% (35% UK + 9% Scottish)

(Based on the assumption that UK Income Tax rates remain unchanged)

The Scottish Rate of Income Tax will apply to all of a Scottish taxpayer's income except:

- Dividends
- Interest and other savings income
- Income from Real Estate Investment Trusts or Property Authorised Investment Funds

Hence, the Scottish Rate of Income Tax will apply to all of a Scottish taxpayer's property rental or trading income, regardless of where their properties are located.

In other words, a Scottish taxpayer will pay the Scottish Rate of Income Tax on income derived from property both within and outside Scotland; other taxpayers will not pay the Scottish Rate of Income Tax on any of their income.

Who Will Be A Scottish Taxpayer?

In most cases, an individual will be classed as a Scottish taxpayer if their main residence is located in Scotland.

The individual's main residence must be determined as a question of fact: it will not be possible to elect which property is to be treated as their main residence for this purpose.

If it is not clear whether an individual's main residence is located in Scotland for any given tax year then the question of whether they are a Scottish taxpayer for that year will be based on where they have spent the most days. This will also apply to any individual who has moved to or from Scotland during the tax year.

An individual must be UK resident to be a Scottish taxpayer. Non-UK residents will not pay the Scottish Rate of Income Tax.

Planning for the Scottish Rate of Income Tax

The Scottish Parliament will set the Scottish Rate of Income Tax on an annual basis, beginning with 2016/17. However, as yet, we have no idea what the rate is likely to be.

From a planning point of view, it may be beneficial to move house by 4 October 2016. But I cannot yet tell you which way to go!

Chapter 8

Advanced Tax Planning

8.1 INTRODUCTION TO TAX PLANNING

In the previous chapters we have looked at the mechanics of the UK tax system as it applies to the individual property investor.

A great many planning ideas and principles have already emerged and doubtless, by now, some readers will have begun to form ideas of their own.

In this chapter we will take a look at some more advanced aspects of UK property taxation and some further useful planning strategies for property investors. These strategies relate in the main to those investors who continue to hold their property investments personally.

In many cases, the best tax-planning results will be obtained through the use of a combination of different techniques, rather than merely following any single one.

Each situation is different and the optimum solution only comes through a detailed analysis of all the relevant facts.

Tax planning should therefore never be undertaken without full knowledge of the facts of the case and the exact circumstances of the individuals and other legal entities involved.

For this reason, the techniques laid out in this chapter, which are by no means exhaustive, are intended only to give you some idea of the tax savings which can be achieved through careful planning.

If and when you come to undertake any tax-planning measures of your own you should seek professional advice from someone fully acquainted with your situation.

Remember also that tax law is constantly changing and a technique which works well now may later be undermined by changes made in Parliament or decisions made in Court.

In this context, it is important to be aware of the new General Anti-Abuse Rule which came into force with effect from 16ᵗʰ July 2013. We will look at the implications of this new rule a little further in Section 8.34.

Bayley's Tax Planning Law

All tax planning should be based on these four guiding principles:

- Hope for the best,
- Plan for the worst,
- Review your position constantly, and
- Expect the unexpected!

The Budgets, Pre-Budget Reports and Autumn Statements which we have seen over the last few years have provided some of the best arguments for these principles that I have ever seen. Especially the last one!

8.2   THE BENEFITS OF JOINT OWNERSHIP

Owning property jointly with one or more other people can be highly beneficial for tax purposes.

In this section, we will look at joint ownership benefits which are available to anyone. In the next section, we will concentrate on married couples.

A number of important tax reliefs and tax bands are available on a 'per person' basis, these include:

- The personal allowance
- The annual exemption for Capital Gains Tax
- Private letting relief
- Entrepreneurs' relief
- The basic rate tax band
- The £100,000 threshold for withdrawal of personal allowances
- The £150,000 'super tax' threshold
- The small earnings exception for National Insurance
- The National Insurance earnings threshold
- The nil rate band for Inheritance Tax

Furthermore, as discussed in Section 4.8, it is also possible to structure investments so that the annual investment allowance effectively operates on a 'per person' basis.

The value of these allowances, bands and reliefs can effectively be doubled in the case of properties held jointly by two people (or tripled for three joint owners, etc.).

How Much Is At Stake?

Sticking with two joint owners, the maximum tax savings which joint ownership can generate in 2014/15 alone are:

- £6,266 on most capital gains
- £17,466 on capital gains with private letting relief
- £1,803,080 on capital gains with entrepreneurs' relief (but see the 'wealth warning' in Section 6.28)
- £16,873 in Income Tax on rental income
- £14,515 in Income Tax and National Insurance on trading profits
- £226,500 in additional Income Tax savings (or even repayments) when claiming the annual investment allowance on commercial property, qualifying furnished holiday accommodation, or assets within 'communal areas' (see Sections 4.8 and 8.15)
- £130,000 in Inheritance Tax

The maximum Income Tax savings described above are based on taxpayers with very high levels of income such that joint ownership can be used, in each case, to reduce their taxable income down to £100,000. Most higher-rate taxpayers can still achieve considerable savings, however.

Wealth Warning

Not every tax relief or band is given on a 'per person' basis. Exceptions to be wary of include:

- All Corporation Tax rate bands
- All Stamp Duty Land Tax bands
- The VAT registration threshold
- Rent-a-room relief
- The landlord's energy-saving allowance

Additionally, in the case of the upper earnings limit for National Insurance, the fact that this works on a 'per person' basis will actually work against joint owners in a trading situation (although this is usually outweighed by Income Tax savings).

Non-Equal Splits

When considering the benefits of joint ownership, remember that it is possible to have any split of beneficial ownership which you desire, as long as the correct form of joint ownership is in place (see Section 2.13).

216

In this context, it is worth mentioning that a joint tenancy can be changed fairly easily into a tenancy in common. This change is not treated as a disposal for Capital Gains Tax purposes unless at the same time there is also a change to a non-equal split of beneficial ownership.

Changing the Split

Where the joint owners are not a married couple, it is difficult to transfer any share in the property across to the other person without incurring Capital Gains Tax or other charges. In Section 8.7, however, we will look at a possible way around this.

Nevertheless, for joint owners other than married couples, it is generally advisable to get your ownership structure right from the outset.

Optimising Rental Income Shares

Joint owners who are not a married couple may agree to share rental income in different proportions to their legal ownership of the property (perhaps because one of the investors is carrying out the management of the jointly held portfolio). The Income Tax treatment should follow the agreed profit-sharing arrangements. It is wise to document your profit-sharing agreement in order to avoid any dispute, however.

Sales by Former Joint Owners

For the purposes of calculating the principal private residence exemption, a former joint owner's period of ownership of the whole property is treated as commencing with the date on which they first acquired any beneficial ownership of any part of the property.

8.3   USING YOUR SPOUSE OR CIVIL PARTNER

Putting property into joint names with your spouse can generate considerable tax savings, just like any other joint owners, as we have seen in the previous section. In some cases, an outright transfer of the whole property may even be more beneficial.

The major difference between those who have legally 'tied the knot' and the rest of us, however, is the fact that the transfer itself is free from tax and will not normally result in any loss of existing reliefs, such as the principal private residence exemption (but see further below).

The example of George and Charlotte in Section 6.32 already demonstrates the potential Capital Gains Tax savings. However, it is normally immaterial whether the property was in joint ownership throughout, or was only transferred into joint ownership at a later date, prior to the ultimate sale (often known as a 'pre-sale transfer'). The effect on the couple's final tax liabilities usually remains exactly the same.

As we saw in Section 6.32, the potential Capital Gains Tax saving on a typical investment property is now up to £6,266. However, the position will differ from one couple to another, so investors need to weigh up the costs of any 'pre-sale transfer' against the saving available in their own particular case.

Far greater savings may be available where the property is eligible for private letting relief (see Section 6.14). It is possible to double the maximum amount of relief available (from £40,000 to £80,000) by putting the property into joint names prior to sale. This can lead to total savings of up to £17,466 and is therefore often worth considering.

Three key provisos must be made here however:

a) The transferee spouse must be beneficially entitled to his/her share of the sale proceeds. Any attempt to prevent this could make the transfer invalid for tax purposes.

b) An interim transfer of property into joint names prior to sale must take place early enough to ensure that the transferee spouse genuinely has beneficial title to their share. If it is left until the ultimate sale is a contractual certainty, it may be too late to be effective for tax purposes.

c) HM Revenue and Customs' interpretation of the law is that a spouse will not be entitled to any principal private residence relief or private letting relief on their portion of a capital gain if the property in question was NEVER their only or main residence during the couple's ownership.

I am not sure that I agree with HM Revenue and Customs' interpretation at (c) above, but it would perhaps be foolish to plan your affairs on any other basis.

Example

Caleb has lived in his house in Liverpool for many years as his main residence. In September 2014 he moves out to be closer to his partner David in London and begins to rent the property out. In March 2015, Caleb and David marry and Caleb decides to put his Liverpudlian property into joint names in order to save some Income Tax.

In February 2016, Caleb decides to sell the house in Liverpool. Caleb will be fully exempted by principal private residence relief on his share of the capital gain. David, however, would be fully taxable on his share as the property was never his only or main residence.

There are one or two ways in which Caleb and David might get around this dilemma. The easiest method might simply be to transfer the property back into Caleb's sole ownership. Alternatively, they could both move back into the property for some reasonable period prior to the sale, so that it could qualify as David's main residence for principal private residence relief purposes.

Under the second scenario, David would be entitled to the same principal private residence relief and private letting relief as Caleb, even though he didn't live there all of the time that Caleb did.

Timing

Where a transfer to a spouse prior to sale is planned, the following guidelines may assist in making it effective for tax purposes. Bear in mind always, though, that the transferee must have beneficial ownership for the transfer to work as intended.

- It is preferable to do the transfer as soon as possible.
- Ideally, it should be before the property is put on the market.
- A transfer at any time after there is a contract for sale to a third party is likely to be ineffective in providing the transferee with the requisite beneficial ownership.

But Joint Ownership Is Not Always Beneficial

A transfer into joint names prior to sale is not always beneficial. Sometimes, it is preferable to have the property in the sole name of one spouse at the time of sale. This may arise, for example, if:

- One spouse's annual exemption will be used on other capital gains in the same year, whilst the other's annual exemption remains fully available,
- Some or all of one spouse's basic rate band is available but the other spouse is a higher rate taxpayer,
- Only one spouse is entitled to principal private residence relief on the property (as in the example of Caleb and David above),
- Only one spouse is entitled to entrepreneurs' relief on the property (see Section 6.28), or
- One spouse has capital losses available to set off against the gain on the property.

If the best spouse to hold the property at the time of the sale is not the one who already holds it, a pre-sale transfer could generate considerable savings. The same provisos as set out above apply equally here.

In summary, when a sale is in prospect, it is well worth assessing whether a transfer into joint ownership, or to the other spouse outright, might result in a significant Capital Gains Tax saving. Always remember, however, that whoever has title to the property at the time of the sale must be entitled to the proceeds!

Lastly, it is also worth remembering that joint ownership does not have to mean equal shares and any other allocation is also possible.

8.4   HAVE YOUR CAKE AND EAT IT

Income Tax savings can also be generated by transferring investment property either into joint names with your spouse or into the sole name of the spouse with the lower overall income. In the right circumstances, moving income from one spouse to another in this way could save a higher-rate taxpayer over £10,000 in Income Tax in 2014/15 alone.

As we saw in Section 8.2, some taxpayers could even save almost £17,000 in 2014/15.

However, as explained in Section 8.3 above, this form of tax planning is not effective unless beneficial title in the property is genuinely transferred. But not everyone trusts their spouse enough to simply hand over the title to their property!

For Income Tax purposes, at least, there is a way to solve this dilemma. Where property is held jointly by a married couple, there is an automatic presumption, for Income Tax purposes, that the income arises in equal shares. This 50/50 split will continue to be applied unless and until the couple jointly elect for the income to be split in accordance with the true beneficial title in the property.

Hence, where a married property owner wants to save Income Tax on their rental profits without giving up too much of their title to the property, what they should do is:

- Transfer the property into joint names with their spouse.
- Retain 99% of the beneficial ownership and transfer only 1% to their spouse.

AND

- Simply never elect for the income to be split in accordance with the true beneficial title.

220

Conversely

Conversely, of course, there will be cases where the actual beneficial ownership split is preferable for tax purposes. In these cases, the election to split the income on an actual basis should usually be made.

Beware though that, once made, this election is irreversible.

8.5   MARRIAGE, DIVORCE AND CIVIL PARTNERSHIPS

Getting married alters your tax status dramatically. One major aspect of this for property investors is the fact that, from that date onwards, the couple can only have one main residence between them for principal private residence relief purposes.

When the 'happy day' comes, there are some important tax-planning points to bear in mind:

i)   If more than one private residence is available to you as a couple, you should elect which one is to be your main residence (see Section 6.22). In these circumstances, the election must be done within two years of the date of marriage.

ii)   You will normally have at least eighteen months during which the residence which is no longer regarded as a main residence continues to be exempt under the principal private residence exemption.

In most cases, where each member of the couple had their own main residence prior to the marriage, the best way to maximise your overall tax reliefs would be to take the following steps *after* you marry:

i)   Put both of your former main residences into joint names.
ii)   Both live in each property as your main residence (together) at some period, or
iii)   If both properties continue to be your private residences (i.e. not let out, etc), use main residence elections to ensure that each property has main residence status for you both at some time (but see Section 6.22 regarding the potential withdrawal of the main residence election facility in the future).

Divorce and Separation

Once you get separated or divorced your married status for tax purposes ends. 'Separated' in this context means either legally separated under the terms of a court order or separated in circumstances which are likely to be permanent. The good news is that, once again, you will be able to have your own individual main residence for principal private residence relief purposes.

Alternatively, if you have not claimed any principal private residence relief on another property in the interim, nor made any main residence election in favour of another property, your former marital home may continue to be exempt as long as your ex-spouse continues to use it as their main residence.

However, this extension to the principal private residence exemption only applies in the case of a subsequent transfer of the former marital home, or a share in it, to the former spouse, as part of a financial settlement.

8.6 INHERITED PROPERTY

In Section 6.11 we looked at the base cost of inherited property and saw that this is generally based on the property's value at the date of the previous owner's death.

In many cases, this is pretty much all there is to tell and the new owner is treated in every respect as if they had purchased the property on the date of the previous owner's death.

There are a few areas of complication which we need to consider, however.

Firstly, there is the fact that during the period of administration the deceased's estate is treated as a separate legal person, rather like a trust.

Like trusts, estates pay Capital Gains Tax at a single flat rate of 28% (except where entrepreneurs' relief is available).

The estate has its own annual exemption equal to the amount given to individuals. The exemption applies for the tax year of death and the following two tax years.

If a property is sold by the deceased's estate, it is treated as if it had been acquired on the date of the deceased's death for its market value on that date. Where 75% or more of the sale proceeds are to go to one or more beneficiaries who occupied the property as their main residence at the time of the deceased's death, the principal private residence exemption will apply to any gain arising.

Transfers of property from the estate to the beneficiary are exempt from Capital Gains Tax.

Secondly, where the new owner of the whole property was already a joint owner prior to the deceased's death, the calculation of principal private residence relief is based on their whole period of ownership (see Section 8.2).

HM Revenue and Customs' view, shared by some commentators, is that a surviving joint owner cannot claim private letting relief on the deceased's share of an inherited property in respect of lettings made prior to the deceased's death.

Widows, Widowers and Surviving Civil Partners

Further complications arise where property passes to a surviving spouse. In the common situation where the surviving spouse was already a joint owner prior to the deceased's death, the points set out below are subject to those made above regarding joint owners which continue to apply.

The main point to note is that for the purposes of calculating principal private residence relief, the survivor is treated as if they had owned the property from the date that it was acquired by the deceased spouse. This does not alter the basic rule regarding the inherited property's base cost, but only acts to determine what **proportion** of the gain is covered by the relief.

The survivor is not, however, eligible for any private letting relief in respect of a letting made by the deceased.

If the couple were separated at the date of the deceased's death (see Section 8.5), the survivor is treated like an unmarried partner for all Capital Gains Tax purposes.

8.7   TAX-FREE PROPERTY TRANSFERS

As we have already seen, married couples are able to transfer property from one spouse to the other free from Capital Gains Tax.

However, transfers of property, or shares in property, to other people, such as an unmarried partner or adult child, present us with a problem.

In principle, such a transfer must be treated as if the property, or property share, had been sold for its open market value.

In many cases, this would produce a significant Capital Gains Tax liability. (There are some important exceptions of course: including the transferor's main residence and property used in the transferor's trading business.)

However, where a property owner makes a lifetime transfer of property into a trust, they may elect to 'hold over' the capital gain arising. At a later date, the trust can then transfer the property to the intended recipient and the trustees may again elect to 'hold over' the gain. In this way, Capital Gains Tax may be avoided on both transfers.

The end result is that the transferee is treated as if they had purchased the property for the same price as the transferor.

However, they are **not** treated as if they acquired the property at the same time as the transferor. For all other Capital Gains Tax purposes the date of purchase is the date that the property is finally transferred out of the trust to the transferee.

This technique does not work where the trust is a 'settlor-interested trust' (see Section 6.11) and should not generally be used where principal private residence relief is available (see Section 6.20).

Furthermore, 'hold over' relief is only available for Capital Gains Tax purposes and would not apply to a property classed as trading stock!

Transferring property to a trust has significant Inheritance Tax implications. Problems can usually be avoided, however, where the property is not worth in excess of £325,000 and the ultimate transfer to the transferee individual takes place within ten years. The full tax-saving potential of this planning technique is examined in the Taxcafe.co.uk guide 'How to Save Inheritance Tax'.

8.8   WHY 'LET TO BUY' BEATS 'BUY TO LET'

When a person lets out their existing home in order to fund the purchase of a new property, we call this 'Let to Buy'. From a tax perspective, 'Let to Buy' scores heavily over 'Buy to Let' for two main reasons:

- Both properties will attract principal private residence relief, and
- Equity in the former home can be released and used for any purpose whilst still attracting Income Tax relief on the interest arising.

Example – Buy to Let

Gregor bought his current home in 1999 for £50,000 and in 2014 it is worth £200,000. Eventually, in 2024, he sells the house for £400,000. Naturally, it is fully exempt from Capital Gains Tax as it has been his main residence throughout his ownership.

Gregor also buys a 'Buy-to-Let' property for £200,000 in 2014. This property is also sold for £400,000 in June 2024. Gregor is a higher rate taxpayer for 2024/25.

After his annual exemption for 2024/25 of £14,000 (say), Gregor has a taxable gain of £186,000 and a Capital Gains Tax bill, at 28%, of £52,080.

Example – Let to Buy

The situation is exactly as before except that, on acquisition of the second property in 2014, Gregor moves out of his former home, begins to rent it out and adopts the new property as his main residence.

Gregor's former home produces an overall gain of £350,000. Sixteen and a half years out of his total ownership period of 25 years is exempted by principal private residence relief. This represents the 15 years of occupation of the property as Gregor's main residence plus his last eighteen months of ownership. Gregor's principal private residence relief thus amounts to £231,000.

Gregor is also entitled to private letting relief of £40,000, bringing his gain down to £79,000 before his 2024/25 annual exemption of £14,000 (say). The taxable gain is thus a mere £65,000, giving him a Capital Gains Tax bill at 28% of just £18,200.

Gregor therefore saves £33,880 simply by moving house!

Added Benefits

In addition to Gregor's huge Capital Gains Tax saving, he could also save substantial amounts of Income Tax on his rental income by maximising the mortgage on his original home (see Section 4.4).

Gregor's Income Tax relief would be unaffected even if he used any additional borrowings for the deposit on his new home. Gregor might even manage to avoid the need to take out any mortgage on his new home, thus confining any risk to his rental property alone.

8.9   CLIMBING THE LADDER

In Chapter 6 we saw how far the principal private residence exemption can be extended.

This can be used to great effect to enable a taxpayer to build up a property portfolio virtually free of any Capital Gains Tax. The basic method is best explained by way of example.

Example

Malcolm buys a small flat (Flat A) in July 2014. He moves in and it becomes his main residence. A year later, he buys another, larger, flat (Flat B). He does not immediately move into the new flat but spends a year renovating it. He moves into Flat B in July 2016, just before the anniversary of its purchase, and then starts renting out Flat A.

Malcolm now has two flats, both of which will be fully exempted by principal private residence relief until at least January 2018. Private letting relief may also further extend Flat A's tax-free status until July 2021 (depending on the ultimate sale price).

Example Continued

In July 2017, Malcolm buys a house (House C). Again, he does not move in immediately but spends a year renovating the house before moving in just before the anniversary of its purchase. He now starts renting out Flat B.

The Story So far (2018)

Flat A may be exempt from any Capital Gains Tax until July 2021, Flat B will be fully exempted until at least January 2020, quite possibly until July 2024, and House C will be fully exempted until at least January 2020, possibly until July 2022. All of this without even considering the annual exemption!

Eventually some of the earlier acquisitions will begin to be exposed to Capital Gains Tax. As illustrated in Chapter 6, however, this may take several years. When that point is reached, Malcolm can sell off the properties one at a time in order to make best use of his annual exemptions.

Potential Drawbacks

Many people have successfully followed a strategy similar to Malcolm's but there are one or two potential problems to be wary of.

Firstly, HM Revenue and Customs has the power to overturn the principal private residence exemption if they perceive that the taxpayer is carrying on a trade of property development or is acquiring properties with the primary motive of realising a profit on their sale.

Hence, Malcolm's strategy does carry some degree of risk. The longer he retains the properties after his original renovation and occupation periods, however, the more this risk will diminish.

Relying On The Principal Private Residence Exemption

In any planning scenario which places reliance on the principal private residence exemption, it is essential to ensure that the property or properties concerned genuinely become your private residence. There is no 'hard and fast' rule as to how long you must reside in a property to establish it as your private residence for Capital Gains Tax purposes. It is the quality of occupation that counts, not the length. Hence, it is recommended that you (and your spouse or partner and/or family, if applicable):

i) Move into the property for a substantial period.
ii) Ensure that all relevant institutions (banks, utilities, HM Revenue and Customs, employers, etc) are notified.
iii) Inform family/friends.
iv) Furnish the property for permanent occupation.
v) Register on the electoral roll for that address.
vi) Do not advertise the property for sale or rent until after the expiry of a substantial period.

It is not possible to provide a definitive view of what would constitute a 'substantial period'. What matters is that the property genuinely becomes your 'permanent home' for a period. In this context, 'permanent' means that it is intended to be your residence, rather than a temporary abode. You must move into the property with no clear plans for moving out again.

As a rough guide only, you should plan your affairs on the basis that you will be residing in the property for at least a year.

However, as already stated, the question would ultimately be decided on quality of occupation, rather than length. Where you are looking to use the principal private residence exemption on a property, you must embark upon occupying that property wholeheartedly; a mere 'sham' occupation will not suffice.

In some instances, you may be able to establish the desired result merely by electing for the property to be treated as your main residence (see Section 6.22). However, it can only be your main residence if it is indeed your private residence and the safest way to ensure that a property is accepted as being your private residence is to make it your main residence, or even your only residence, by following the measures set out above.

Furthermore, as explained in Section 6.22, the facility to make main residence elections may be withdrawn in the near future.

8.10 GENERAL ELECTIONS

As explained in Section 6.22, where a taxpayer has two or more private residences, it is currently possible to elect which is to be regarded as their main residence. In fact, it is more than possible, it is **highly advisable**, even when it seems obvious which property should be regarded as the main residence.

Example

Diana owns a house in London purchased in 2009 for £300,000. In July 2012, she buys a small cottage in Sussex for £100,000, as her 'weekend retreat'.

In early 2016, plans for a new motorway junction to be built only half a mile from Diana's cottage are announced. Simultaneously, the value of her property increases dramatically, whilst her own desire to use the place herself rapidly diminishes. A few months later, in July, she sells it for an astonishing £400,000.

Now, fortunately for Diana, her accountant had insisted that she make a main residence election in January 2014. At the time, she naturally elected that her London house was her main residence, since it seemed far more likely to produce a significant capital gain.

Because of this earlier election, however, Diana was able to make a new election in January 2015, stipulating her Sussex cottage as her main residence. She did this due to concerns about the potential withdrawal of the facility to make main residence elections (see the 'Major Wealth Warning' in Section 6.22).

A week later, Diana made a third election stipulating her London house as her main residence once more. This seemed sensible at the time as the London house still seemed likely to produce a larger capital gain and Diana wished to keep her Capital Gains Tax exposure on that property to a minimum.

Nonetheless, as a result of the Sussex cottage having main residence status for a week, it is covered by the principal private residence exemption for the last eighteen months of Diana's ownership. This exempts her from Capital Gains Tax on £112,500 out of her total gain of £300,000 and produces a saving of £31,500! (£112,500 x 28% = £31,500)

Furthermore, her London house will only lose its principal private residence exempt status for a week.

The moral of the story: always, always, **always** make the main residence election where applicable.

Tax Tip

A property only has to be classed as your main residence for **any** period, no matter how short, in order for your last eighteen months of ownership to be exempted under the principal private residence exemption.

Hence, in order to minimise the impact on the principal private residence relief available to another property, it is only necessary to elect in favour of the new 'main residence' for a very short period.

In Diana's case, she was able to preserve most of the principal private residence exemption on her London house by making another revised 'main residence' election in favour of that property a week after she had made the election in favour of her Sussex cottage.

Wealth Warning

Electing for an existing private residence to be your 'main residence' for just a week is fine.

Do not confuse this, however, with the need to establish the property as being your private residence in the first place (as explained in Section 8.9 above), where a considerably longer period of occupation is recommended.

Another Wealth Warning

The planning outlined in this section may no longer be available after 5ᵗ April 2015 (see the 'Major Wealth Warning' in Section 6.22).

Any main residence elections should therefore be made, and submitted to HM Revenue and Customs, before that date.

8.11 DEVELOPING YOUR HOME

As we have seen, the principal private residence exemption provides many opportunities to make large capital gains with little or no exposure to Capital Gains Tax.

Many people are able to enhance the amount of the tax-free capital gain on their home by making improvements to the property.

However, where expenditure is incurred specifically for the purpose of realising a profit on the sale of the property, HM Revenue and Customs is able to deny part of the principal private residence exemption.

Example

Harry bought his house in 1999 and has used it as his main residence ever since. In August 2014, the house is worth £400,000. Harry now decides to sell the house and realises that he can make more money if he has a swimming pool built. Harry and his family therefore move out of the house into a new home and he has the pool built at a cost of £30,000.

With its new swimming pool, Harry is able to sell the house for £500,000. He has therefore made an extra profit of £70,000 as a result of building the pool.

Harry's extra profit of £70,000 will not be covered by his principal private residence exemption. It will, however, still be eligible for the annual exemption (£11,000), leaving Harry with a taxable gain of £59,000 and a Capital Gains Tax liability of something between £13,334 and £16,520.

In practice, Harry might be able to argue that some of the extra £70,000 profit was just down to getting a good offer, or was due to a general increase in property values over the period since work began on the pool.

In other words, don't just accept that the whole of the extra gain is taxable: take other factors into account.

Many readers will be horrified by this last example but let me reassure you that HM Revenue and Customs generally only tends to use this power when major capital expenditure is blatantly carried out for no reason other than to make an extra profit on the sale of the property.

If Harry and his family had continued using the property after the pool was built and only sold it perhaps a year or two later, it is highly unlikely that there would have been any restriction to his principal private residence exemption.

Hence, in general, homeowners can enhance the value of their property by making capital improvements and still retain their principal private residence exemption: as long as there is a reasonable delay between those improvements being carried out and the property being put up for sale.

In the more common situation where homeowners carry out minor renovation work in order to prepare a property for sale, there is not usually any restriction in their principal private residence relief.

Furthermore, in practice, HM Revenue and Customs will not restrict principal private residence relief simply because a homeowner has obtained planning permission for conversion or improvement work.

Home Conversions

Where a property undergoes extensive conversion work, it may no longer remain a single dwelling for tax purposes. This is what HM Revenue and Customs refers to as a 'Change of Use' and it has a far wider-ranging impact than merely letting out part of your home.

Example

David bought a large detached house for £160,000 in December 2002. He lived in the whole house for one year and then converted it into two separate, semi-detached, houses. He continued to live in one of these, but rented the other one out. The conversion work cost £40,000, bringing his total costs up to £200,000.

In December 2014, David sold both houses for £300,000 each, making a total gain of £400,000.

David's gain must be apportioned between the two houses. As they each sold for the same price, it is reasonable to assume that the gain should be split equally between them (but see Section 5.2 for other allocation methods which might be used).

The £200,000 gain on the house which David retained as his own home will be fully covered by the principal private residence exemption.

However, David's £200,000 gain on the other house will only be covered by the principal private residence exemption for one year out of his twelve years of ownership. His principal private residence exemption on this house thus amounts to only £16,667, leaving a taxable gain of £183,333 (before the annual exemption).

There are two very important differences here to the situation in Section 6.26 where part of the property was let out, both of which occur because the rented house is no longer a part of the same dwelling:

i) The principal private residence exemption is not available for the last eighteen months of ownership.
ii) No private letting relief is available.

Tax Tips

David would have improved his position dramatically if he had spent some time living in the other semi-detached property after the conversion.

Taxpayers in this sort of situation may also sometimes find it more beneficial to treat the gains arising before and after the conversion as two separate gains. In David's case, for example, this would have been more beneficial for him if the original property had already increased in value by more than £33,334 before the conversion work began. This gain would have been completely exempt, half of which related to the house which was subsequently rented out.

Both approaches are equally acceptable and we will look at the alternative method in more detail later in this section.

Conversion for Sale

In our previous example, David did enough conversion work to mean that he had created two new 'dwellings' and this radically altered the amount of principal private residence relief available to him.

David did, however, retain both new properties long enough for them to remain capital assets in his hands under basic principles.

Where conversion work is carried out as a prelude to a sale, however, basic principles would usually dictate that the property has become trading stock. The profit arising on the development would then be treated as a trading profit and the principles examined in Chapter 5 would apply.

Nevertheless, there are some situations where a homeowner may develop part of their property for sale and still retain the more beneficial Capital Gains Tax treatment.

This is because HM Revenue and Customs cannot deem a former main residence to be trading stock unless they can also show that the owner has a property development trade. This means that 'one-off' developments which homeowners carry out on their own property may sometimes continue to be subject to Capital Gains Tax instead of Income Tax.

Example

Spencer inherited a large house from his Uncle Charles in March 2009 when it was worth £700,000. Spencer adopted the house as his main residence and

232

lived there until September 2014, at which point it was worth £900,000. Spencer then had the house converted into five flats at a total cost of £300,000.

Spencer moved into one of the flats and adopted it as his home. He then sold the other four flats for £350,000 each in March 2015. Spencer is a higher rate taxpayer for 2014/15 and his Capital Gains Tax liability on the sale of the flats is calculated as follows:

	£
Sale proceeds (4 x £350,000)	*1,400,000*
Less:	
Value prior to conversion (4/5 x £900,000)	*720,000*
Conversion costs (4/5 x 300,000)	*240,000*

Gain made on the development:	*440,000*
Less:	
Annual exemption	*11,000*

Taxable gain	*429,000*
	========
Capital Gains Tax at 28%:	*£120,120*

For the sake of illustration, I have taken a very simplistic approach to the allocation of costs here by assuming that the flats were all equal in size. In reality, a more sophisticated method will usually be appropriate, perhaps based on floor area or, better still, using accurate calculations prepared by a surveyor.

It is worth noting that Spencer's capital gain is based on the extra value created as a result of the conversion.

The property's previous increase in value from £700,000 in 2009 to £900,000 immediately before Spencer began his conversion work continues to be exempt because the whole property was his main residence during this period.

In this particular situation, Spencer does not appear to have a property development trade. His non-trading status is strengthened here by the fact that he had inherited the property.

The situation might be different if he had purchased the property within one or two years before commencing the conversion work or had carried out any similar developments in the past. Furthermore, if Spencer already had a property development trade, it is likely that this conversion would be seen as part of that business.

In practice, each situation has to be looked at on its own merits and HM Revenue and Customs will frequently argue that a trading activity exists.

If Spencer were deemed to have a property development trade, the gain of £440,000 made on the development would be taxed as a trading profit and could give rise to Income Tax of up to £199,500 and National Insurance of somewhere between £8,800 and £11,317.

(The maximum Income Tax cost of £199,500 arises if Spencer has other existing taxable income of £100,000 before taking the gain into account.)

Spencer's total tax liability could therefore be increased by up to £90,697.

Furthermore, if Spencer were treated as a developer, HM Revenue and Customs might also argue that the development profit of £110,000 on the flat which he retained should also be taxed as a trading profit, giving him a further tax bill of up to £51,700!

One drawback to treating the development as a capital gain, however, is that Spencer would not be able to deduct any interest or other overheads from his profit, only direct costs. This seems a small price to pay in Spencer's case but, in some other cases, it may actually be more beneficial if the development is treated as a trading activity.

The New Residence

The flat Spencer retained for personal use has now become his main residence and will continue to be eligible for principal private residence relief. To see how this works in practice, let's return to the example.

Example Continued

Spencer moves out of the flat in September 2019 and then rents it out before eventually selling it in March 2023 for £550,000. His Capital Gains Tax calculation is as follows:

	£
Sale proceeds	*550,000*
Less:	
Value when inherited (1/5 x £700,000)	*140,000*
Conversion costs (1/5 x 300,000)	*60,000*

Capital Gain before reliefs	*350,000*
Less:	
Principal private residence relief (£350,000 x 12/14):	*300,000*
(March 2009 to September 2019 + last 18 months	
=12 years out of 14)	
Private letting relief (maximum)	*40,000*

Gain before annual exemption	*10,000*
	======

After deducting his annual exemption, Spencer is unlikely to have any Capital Gains Tax to pay.

The new flat is not the same 'dwelling' as the original house prior to the conversion work, but in our example they were both used as Spencer's main residence. He is therefore able to claim principal private residence relief on the appropriate proportion of the gain both before and after the conversion work.

The calculation set out above is not the only valid method. The law only requires a method which is 'just and reasonable'. An alternative method might be to view the gain on the first 'dwelling' from March 2009 to September 2014 as wholly exempt and then compute the gain on the second dwelling (the flat) as follows:

	£
Sale proceeds	*550,000*
Less:	
Value before conversion (1/5 x £900,000)	*180,000*
Conversion costs (1/5 x 300,000)	*60,000*

Capital Gain before reliefs	*310,000*
Less:	
Principal private residence relief (£310,000 x 6½/8½):	*237,059*
September 2014 to September 2019 + last 18 months	
(= 6½ years out of 8½)	
Private letting relief (maximum)	*40,000*

Gain before annual exemption	*32,941*
	======

This method produces a larger capital gain and is therefore likely to be favoured by HM Revenue and Customs. Nevertheless, the first method may also be regarded as 'just and reasonable'.

At this point, I can only advise you to be aware of the alternative methods. Use the one which is best for you, but be prepared for an argument!

Lastly, there is also the possibility discussed above that the development gain on this flat may have been taxed already as a trading profit. In this case, the capital gain on the sale of the flat in 2023 would be just £200,000 (£550,000 - £350,000), the principal private residence relief (6/8ths) would be £150,000, private letting relief would remain £40,000, and the remaining gain of £10,000 would most likely be covered by Spencer's annual exemption.

(If you're wondering why the principal private residence relief is 6/8ths in this last calculation when we used 6½ years out of 8½ in the previous one, it's because Spencer was able to treat the flat as his main residence from September 2014 in the earlier calculation (see Section 6.17), but would only be regarded as re-adopting it as a capital asset in March 2015 if it had been treated as trading stock during the development period.)

8.12   SOMETHING IN THE GARDEN

It's a common scenario: a taxpayer has a large garden, so he or she sells part of it off for property development. (See Section 6.16 for general guidance on the limitations of the principal private residence exemption in these circumstances.)

There are the right ways to do this and there are other ways, which are very, very wrong.

The Wrong Ways

DO NOT:

- Sell your house first before selling the development plot.
- Fence the development plot off or otherwise separate it from the rest of your garden before selling it.
- Use the development plot for any purpose other than your own private residential occupation immediately prior to the sale.
- Allow the development plot to fall into disuse.

Each of these will result in the complete loss of your principal private residence exemption for the development plot. And, furthermore, do not assume that the plot is covered by the principal private residence exemption if the total area of your house and garden exceeds half a hectare.

Practical Pointer

Fencing off the plot alone may not necessarily lead to the loss of your principal private residence exemption on the plot; provided that the plot continues to be used for your own private residential occupation up to the point of sale. Nonetheless, there remains some doubt over this issue, so it is wise to avoid any separation of the plot from the rest of the garden prior to sale.

The Right Ways

First, the simple way:

Carefully ensuring that you do not commit any of the cardinal sins described above, you simply sell off the plot of land. This sale will now enjoy the same principal private residence exemption as applies to your house itself. (E.g., if 90% of a gain on your house would have been exempt, then 90% of the gain on the plot of land will be exempt.)

The Other 'Right Way'

The only drawback to the simple way is that you do not get to participate in any of the profit on the development of the plot.

But, what if you hang on to the plot and develop it yourself? Yes, at first this looks like we've gone the wrong way, but not if you then proceed to move into the new property and adopt it as your main residence.

Your old house can safely be sold at any time up to eighteen months after the date you move out and still be covered by the principal private residence exemption.

The new house should be fully covered by the principal private residence exemption as long as you moved in within a year of the date that development started.

As in Section 8.9, there are some potential dangers here, but the exemption should be available if you genuinely adopt the new house as your new main residence.

Wealth Warning 1

Although the new house will be covered by the principal private residence exemption, there is an argument that any gain on the land comprised in the development plot arising prior to the point that development commenced is not covered.

For example, if the cost of the land were £10,000 (based on an allocation of the original house's purchase price) and it was worth £20,000 immediately prior to the commencement of the development of the new house, there would be a gain of £10,000 which was not covered by principal private residence relief. Such a small gain would probably be covered by the owner's annual exemption, but larger gains would lead to a Capital Gains Tax liability.

Wealth Warning 2

More worryingly, some commentators argue that the gain on the new house would have to be calculated on a 'time apportionment' basis, with principal private residence relief only applying to the period of occupation.

For example, if the land had originally cost £10,000 (as above) in 2004; the development had taken place in 2014 and cost £140,000; and the house was then occupied as a main residence until eventually being sold for £300,000 in 2024; the principal private residence relief would then be restricted to just £75,000, leaving a taxable gain of £75,000 (before the annual exemption).

At present, it is not clear which of the above interpretations is correct. Personally, however, I would argue strongly in favour of either full principal private residence exemption or the 'just and reasonable' allocation under 'Wealth Warning 1' above, as permitted by the relevant tax legislation.

What is beyond doubt, however, is that if the newly developed property were sold straight away, this would give rise to a trading profit (see Chapter 5).

8.13 STUDENT LOANS

Each unmarried adult is entitled to have their own main private residence which is exempt from Capital Gains Tax.

Once your children reach the age of 18 therefore, it is possible to put some tax-free capital growth into their hands. (They do not actually have to be students by the way – it works just as well if they are in employment or even just living a life of leisure at your expense, as many teenagers seem to do!)

The basic method is fairly straightforward: all that you need to do is purchase a property in their name which they then move into and adopt as their main residence.

Financing can be achieved in a number of ways, but the important point is that they must have legal and beneficial title to the property. (Hence this simple technique should only be undertaken if you are prepared to pass wealth on to the children.)

The purchase of the property has possible Inheritance Tax implications but these are avoided simply by surviving for seven years.

Wealth Warning

You should also be careful not to make any use of the property yourself, since, if you have provided the funds for its purchase, any subsequent occupation by you or your spouse may give rise to an Income Tax charge under the 'pre-owned assets' regime.

Keeping the Capital Growth Yourself

Alternatively, if you would prefer to keep the wealth to yourself for the time being, you may want to use the trust method set out in the next section.

8.14 USING A TRUST FOR EXTRA PRINCIPAL PRIVATE RESIDENCE RELIEF

As explained in Section 6.20, a trust is exempt from Capital Gains Tax on a property occupied as a main residence by one of the trust's beneficiaries.

Although this exemption does not apply where a capital gain on a property has been held over on a transfer into the trust, there is no problem where the property is purchased by the trust in the first place (or is transferred to the trust with no hold over claim).

Hence, it is possible to obtain principal private residence relief on an additional property using the following method:

i)   Set up a trust with another person (or persons) as the beneficiary (but not your spouse)
ii)   Purchase a residential property through the trust
iii) The beneficiary adopts the property as their main residence (remember that, like everyone else, they can only have one main residence and the usual rules apply if they are married)

You retain the reversionary interest in the trust. This means that the trust assets will ultimately revert to you. As explained in Section 6.11, this means that the trust is a 'settlor-interested' trust and hold over relief is not available on any transfer of property into the trust. This is not a problem – you don't want hold over relief anyway!

Some years later, but within eighteen months of when the property ceases to be the beneficiary's main residence, the trust can either sell the property or transfer it to you.

Either way, the gain arising will be exempt from Capital Gains Tax and you can either retain the property or enjoy the tax free sales proceeds.

Wealth Warnings

This method has potential Inheritance Tax implications which are explained in detail in the Taxcafe.co.uk guide *'How to Save Inheritance Tax'*.

In general, however, it is usually possible to avoid any problems by restricting the value of property held in the trust to no more than the amount of the Inheritance Tax nil rate band (currently £325,000). A couple can effectively double this amount as long as they structure their investments carefully.

Once again, you should also be careful to ensure that neither you nor your spouse makes any use of the property whilst it is held by the trust as this may give rise to Income Tax charges under the 'pre-owned assets' regime.

8.15 FURNISHED HOLIDAY LETTINGS

Prior to the General Election in 2010, the old Labour Government had been planning to abolish the beneficial tax regime for furnished holiday lettings. Thankfully, the then opposition managed to secure a last minute reprieve and the current Coalition Government has confirmed that the regime will be retained for the foreseeable future.

The current Government has, however, made some amendments to the regime which have restricted its benefits and which also now make it more difficult for properties to qualify.

Benefits of Furnished Holiday Lettings

For many years, furnished holiday lettings have enjoyed the best of all worlds. They continue to be treated as investment properties whenever that is more beneficial but get treated like a trade whenever many trading reliefs are up for grabs.

They can sometimes qualify as private residential accommodation and yet still get so many of the advantages generally reserved for commercial property.

Even despite the recent changes, getting one of your properties to qualify as furnished holiday accommodation is the property tax equivalent of winning the lottery! (Albeit with the proviso that the winnings are not quite as great as they used to be and the chances of winning have been reduced!)

In essence, properties qualifying as 'furnished holiday lettings' enjoy a special tax regime, which includes many of the tax advantages usually only accorded to trading properties. At the same time, however, the profits derived from furnished holiday lettings are still treated as rental income.

The current taxation benefits of qualifying furnished holiday lettings include the following:

- Entrepreneurs' relief
- Rollover relief on replacement of business assets
- Holdover relief for gifts
- Capital allowances for furniture, fixtures, fittings and integral features (see Section 4.8)
- Despite its 'trading-style' advantages, National Insurance should not usually be payable in respect of income from furnished holiday accommodation (but see Section 7.14)
- A non-UK resident investing in UK furnished holiday accommodation would usually continue to be exempt from Capital Gains Tax on gains arising up to 5ᵗʰ April 2015

The letting of holiday accommodation is, however, standard-rated for VAT purposes (whether or not the qualifying conditions set out below are met). The landlord must therefore register for VAT if gross annual income from UK holiday lets exceeds £81,000. Foreign VAT registration will also often be required in respect of holiday lettings elsewhere within the European Union (see Appendix D).

A furnished holiday letting business might also be exempt from Inheritance Tax where the lettings are generally short-term and the owner (or their employees) was substantially involved with the holidaymakers' activities.

The available reliefs extend to any property used in a furnished holiday letting business. This will include not only the holiday accommodation itself but also any office premises from which the business is run.

Loss Relief

From 2011/12 onwards, losses arising in a furnished holiday letting business may only be carried forward for set off against future profits from the same furnished holiday letting business.

For this purpose, all of a landlord's UK furnished holiday lettings are regarded as one business but any furnished holiday lettings elsewhere in the European Economic Area (EEA) are regarded as a different business.

(All furnished holiday lettings within the EEA but outside the UK are regarded as the same business.)

See Appendix D for a list of countries within the EEA.

Qualification

The current qualification requirements for a property to be regarded as a furnished holiday letting are set out below. The previous requirements for 2011/12 and earlier years are included in brackets.

    i)   The property must be situated in the EEA (see Appendix D)
    ii) The property must be furnished (to at least the minimum level which an occupier would usually expect)
    iii) It must be let out on a commercial basis with a view to the realisation of profits
    iv) It must be available for commercial letting to the public generally for at least 210 days in a 12-month period (140 days up to 2011/12)
    v)   It must be so let for at least 105 such days (70 days up to 2011/12)
    vi) The property must not normally be in the same occupation for more than 31 consecutive days at any time during a period of at least seven months out of the same 12-month period as that referred to in (iv) above

The 12-month period referred to in (iv) and (vi) above is normally the tax year.

From 2011/12 onwards, landlords can elect for properties which qualified for the furnished holiday letting regime under the above criteria in the previous year to stay within the regime for up to two further tax years despite failing to meet the test under (v) above. In effect, this means that properties will generally only need to meet this test once every three years. The property will still need to meet all of the other tests, however, and the landlord must make genuine efforts to meet the test under (v) every year.

A taxpayer with more than one furnished holiday letting property may also use a system of averaging to determine whether they meet test (v). This extension cannot, however, be used in conjunction with the two year extension described above: properties must qualify in their own right before the two year extension can be claimed.

Other Qualification Issues

Whilst the property need not be in a recognised holiday area, the lettings should strictly be to holidaymakers and tourists in order to qualify.

Where a property qualifies, as set out above, then it generally qualifies for the whole of each qualifying tax year, subject to special rules for the years in which holiday letting commences or ceases.

Where, however, there is some other use of the property during the year, the Capital Gains Tax reliefs described above will be restricted accordingly.

Nevertheless, it remains possible for the taxpayer and their family to use the property privately as a second home during the 'off season' and still fit within the rules described above.

However, the overall position must still fit in with rule (iii) above and hence, in practice, the property must be made available for letting to third parties for a sufficiently large proportion of the year to give its owners a realistic expectation of profits.

The result of failing to meet this test would be the loss of furnished holiday letting status and hence the consequent loss of all the additional reliefs which that status provides.

Tax Tip

Preparing a credible business plan when you first acquire the property would provide valuable supporting evidence that you had a reasonable expectation of profit.

A documented annual review of the plan will also be useful, as the 'profit expectation' test must be met every year.

A business plan will not help you, however, if it clearly bears no resemblance to your actual behaviour in respect of the property.

Interaction with Other Reliefs

A property which qualifies as furnished holiday accommodation and which has qualified as the owner's main residence at some time during their ownership, will also be eligible for private letting relief.

This could produce a quite remarkable combination of tax reliefs.

Example

In Section 6.21 we met Bonnie who had a small cottage on Skye which, for ten years, she rented out as furnished holiday accommodation for 48 weeks each year and occupied herself for the remaining four weeks. The property also qualified as Bonnie's main residence (perhaps by election).

When, on 1 April 2015, Bonnie realised a capital gain of £104,000 on her sale of the property, we saw that she obtained principal private residence relief of £22,400 and private letting relief of £22,400, thus reducing her gain to just £59,200. But it doesn't end there!

Bonnie would then be entitled to entrepreneurs' relief (see below) on 48/52nds of this gain, i.e. £59,200 x 48/52 = £54,646.

This leaves only £4,554 exposed to Capital Gains Tax at the normal rate of either 18% or 28%. However, as Bonnie can allocate her annual exemption in the most beneficial way, she can exempt this amount altogether.

The taxable gain of £48,200 remaining after deducting her annual exemption of £11,000 is therefore wholly eligible for entrepreneurs' relief, giving Bonnie a Capital Gains Tax bill of just £4,820 (£48,200 x 10%), or a mere 4.6% of her total gain.

Note, in this example, that Bonnie's entrepreneurs' relief claim is restricted due to her private use of the property for four weeks per year (although the restriction did not actually affect her in this case).

A similar restriction would apply if she attempted to claim rollover relief on a replacement of the property or holdover relief on a gift of it.

These restrictions apply whenever the owner makes any private use of the property, whether it qualifies as their main residence or not.

In the case of entrepreneurs' relief, however, it could be fairly easy to avoid any such restriction, as we shall see in Section 8.18.

Entrepreneurs' Relief on Furnished Holiday Accommodation

In the above example, I assumed that entrepreneurs' relief would be available on Bonnie's sale of her cottage.

As explained in Section 6.28, entrepreneurs' relief is available when a qualifying business or part of a qualifying business is sold or when assets used in a qualifying business are sold within three years of that business's cessation.

As also explained in Section 6.28, a 'part' of a qualifying business must be capable of being run as a going concern in its own right in order to qualify for these purposes.

In my view, most properties which qualify as furnished holiday accommodation must be a 'part' of a business capable of being run independently of any other part of the business. Hence, my interpretation of the entrepreneurs' relief legislation is that a capital gain on the sale of qualifying furnished holiday accommodation should generally qualify for entrepreneurs' relief as long as:

a)   The property is still being used as qualifying furnished holiday accommodation at the time of sale, or

b)   The property was being used in a qualifying furnished holiday accommodation business at the time of the cessation of that business and is sold within three years thereafter.

However, I have now become aware that HM Revenue and Customs is applying the entrepreneurs' relief legislation in a more restrictive manner, arguing that the sale of a single furnished holiday letting property does not constitute the sale of a qualifying 'part' of a business when the owner also continues to operate other furnished holiday letting properties.

HM Revenue and Customs' view seems to be that advertising the properties together (e.g. through the same website) makes them a single indistinguishable business.

This is a new and developing area of tax law, so it is difficult to provide any definitive guidance until we see a suitable case in court. In the meantime, each case will have to be argued on its own merits. The more steps which the owner takes to separate the way in which the different properties are run, the better their chances are likely to be. Useful steps may include:

- Advertising each property separately
- Ensuring that each property has its own website
- Keeping separate sets of books and records for each property
- Using different cleaners, gardeners, etc.
- Using significantly different names for each property

Naturally, the commercial impact of these steps needs to be weighed against the potential Capital Gains Tax savings: which may be remote and uncertain when no sales are anticipated in the foreseeable future.

Tax Tip

A more certain approach might be to separate out the property which is intended for sale by initially transferring it into different ownership, such as the owner's spouse or adult child, or a trust. As long as the property is a qualifying furnished holiday let at the time of the transfer, it should be possible to carry this out free from Capital Gains Tax. The new owner would then need to operate the property as a furnished holiday let for at least a year, but could then sell it with the certainty of obtaining entrepreneurs' relief (provided that they did not have any other furnished holiday lets themselves!)

Subject to the uncertainty created by this issue, a property investor might be able to realise total capital gains of up to £10m on qualifying furnished holiday accommodation at a maximum effective Capital Gains Tax rate of just 10%. Furthermore, as explained in Section 6.28, a couple investing in property jointly may be able to benefit from this rate on total gains of up to £20m.

8.16   TAX-FREE HOLIDAY HOMES

There is a fairly easy way to shelter the entire capital gain on a qualifying furnished holiday letting property.

If the property has never been used for any other purpose then the entire capital gain arising on a gift of the property can be held over where a joint election is made by the transferor and the transferee.

If the transferee then adopts the property as their main residence, any capital gain arising when they sell it, including the original held over gain, will be fully exempt.

At present, it may sometimes be possible for the transferee to establish the property as their main residence by way of election. However, as explained in Section 6.22, this facility may be withdrawn in the near future. The transferee would then need to establish the property as their main residence as a question of fact (see Section 6.22 for the factors to be considered).

The transferee must also retain the property for a long enough period to ensure that it is treated as a capital asset in their hands.

The transferor should avoid any personal use of the property after the transfer, as this could give rise to an Income Tax charge.

8.17   HOTELS AND GUEST HOUSES

Small hotels and guest houses which continue to be the owner's main residence, despite also being a business property, are in a rather special situation.

This is because hotel or guest house accommodation counts as private residential accommodation for the purposes of private letting relief.

Hence, in many cases, up to £40,000 (per person) of any gain arising as a result of the business use of the property can be relieved.

HM Revenue and Customs accepts that this approach is correct in respect of any part of the property which has had some private use by the owner.

Many commentators also argue that private letting relief should even extend to parts of a hotel or guest house which have only ever had exclusive business use.

8.18   ENTREPRENEURS' RELIEF ON INVESTMENT PROPERTY

As explained in Section 6.28, entrepreneurs' relief is available on the disposal of a property used in a qualifying business carried on by the property's owner for at least a year prior to:

a) The disposal of the property as part of the sale of the business (or a part of the business which is capable of operating as a going concern in its own right), or
b) The cessation of the business.

In the latter case, the property must be sold within three years of the cessation.

In Section 6.28, we also saw that there were restrictions on entrepreneurs' relief for a property used by the owner's 'personal company', or a partnership in which they are a partner, where the property was not so used throughout their ownership.

However, no such restrictions apply where the property is used in the owner's own qualifying business, such as a trade, profession, or as qualifying furnished holiday accommodation, and it appears that full relief is available provided that the property is in the appropriate use at the time of disposal, or cessation of the business, as the case may be.

Where the owner has an existing qualifying business, it even appears that there is no minimum period for which the property must be used in that business, provided that the owner runs the business itself for at least a year.

For those without an existing qualifying business, it will be necessary to set one up and run it for at least a year in order to benefit.

Example

In 1982, Abdul bought a shop as an investment property for £30,000. It is now worth £330,000 and he would like to sell it.

Before selling the property, however, Abdul adopts it as his own trading premises for thirteen months. He then ceases trading and sells the property, making a gain of £300,000.

Because Abdul used the property in his own trade, he will be entitled to entrepreneurs' relief, reducing the Capital Gains Tax due on his sale from £84,000 to £30,000 (ignoring the annual exemption and assuming that Abdul is a higher rate taxpayer).

He still gets the relief despite the fact that the entire gain arose before he adopted the property as his own trading premises!

Note that Abdul would need to use the property in his own qualifying trade – e.g. as a shop with him as sole proprietor. Using it as the office for his investment business will not suffice. He can, however, employ a manager to run the shop for him if he wishes.

A similar approach might work with residential property by adopting it as a furnished holiday let for a year or more. Where the owner already has an existing furnished holiday letting business, it might even be possible for them to obtain entrepreneurs' relief on a residential investment property by letting it out as qualifying furnished holiday accommodation for a shorter period before sale.

As explained in Section 8.15, however, it is not clear whether this would work when the owner does not also either sell their other furnished holiday letting properties or cease their furnished holiday letting business altogether.

8.19   ENTERPRISE INVESTMENT SCHEME SHARES

Capital Gains Tax liabilities can be deferred by reinvesting some or all of a capital gain in Enterprise Investment Scheme shares. To obtain relief, the investment must take place within the period beginning a year before, and ending three years after, the date of the disposal which gave rise to the gain.

Furthermore, Capital Gains Tax reinvestment relief is still available even when the investor is connected with the company issuing the shares. Hence, it is even possible to defer Capital Gains Tax on your property gains by investing in your own trading company!

Unfortunately, however, companies engaged in any form of property business are generally ineligible to issue Enterprise Investment Scheme shares.

Alternatively, products are available which enable taxpayers to utilise a 'portfolio' approach when investing in these intrinsically risky investments. This does not totally eliminate the risk, but it certainly improves the odds!

There is no limit on the amount which can be invested in Enterprise Investment Scheme shares for Capital Gains Tax deferral purposes.

Gains held over on reinvestment into Enterprise Investment Scheme shares become chargeable to Capital Gains Tax when those shares are sold.

Qualifying investments of up to £1m per year in Enterprise Investment Scheme shares issued by an unconnected company also carry an Income Tax credit of up to 30% of the amount invested.

Investments may also be carried back to the previous tax year for Income Tax credit purposes.

Combining the Income Tax credit with the Capital Gains Tax deferral outlined above gives a potential for total tax savings of up to 58% of the amount invested.

8.20 SWEET SHOP COMPANIES

The 'sweet shop principle' is a method which enables property investors to defer Capital Gains Tax using Enterprise Investment Scheme shares.

The idea is that you find a very simple, low risk trading business, like a sweet shop, which requires business premises.

Then you set up 'Sweet Shop Company Limited' to run the shop. This company issues Enterprise Investment Scheme shares to you in exchange for the cash proceeds of a property sale. The company then uses this cash to buy its retail premises.

In this way, you are effectively able to roll over any capital gain into the purchase of the business premises, via the medium of the sweet shop company. This is probably the least risky way to secure a Capital Gains Tax deferral with Enterprise Investment Scheme shares.

It doesn't necessarily have to be a sweet shop, but it must not be any of the types of trade or business which are specifically excluded in the legislation and, as I explained in the last section, this covers most types of property business. Even hotels and guest houses are excluded.

8.21 THE SEED ENTERPRISE INVESTMENT SCHEME

The Seed Enterprise Investment Scheme provides Income Tax relief at 50% to individuals investing up to £100,000 per tax year in qualifying companies.

Qualifying investments may be carried back to the previous tax year for tax relief purposes (but cannot be carried back prior to 2012/13, the first year of the scheme).

Capital gains arising in 2012/13 which are reinvested in Seed Enterprise Investment Scheme shares for which Income Tax relief is claimed in 2012/13 are completely exempted from Capital Gains Tax. This includes gains reinvested in shares issued during 2013/14 for which Income Tax relief is claimed in 2012/13. This is considerably better than the Enterprise Investment Scheme, where capital gains are only deferred until the shares are sold.

Capital gains arising in 2013/14 or later years which are reinvested in Seed Enterprise Investment Scheme shares are given a 50% exemption from Capital Gains Tax.

This again compares well with the Enterprise Investment Scheme, although half of the gain does remain exposed to Capital Gains Tax.

The combination of Income Tax and Capital Gains Tax reliefs provides the opportunity to obtain up to 78% tax relief on gains arising in 2012/13 and up to 64% on gains arising in 2013/14 and later years – leaving only a small part of the amount invested exposed to the inherent commercial risk of investing in small businesses.

Furthermore, since Income Tax loss relief would be available on 50% of the investment should the Seed Enterprise Investment Scheme company fail, the ultimate amount at risk for a higher rate taxpayer may be as little as:

- 2% where a gain arising in 2012/13 is reinvested, or
- 16% where a gain arising in 2013/14 or later years is reinvested

Investors with annual income over £150,000 who reinvested a gain arising in 2012/13 could even potentially make a profit out of a failed investment!

Such investors would also ultimately lose just 13.5% of a failed investment where they had reinvested a gain arising in 2013/14 or later years.

Scheme Restrictions

There is a cumulative limit of £150,000 for the total amount raised by a company under the scheme. In fact, this limit actually applies to the **total** amount of state aid received by the company, **including** the value of shares issued under the scheme.

The main drawback, however, is that the scheme is targeted at new, small, 'start-up companies'. Broadly speaking, this means that the company issuing the shares must have:

- Total assets worth no more than £200,000 (before issuing the shares)
- Less than 25 employees (or full-time equivalents)
- Been in business for no more than two years (and not carried on any other business previously)

Investors must not be employees of the issuing company (but may be directors) and, together with their 'associates', must not hold, nor be entitled to acquire, an interest of more than 30% in the company's share capital. 'Associates' for this purpose include the investor's spouse, parents, grandparents, children, grandchildren, trusts set up by the investor or any of these relatives, and business partners of the investor.

There are many, many, further restrictions, including the fact that the company must be carrying on a qualifying trade or research and development, so professional advice is essential!

8.22 THE TENDER TRAP: THE BENEFITS AND PITFALLS OF RE-MORTGAGING (A.K.A 'EQUITY RELEASE')

"What, no tax at all? That's amazing! Well, thanks a lot, that's wonderful news."

This is the kind of reaction I often get when people ask me about the tax consequences of re-mortgaging their properties, or 'equity release', as it is often called.

The situation is a pretty common one. You have a property which has risen significantly in value since you bought it. Rather than sell the property, you can realise the 'profit' from this growth in value by re-mortgaging and thus obtain the cash value of your equity by different means.

Initially, this is a good way of avoiding tax on the growth in value of your investment properties, but there are some long-term dangers inherent in this strategy which could ultimately prove to be your downfall if you are not prepared for them.

The combination of the initial benefits of re-mortgaging and the potential long-term pitfalls of the strategy is what leads me to call it 'The Tender Trap'. It's tender because of its initial benefits, but it can prove to be a costly trap from which it is difficult to escape.

More about the trap later. To begin with, let's look at the benefits.

In the short term, this method works extremely well. Potentially, in fact, realising equity value through re-mortgaging can produce benefits under three major taxes: Capital Gains Tax, Income Tax and Inheritance Tax. To illustrate these benefits, let's look at an example.

Example Part 1

Steve has a buy-to-let property in Essex which has grown significantly in value since he bought it for £25,000 in 1998. In fact, by March 2015, the property is valued at £85,000.

However, Steve feels that property values in Essex are unlikely to show any significant increase in the foreseeable future and he now wishes to invest in some new developments in Leeds.

In order to pursue his new investment opportunity in Leeds, Steve will need to 'cash in' his equity in his Essex property. Initially he considers selling the Essex property, but is horrified to learn that he would have a Capital Gains Tax bill of £16,800 (he is a higher rate taxpayer and has already used his annual exemption).

Instead of selling the Essex property, therefore, Steve decides to re-mortgage it. His new mortgage is at 85% of current value, £72,250. Hence, after repaying his original mortgage of £20,000, Steve has freed up £52,250 of equity value in cash. What's more, he still has the rental income from his original property.

Benefit 1: Capital Gains Tax

Capital Gains Tax can generally only be charged where there is a disposal of an asset. If you sell a property, you have made a disposal and hence there will usually be Capital Gains Tax to pay.

On the other hand, however, when you re-mortgage a property, you have not actually made any disposal, as you still own the property. Hence, although you will have realised some of your capital, you cannot be charged any Capital Gains Tax.

Although, in our example, Steve did this for investment purposes, this Capital Gains Tax benefit remains equally true whatever your reason for re-mortgaging a property.

Example, Part 2

Steve uses the £52,250 which he generated by re-mortgaging his Essex property as a deposit on a buy-to-let development in Leeds.

However, when he is completing his next tax return, he's uncertain what to do about the mortgage interest he is now paying on the Essex property. Fortunately, his friend Matthew (a Chartered Accountant) is able to point him in the right direction.

Matthew explains that the portion of the interest which relates to the original £20,000 loan (i.e. 20,000/72,250ths or 27.7%) should continue to be claimed against the rental income from the Essex property and the remainder (52,250/72,250ths or 72.3%) can be claimed against rental income from the Leeds properties.

"In fact," Matthew explains, "you could even claim the interest on the new borrowings if you re-mortgaged your own home instead because you're using the money for business purposes."

Benefit 2: Income Tax

Where the funds generated by re-mortgaging an existing property are used to purchase new investment properties, the interest on the new borrowings can be claimed against the income from the new properties. This applies even if the re-mortgaged property is the borrower's own home. The interest relief remains available as long as the funds are invested for business purposes.

Sometimes, however, the borrower will re-mortgage a property for other reasons – perhaps simply to provide living expenses. Whilst this will still produce the Capital Gains Tax benefit described above, only interest on borrowings against a rental property up to the value of the property when first rented out (plus other capital invested in the business) will be eligible for Income Tax relief under these circumstances (see Section 4.4 for further details).

Example, Part 3

For the next ten years, Steve continues to re-mortgage his existing properties and invest his realised capital growth in new buy-to-let developments.

By March 2025, he has 12 properties in Essex, Leeds and Newcastle worth a total of £2,500,000.

His borrowings at this stage amount to £1,400,000 in total, giving him a total net equity value in his property portfolio of £1,100,000.

Steve happens to bump into his old friend Matthew, who he hasn't seen in years, and tells him how well his property portfolio has grown. "That's great", says Matthew. "Have you done anything about the Inheritance Tax though?"

Once again, Steve is horrified to discover that he has a huge potential tax bill on his properties – this time Inheritance Tax of £440,000. "Well, I'm wealthy enough now," he thinks. "I'll stop investing in new properties, live off the existing ones and give away as much as I can to my family."

For the next ten years, Steve continues to re-mortgage his properties up to 85% of their market value and he spends or gives away the proceeds. By 2035, his portfolio is worth £5,000,000, but he has total borrowings of £4,250,000, leaving him with a net equity value in his portfolio of only £750,000 and thus reducing his potential Inheritance Tax bill to only £300,000.

Benefit 3: Inheritance Tax

Re-mortgaging your properties as much as possible is an effective way to limit the net value of your estate for Inheritance Tax purposes. Rather than selling properties, which creates Capital Gains Tax liabilities, this enables you to give away some of the value of your assets, hopefully tax free (as long as you survive for seven years after making the gift).

Of course, to save Inheritance Tax, you will need to spend or give away the proceeds of re-mortgaging your properties, so this technique does not allow you to claim Income Tax relief on new borrowings above the original value of your properties plus any other capital invested in your business.

Following this method may also put a severe strain on your cashflow. One of the ways to alleviate this would be to use some of the funds realised through re-mortgaging to purchase annuities, thus keeping the value of your estate down for Inheritance Tax purposes, whilst still providing you with an income during your lifetime.

Naturally, you need to be able to afford to spend or give this money away and still be able to pay the interest on your ever-increasing borrowings, so this strategy is not for everyone!

The Trap

So far, we've looked at the 'tender' part of the strategy, namely the potential tax benefits. Now we turn to the trap. The problem in essence is that Capital Gains Tax is based on the difference between sales proceeds and purchase cost. Hence, in order to calculate the capital gain arising when you sell a property, you deduct the original cost of the property from your sale proceeds.

What you **do not** deduct in your capital gains calculation is the outstanding amount of the mortgage over the property!

Naturally, if you have used additional borrowings to make improvements to the property, then these costs may also be deducted from sale proceeds.

However, where your additional borrowings have been spent, given away, or used to invest in other properties, you will have a liability to the lender without a corresponding deduction in your capital gains calculation. This is what creates the trap and we will go back to our friend Steve to see it in action.

Example, Part 4

In 2036, there is a sudden downturn in the property market with property values typically falling by around 10%. Steve runs into some financial difficulty and decides that he needs to sell one of his properties. The rental yield of his original Essex property has been pretty poor lately, so he sells this property for £324,000.

Steve's borrowings against this property now amount to £306,000 (i.e. 85% of the property's value before the downturn), so he realises net proceeds of only £18,000 (even before any sale expenses).

However, as Steve's original cost for the property was only £25,000, he realises a capital gain of £299,000. His Capital Gains Tax bill at 28% may therefore be up to £83,720.

*After tax, Steve's sale of the Essex property has therefore actually generated an overall net **cost** of £65,720!*

*In fact, if Steve were to sell his entire portfolio for its post-downturn value of £4,500,000, he would suffer an overall net **cost** of over £500,000!*

Escaping the Trap

Steve's story is a lesson to us all. It's only an example, I know, but I have met property investors who could easily end up in a very similar position.

Escaping the trap is possible, but does require some drastic action. The first option is to hang on to the properties until you die. This resolves the Capital Gains Tax problem and, as we have seen, the level of borrowings keeps the Inheritance Tax bill down.

If Steve had died before selling his properties, the portfolio would have still yielded a net sum of £150,000 for his family after Inheritance Tax, rather than creating an overall cost of over £500,000.

This is all very well, but what if you can't afford to keep the properties? This could happen for a variety of reasons: rental yields could fall or interest rates could rise.

But, at the same time, if you have insufficient other wealth beyond your property portfolio, you may be unable to pay the Capital Gains Tax arising if you sell!

You could end up not being able to afford to keep the properties, nor able to afford to sell them!

Where someone is *currently* in a situation like Steve's, I would probably recommend emigration as their best chance to escape the tender trap (see Section 8.32). It's still quite drastic, but not as bad as the previous option!

In future, however, for the reasons explained in Section 8.33, even this may not work!

Responsible Borrowing

To avoid falling into the 'tender trap', investors need to borrow responsibly, taking account of their potential Capital Gains Tax liabilities.

In theory, with a maximum Capital Gains Tax rate of 28%, this suggests that it should be safe to borrow a sum up to 'original cost plus 72% of any increase in value'.

However, this would still leave the owner highly vulnerable to either a downturn in property values (as we have already seen) or a future increase in Capital Gains Tax rates. Hence, I would tend to suggest reducing this figure by at least a further 10% to safeguard against such 'nasty surprises'.

One would hope that keeping mortgage levels within these more responsible limits should ensure that you will have sufficient net funds on a sale of the property to be able to pay your Capital Gains Tax bill.

In Conclusion

Using a re-mortgaging strategy to build your property portfolio has tremendous potential Capital Gains Tax and Income Tax benefits. Realising your equity through additional borrowings is more tax efficient than selling properties when you intend to reinvest the proceeds in your portfolio.

Re-mortgaging can also be used to reduce the value of your net estate for Inheritance Tax purposes.

However, a trap awaits the unwary and can, in the most extreme cases, put the taxpayer in a quite untenable position. Sticking to responsible levels of borrowing should ensure that you don't fall into this trap.

8.23   NON-DOMICILED INVESTORS

A UK resident but non-UK domiciled taxpayer may opt to only pay UK tax on income or capital gains from foreign properties if and when these sums are remitted back to the UK. This is known as the 'remittance basis' of taxation.

However, an annual charge of £30,000 is levied on any adult resident in the UK for seven or more of the previous nine UK tax years who opts to use the remittance basis (unless their unremitted overseas income and gains for the year total less than £2,000). This charge is increased to £50,000 for adults who have been UK resident for 12 or more of the last 14 years.

Hence, such taxpayers now generally have to either pay tax in full on their overseas income and capital gains or face a heavy annual charge.

In addition, taxpayers paying the £30,000 or £50,000 charge are also subject to Capital Gains Tax at 28% on all capital gains, regardless of the level of their income (except where entrepreneurs' relief applies).

Furthermore, all UK resident taxpayers claiming the remittance basis lose entitlement to their personal allowance and Capital Gains Tax annual exemption if they have unremitted overseas income and gains of £2,000 or more. The effective cost of these further punitive measures in 2014/15 alone could be up to £7,080.

For some taxpayers, the total annual cost of claiming the 'remittance basis' could be almost £60,000!

Even so, in some cases, non-UK domiciled individuals may still be able to make considerable tax savings by investing in foreign property and retaining their income and gains from that property overseas.

Tax Tip

Individuals claiming the remittance basis may claim exemption from UK tax on any funds remitted to the UK after 5ᵗʰ April 2012 for the purpose of making commercial investments in qualifying businesses.

The detailed rules for this new exemption are highly complex, so anyone hoping to benefit should seek professional advice.

Ordinary Residence

Prior to 2013/14, it was also possible for individuals who were classed as not ordinarily resident in the UK to claim the remittance basis. However, the concept of 'ordinary residence' has been largely abolished with effect from 6ᵗʰ April 2013. Anyone likely to be affected should seek professional advice

8.24   USING LEASE PREMIUMS TO GENERATE TAX-FREE RECEIPTS

As we saw in Section 6.34, the granting at a premium of a lease of between two and fifty years' duration gives rise to a capital receipt equal to 2% of that premium for each whole year that the lease exceeds one year. For example, 12% of the premium charged for a seven-year lease will be treated as a capital disposal. Clever investors might consider this a good way to use their annual Capital Gains Tax exemption.

Example

Bob owns a small workshop which Terry wants to lease for 20 years. If Bob charges a premium of £28,947, 38% of this (£11,000) will be treated as a capital disposal. If Bob has no other gains this year, his 2014/15 annual exemption will cover any capital gain, meaning that £11,000 of the premium is received tax free.

Bob and Terry then simply negotiate a level of rent which takes suitable account of the premium Bob has paid.

To keep this example simple, I have ignored any base cost which Bob has in the workshop. (See Section 6.34 for more details.)

8.25   THE RENTAL LOSS – CAPITAL GAIN DILEMMA

Many investors find themselves with rental losses carried forward which they are unable to set against capital gains arising on the same properties.

If the rental losses are likely to be used against other rental income in the foreseeable future (see Sections 4.11 and 4.14 for details) then all well and good: this will save Income Tax at 20%, 40% or even more.

In fact, any foreseeable Income Tax saving is probably better than a maximum Capital Gains Tax saving at 28% at some uncertain date in the future when the property is sold.

However, where it seems unlikely that rental losses will ever be relieved against future rental income, securing Capital Gains Tax relief at up to 28% for some of your expenditure could be your best option.

It is worth bearing this in mind before claiming expenses for Income Tax purposes. Many costs are quite clearly revenue in nature but, in some borderline cases, it may be worth considering whether treating the expense as a capital improvement may actually be better in the long run.

As we saw in Section 4.6, any renovation costs incurred on a new rental property which cannot be claimed for Income Tax purposes will be allowed for Capital Gains Tax purposes.

Hence, it will sometimes be wise to resist the impulse to claim as much as possible at this stage.

Renovation costs which simply increase the amount of carried forward rental losses are of dubious benefit when there is no foreseeable relief for those losses and it may be better to secure some Capital Gains Tax relief instead by classifying costs as capital improvements whenever it is reasonable to do so.

More Tax-Free Lease Premiums

In the previous section, we saw how it was possible to use lease premiums to generate tax free income. Lease premiums also provide a further opportunity for tax-free income when the investor has rental losses brought forward.

As explained in Section 6.34, a proportion of any premium for a short lease of no more than 50 years' duration is treated as income. Hence, where an investor has rental losses brought forward, they could consider granting short leases at a premium instead of selling their property.

The rental losses brought forward can then be set off against part of the lease premium received, leaving a much smaller sum exposed to Capital Gains Tax.

This strategy is generally only worth considering when the investor has a large amount of rental losses available which are unlikely to be relieved against rental income in the foreseeable future, or which are likely to provide future Income Tax relief at no more than 20%.

8.26 WINDING DOWN GRACEFULLY

As discussed in the previous section, many property investors build up large amounts of rental losses.

A simple way to ensure that you utilise your rental losses is to wind down your property business slowly over a number of years.

As you sell properties and use the proceeds to repay borrowings on your remaining portfolio, you will slowly increase your profit levels as your interest costs reduce.

However, because of the rental losses which you have accumulated in the past, you may be able to enjoy many years of tax free rental profits as you wind your business down and prepare for retirement.

This strategy combines very well with the annual Capital Gains Tax exemption. By selling your properties slowly, over many years, you will be able to utilise your annual exemption many times.

In some cases, you may also benefit from the lower Capital Gains Tax rate applying to gains falling within your basic rate tax band each year.

Example

Bill and Kate have a portfolio of 20 jointly held rental properties. The couple have built up their portfolio over many years; each property stands at a capital gain of at least £100,000 with the total capital gain on the whole portfolio amounting to £4m.

The couple have also accumulated rental losses of £500,000. Because of this, they each currently have total taxable income less than the Income Tax personal allowance.

Bill and Kate now wish to close down their property business.

If they sold their entire portfolio straight away, they would lose the benefit of their rental losses and would be fully taxable on any income derived by investing their sale proceeds elsewhere.

This would make them higher rate taxpayers, so they would be subject to Capital Gains Tax at 28% on their entire capital gains of £4m, less their two annual exemptions. They would therefore have a total Capital Gains Tax bill of £1,113,840 (£4m – 2 x £11,000 = £3,978,000 x 28%).

Instead, they start selling just one property each year and use the sale proceeds to reduce their borrowings on the rest of the portfolio.

Conservatively, we can assume that the annual Capital Gains Tax exemption will average at least £12,500 over the 20 year period it takes Bill and Kate to wind down their business. This means that they will benefit from total annual exemptions of at least £500,000 (£12,500 x 2 x 20).

A large part of their capital gains will also fall within their basic rate bands. Certainly, in the first few years, they can expect to have their basic rate bands fully available.

For the sake of illustration, let us assume that their brought forward rental losses keep them in this position for the first 15 years (by ensuring that their taxable income, after deducting the losses brought forward, is less than their personal allowance each).

We will also make a further conservative estimate that the basic rate band will average at least £35,000 over this period. Thus, on average, at least £70,000 (2 x £35,000) of each capital gain will be taxed at just 18% for the first 15 years.

Thereafter, we will assume that they each become higher rate taxpayers.

This strategy therefore reduces the total Capital Gains Tax on the sale of their portfolio as follows:

Total capital gains over 20 years	*£4,000,000*
Less	
Annual exemptions	
£12,500 x 2 x 20	*£500,000*
Taxable gains	*£3,500,000*
Capital Gains Tax payable:	
Gains falling within basic rate bands	
£35,000 x 2 x 15 = £1,050,000 @ 18%	*£189,000*
Remaining taxable gains	
£3,500,000 - £1,050,000 = £2,450,000 @ 28%	*£686,000*
Total	*£875,000*

I have ignored future capital growth in the value of Bill and Kate's properties for the sake of illustration but, in reality, it will only add to the benefit of winding down slowly.

Based on our assumptions, Bill and Kate will therefore save £238,840 (£1,113,840 - £875,000) in Capital Gains Tax by selling up over a long period.

On top of this, as they repay their borrowings, they will generate rental profits. Thanks to their brought forward losses, the first £500,000 of these profits will be tax free. This provides further potential tax savings of up to £225,000 compared with income from other sources.

As we can see, by winding down gracefully, Bill and Kate could be around £400,000 better off from tax savings alone!

Wealth Warning

The above example is based on the assumption that Capital Gains Tax rates will not be subject to any increases in the future.

However, there is no guarantee that such increases will not occur. If Capital Gains Tax rates do increase significantly in future, investors like Bill and Kate could be better off selling the majority of their portfolio now. As we saw in Section 4.11, only one property needs to be retained to preserve the benefit of rental losses.

8.27 COMMERCIAL DEVELOPMENTS IN ASSISTED AREAS

The 'Business Premises Renovation Allowance' provides a 100% first year allowance for costs incurred in renovating or converting disused commercial property in designated 'assisted areas' to bring it back into business use. These areas can be found in the Assisted Areas Order SI 2007/107.

The new 'business use' need not be the same as the building's original use and can include offices and shops. Some businesses are excluded, however, including fisheries, shipbuilding, coal, steel, synthetic fibres and a number of agricultural activities.

The relief is available to both owner-occupiers and landlords letting the property out to qualifying businesses following renovation.

The property must have been vacant for at least a year prior to the commencement of renovation work. Where part of a property has been vacant for a year or more, relief may be claimed for the cost of work on that part of the property.

The relief is confined to the cost of renovation or conversion. Purchase costs and the costs of building any extensions (except where built merely to provide access) are excluded from relief.

Expenditure incurred from April 2014 onwards is excluded from relief where the project also attracts any other form of State aid. Earlier expenditure covered by a grant is also excluded.

The claimant may choose not to claim the first year allowance in full and may, instead, claim the lower of the unrelieved balance or 25% of the qualifying expenditure in each year until the claim is exhausted.

This relief was originally introduced for a fixed period but has now been extended for a further five years, to April 2017.

8.28 ROLLOVER RELIEF

The capital gain arising on the sale of a property used in your own trading business may be rolled over into the purchase of a new trading property within the period beginning one year before, and ending three years after, the date of disposal of the original property.

This effectively defers any Capital Gains Tax liability on the original property until such time as the new property is sold.

Property qualifying under the furnished holiday letting regime is treated as trading property for the purposes of this relief (see Section 8.15 for further details).

Full relief is available only if the old property was used exclusively for 'trading purposes' throughout your ownership, or at least since 31· March 1982, if it was acquired earlier.

Furthermore, for rollover relief purposes, it is the sale **proceeds** of the old property which must be reinvested and not merely the capital gain arising. Any shortfall in the amount reinvested is deducted from the amount of gain eligible for rollover.

If there is less than full trading use of the property then an appropriate proportion of the gain arising may be rolled over.

Example

Stavros sells an office building in June 2014 for £400,000, realising a capital gain of £100,000.

Stavros has owned the building since June 2004 and, up until June 2009, he rented all of it out to tenants. From June 2009 until the date of sale, however, Stavros used two thirds of the building as his own premises from which he ran a property development trading business.

Stavros is therefore eligible to roll over £33,333 (£100,000 x 5/10 x 2/3) of his capital gain into the purchase of new trading premises. The eligible amount has been restricted by reference to both the time that the property was used for trading purposes and also the proportion of the property used for trading purposes.

In August 2014, Stavros buys a small gift shop in Cornwall for £120,000 and begins to use it as his own trading premises.

Stavros is therefore able to claim rollover relief of £20,000. He cannot claim the full £33,333 which was eligible for rollover, because he has not reinvested the whole qualifying portion of his sale proceeds (£400,000 x 5/10 x 2/3 = £133,333).

The new qualifying property does not need to be in the same trade or even the same kind of trade. It could even be qualifying furnished holiday accommodation.

There is no minimum period for which the new property needs to be used for trading purposes, although it must be acquired with the intention of using it for trading purposes.

In our example, Stavros could run the gift shop for, say, two years and then convert it into residential property. His Capital Gains Tax rollover relief would not be clawed back, although he would have a reduced base cost for the property when he eventually came to sell it.

Tax Tip

Where you have a capital gain eligible for rollover relief, it is only necessary to use the replacement property for trading purposes for a limited period.

This might include initially running the new property as a guest house or as qualifying furnished holiday accommodation before later converting to long-term letting or even adopting it as your own home.

What Kinds of Investment Properties Can Qualify?

Rollover relief is generally only available to property investors for:

- Furnished holiday lettings (see Section 8.15)
- The trading premises of a property development, property dealing or property management business
- A property where the owner is providing significant additional services

The latter case would generally require a level of services akin to a guest house, although the owner need not reside there themselves.

Gains on other rental properties may be eligible for rollover relief in certain limited circumstances, such as a compulsory purchase of commercial property, or residential property purchased by a tenant under the Leasehold Reform Act 1967.

Rollover relief is not restricted to property and could also apply where the old asset and/or the new asset is one of several other designated classes of trading assets.

8.29 YEAR END TAX PLANNING

Rental Income

As explained in Chapter 4, for individuals with rental income, it is generally necessary to draw up accounts for the tax year, rather than for any other accounting period. Hence, for these property businesses, 5ᵗʰ April is usually twice as important since, not only is it the end of the tax year, but it is generally also the end of their accounting period.

Where I refer in this section to 'your year end', those with property rental businesses should therefore generally read this as meaning 5ᵗʰ April.

Property Trades

As we saw in Chapter 5, those with property trades may choose their own accounting date.

Where I refer in this section to 'your year end', those with property trades should read this as meaning their own accounting date, rather than the tax year end.

The Tax Year End

Where I refer to 'the tax year end' this means 5ᵗʰ April whatever kind of business you have!

Timing Is Everything

For most property businesses the 'accruals' basis will apply, meaning that income and expenditure must be recognised when it arises, or is incurred, rather than when it is received or paid. Hence, whenever you are expecting to need to make some business expenditure in the near future, it may make sense to ensure that it takes place by your year end, in order to get tax relief in an earlier year, rather than having to wait another 12 months.

Obviously, this does not mean it is worth incurring expenditure just for the sake of it. It is seldom wise to make uncommercial decisions purely for tax reasons! What it does mean, however, is that it can often be worth accelerating some of the expenditure, which is going to be taking place in any case, so that it falls into an earlier accounting year.

Conversely, those who are basic rate taxpayers this year, but expect to be higher rate taxpayers next year, may be better off by delaying business expenditure so that it falls into next year and provides tax relief at 40% instead of just 20%.

Furthermore, in some cases, those expecting total taxable income between £100,000 and £121,000, or over £150,000, next year may also be better off by delaying business expenditure so that it falls into that year and provides tax relief at 45% or 60% (see Section 3.3 and Appendix A). The same may apply to some of those who expect to be subject to the High Income Child Benefit Charge next year (see Section 3.3).

Businesses on a Cash Basis

For smaller businesses operating on a cash basis (see Sections 4.1 and 5.11) the tax-planning objective will usually be to accelerate the actual *payment* of any necessary expenditure to before the accounting year end.

Landlords on the cash basis might also do well to consider setting the due dates for rent receivable to fall shortly after the tax year end.

Any property traders using the new 'cash basis' detailed in Section 5.11 may also want to consider deferring sales until after their accounting year end where possible.

As before, the position may differ if the taxpayer expects a higher level of total taxable income next year.

Capital Allowances

Where capital allowances are available (see Section 3.10 for details), the full allowance is usually given for the year in which the expenditure is incurred. Where expenditure is eligible for capital allowances, therefore, consider making your purchase by your year end.

However, where you have already incurred qualifying expenditure in excess of the annual investment allowance (see Section 3.10) this year, it may be more beneficial to defer any further expenditure in order to get full tax relief for it in your next accounting period rather than a writing down allowance of just 8% or 18%.

Note that any assets bought on Hire Purchase must actually be brought into use in the business by your year end to qualify for capital allowances.

Cars

Some capital allowances may be available on a car which you use in your property business. The allowance is usually restricted by reference to the private use of the car, but nevertheless it is worth noting that:

- A balancing allowance is usually available on the sale of an old car previously used in your property business, and
- A full year's allowance will be given on any new car brought into use in the business by your year end.

Hence, both sales of old cars and purchases of new cars before your year end will often save tax where the vehicles are used in your property business.

Beware, however, that sales of old cars can sometimes give rise to a balancing charge (although a balancing allowance is far more common).

Employees' Bonuses

If you have any employees in your property business, it may be worth considering whether you wish to pay any of them a bonus before your year end. However, bonuses are only worth thinking about from a tax-planning point of view if either:

a) You were going to pay them anyway, or
b) The employee is your spouse, partner or other family member.

Those with a spouse, partner or other family member working in their business may also wish to ensure that these employees receive sufficient salary by the tax year end to utilise their personal allowances.

8.30 USING YOUR BASIC RATE BAND TO SAVE CAPITAL GAINS TAX

As explained in Section 6.4, the rate of Capital Gains Tax applying to most gains now depends on the level of your taxable income for the relevant tax year.

At current rates, savings of up to £3,186 can be achieved by ensuring that your capital gains fall into a tax year in which you have a lower level of income. This saving represents the difference between the 18% and 28% rates of Capital Gains Tax on the current basic rate band of £31,865.

Where you are also able to utilise your annual Capital Gains Tax exemption, the total saving available could be up to £6,266 (£3,186 + £11,000 x 28%).

How Can Property Investors Use These Savings?

We have already seen one example of how property investors may be able to use these savings in Section 8.26, where a property investor couple were benefitting from brought forward rental losses to keep their taxable income at a low level.

This could typically arise where the investor has retired from previous employment or self-employment and is now living purely off their rental income.

Even without the benefit of rental losses, waiting until you retire before you sell your investment properties may enable you to benefit from the lower Capital Gains Tax rate.

Example

Edwina has an investment property which will yield a capital gain of £50,000 when she sells it.

Edwina has a salary of £40,000 in 2014/15 but is due to retire on 31· March 2015. She is also currently making a rental profit of £1,000 per month.

If Edwina was to sell her property shortly before 5· April 2015, she would be subject to Capital Gains Tax at 28% on a gain of £39,000 (£50,000 less her annual exemption of £11,000), giving her a bill of £10,920.

If, however, she was to delay her sale until 6· April 2015, or shortly afterwards, she would pay Capital Gains Tax at just 18% on the first £31,785 of her taxable gain, thus reducing her tax bill to just £7,714 (see note (i) below).

Notes to the Example

i)   The annual Capital Gains Tax exemption and basic rate band for 2015/16 have already been announced as £11,100 and £31,785 respectively. See Appendix A for further details of the tax bands and allowances applying for 2015/16.

ii)   I have assumed that Edwina's total income for 2015/16 will be less than her personal allowance. In reality, she may have pension or investment income which uses up part of her basic rate band, but is still likely to make a considerable saving by waiting until after she retires to sell her property.

iii)   I have also assumed that Capital Gains Tax rates will remain the same in 2015/16.

iv)   Remember that the date of sale for Capital Gains Tax purposes is the date on which there is an unconditional sales contract (see Section 6.6).

The example also demonstrates the fact that selling an investment property early in a tax year means that there is less income from that property to use up your basic rate band, thus potentially producing a Capital Gains Tax saving.

There are many other situations where property investors may be able to reduce their Capital Gains Tax liability by selling property in a tax year in which their taxable income is at a lower level. Examples include:

- Self-employed taxpayers making large capital allowances claims
- Employed taxpayers on career breaks
- Company owners who are able to refrain from taking income out of their company that year
- Furnished holiday letting landlords with large capital allowances claims
- Investors reducing their taxable income by making tax-advantaged investments, such as investment bonds

Remember, however, that there is no guarantee that Capital Gains Tax rates will not be increased in the future.

8.31   AVOIDING THE HIGH INCOME CHILD BENEFIT CHARGE

As explained in Section 3.3, many parents are now suffering a draconian new tax charge, the High Income Child Benefit Charge, on income between £50,000 and £60,000. This creates the truly horrendous tax rates set out in the table in Section 3.3.

Some property investor couples may, however, be able to avoid the High Income Child Benefit Charge by redistributing their income.

Example

Salvatore and Cherilyn are a married couple with a portfolio of rental properties which yield total annual profits of £90,000. Cherilyn owns more properties than Salvatore, so she receives £60,000 of this profit.

The couple also have three young children and are therefore eligible to claim £2,475 per year in Child Benefit (at current rates). However, Cherilyn's profit share means that she will effectively have to repay the Child Benefit by way of an additional Income Tax charge of £2,475.

The answer to this problem is simple: Cherilyn should transfer some of her properties to Salvatore.

If, as a result, Cherilyn's share of the couple's profits is reduced to £50,000 or less, she will not be subject to the High Income Child Benefit Charge – thus saving the couple £2,475 per year (at current rates).

Ideally, in fact, it would generally be best if the couple owned all their properties jointly. They would then have profits of £45,000 each. Not only would they avoid the High Income Child Benefit Charge, they would also make further savings by making full use of Salvatore's basic rate tax band.

In short, many property investor couples can avoid some or all of the High Income Child Benefit Charge simply by evening up, or equalising, their income – and the easiest way to do that is to own all their properties jointly.

Unmarried Couples

For unmarried couples, the solution is not so simple, as a direct transfer of properties from one partner to the other, or into joint names, will generally lead to a Capital Gains Tax charge. This can often be avoided, however, by using the technique set out in Section 8.7.

Joint Income over £100,000

A couple with total joint income over £100,000 may not be able to avoid the High Income Child Benefit Charge altogether but, if your total joint income is less than £120,000, you could still minimise the overall impact by equalising your income as discussed above.

Alternatively, you could avoid the High Income Child Benefit Charge by transferring properties into a trust or a company. These strategies have many further tax implications and require professional advice.

8.32   EMIGRATION

At present, subject to the points covered below and in Section 6.3, non-UK residents are exempt from UK Capital Gains Tax.

Under current Government proposals, however, non-UK residents will be subject to capital gains arising on UK residential property after 5ᵗʰ April 2015.

Nonetheless, it is important to note that:

- These proposals only apply to UK residential property
- Only the increase in the property's value after 5ᵗʰ April 2015 will be subject to UK Capital Gains Tax

The implications of these proposals are explored further in Section 8.33.

In this section, we will concentrate on the issue of achieving non-UK residence in the first place!

The Benefits of Emigration

Investors facing substantial Capital Gains Tax liabilities sometimes avoid them by emigrating. However, merely going on a world cruise for a year will not be sufficient, as it is necessary to become non-UK resident for more than five years in order to avoid UK Capital Gains Tax.

This is a complex field of tax planning, which really requires a separate guide in its own right. Furthermore, matters have been further complicated by the introduction of a new statutory residence test which applies from 2013/14 onwards. In this section, I am therefore only going to give you a flavour of what is involved: there are many other factors and considerations to be taken into account which I simply do not have space to cover here.

Nonetheless, the main points worth noting are:

- Emigration must generally be permanent, or at least long-term (a period of more than five years is required for those emigrating after 5 April 2013; a period of at least five complete UK tax years is required for those who emigrated earlier).
- Disposals should be deferred until non-residence has been achieved.
- Limited return visits to the UK are permitted (see below).
- Resuming UK residence (under the new statutory residence rules) before the expiry of the required period discussed above may result in substantial Capital Gains Tax liabilities.
- It is essential to ensure that there is no risk of inadvertently becoming liable for some form of capital taxation elsewhere. (There is no point in 'jumping out of the frying pan and into the fire!')

Emigration to avoid UK tax is a strategy which is generally only worth contemplating when the stakes are high. Naturally, therefore, detailed professional advice is always essential.

The following example illustrates the broad outline of what is involved.

Example

Eleanor has been a highly successful UK property investor for many years. By early 2015, she has potential Capital Gains Tax liabilities on her UK investment property portfolio of over £2,000,000.

She therefore decides to emigrate and, on 3ʳᵈ April 2015, she flies to Utopia where she settles down to a new life.

During the 2015/16 UK tax year, Eleanor sells all her UK properties, but is mostly exempt from UK Capital Gains Tax as a non-resident. Her only exposure to UK Capital Gains Tax arises from any increases in the value of her UK residential property between 5ᵗʰ April 2015 and the date of disposal of the properties (see Section 8.33 for further details).

Eventually, however, Eleanor decides that she wants to return home and, on 8ᵗʰ April 2020, she comes back to the UK to live.

As Eleanor was non-resident for over five years, she will remain exempt from UK Capital Gains Tax on the remaining, more substantial, part of her capital gains.

Notes to the Example

i)   Utopia does not exist. Real countries have their own tax systems and may potentially tax immigrants like Eleanor on their UK capital gains. It is therefore always essential to take detailed local professional advice in the destination country.

ii) The sales giving rise to capital gains must be deferred until after non-residence has been achieved. From 2013/14 onwards, 'split year' treatment is available, meaning that, under certain circumstances, the emigrant may effectively be regarded as non-resident from the day after the date of departure. Nonetheless, the position will often be uncertain and it will therefore generally be wiser to defer sales until the UK tax year after the year of departure (e.g. until at least 6ᵗʰ April 2015 in Eleanor's case).

iii) If Eleanor had returned to the UK to live within five years or less, all of her property disposals in 2015/16 would have become fully liable to UK Capital Gains Tax. The gains would then be treated as if they had arisen in the tax year in which Eleanor returned to the UK (apart from the small element already taxed during 2015/16). To avoid this, the emigrant must remain non-UK resident for at least five years and a day. My suggestion would thus be to ensure that there is a clear period of at least five years and a day between the date of departure and the date of return (e.g. Eleanor should not return until at least 5ᵗʰ April 2020: five years and two days after her date of departure) – but see also points (iv) and (v) below.

iv) For those emigrating after 5ᵗʰ April 2013, 'split year' treatment is again available on their return to the UK in order to determine if they have achieved the requisite period of non-residence. However, achieving 'split year' treatment requires the taxpayer to adhere to certain circumstances as prescribed by a highly complex set of rules so the position will often remain uncertain. For this reason, I would generally suggest that it is safer to remain non-UK resident until after the end of the UK tax year in which the fifth anniversary of the day after the date of departure falls (e.g. until at least 6ᵗʰ April 2020 in Eleanor's case).

v) As explained above, those who emigrated before 6ᵗʰ April 2013 must remain non-UK resident for at least five complete UK tax years and cannot use 'split year' treatment to determine whether their period of non-UK residence has been sufficiently long. The question of whether such emigrants have retained their non-UK residence in 2013/14 and later years will be determined using the new statutory residence test.

Return Visits

Limited return visits to the UK are permitted. For 2013/14 onwards, the maximum amount of return visits is based on a highly complex set of rules included within the new statutory residence test.

Set out below is a rough guide to the maximum amount of return visits which an individual can usually make to the UK without losing their non-UK resident status. As explained above, however, there are many other factors and considerations which need to be taken into account, so professional advice is essential.

Ties

The maximum number of days which a non-UK resident may spend in the UK generally depends on how many 'ties' they have with the UK for the relevant tax year. The 'ties' taken into account for this purpose are:

i)   The Family Tie
The individual has a spouse, civil partner, common-law partner, or minor child who is resident in the UK. A minor child need only be counted if the individual sees them on more than 60 days in the tax year. Separated spouses and civil partners do not need to be counted.

ii)   The Accommodation Tie
The individual has a home or other accommodation available to them in the UK for at least 91 consecutive days during the tax year and spends at least one night there during the tax year (or spends at least 16 nights

there during the tax year if the available accommodation is the home of a close relative).

iii)   The Work Tie
The individual works in the UK for more than three hours on at least 40 days during the tax year.

iv)   The 90-Day Tie
The individual spent more than 90 days in the UK in either of the two previous tax years.

v)   The Country Tie
There is no other country where the individual was present at midnight on more days during the tax year than in the UK.

Maximum Visits

The maximum permitted return visits also depend on whether the individual was UK resident in any of the three previous UK tax years, as follows:

Maximum Visits If UK Resident in One or More of the Previous Three Years

No. of Ties	Maximum Visits
0	182 Days
1	120 Days
2	90 Days
3	45 Days
4 or 5	15 Days

Maximum Visits If Not UK Resident in Any of the Previous Three Years

No. of Ties	Maximum Visits
0 or 1	182 Days
2	120 Days
3	90 Days
4	45 Days

(The 'country tie' is disregarded in this case.)

Practical Implications

Every individual will face a different set of circumstances, so it is difficult to provide definitive advice which works in every case.

Generally, however, the above tables tell us that an individual can almost always achieve non-UK residence by limiting return visits to the UK to 15 days or less for the first three UK tax years after departure and to 45 days or less per year thereafter.

Typically, a UK property investor seeking to avoid UK Capital Gains Tax by emigrating will usually be able to avoid the 'work tie' and the 'country tie' but will often be subject to the 'accommodation tie', especially if they still have any family in the UK. The '90-day tie' will also generally be unavoidable for the first two years after departure. Whether the 'family tie' applies will depend very much on personal circumstances.

Hence, we can generally expect most property investors to have two or three 'ties' in the first two years after departure, meaning that return visits would need to be limited to a maximum of either 45 or 90 days in each UK tax year.

From the third year onwards, this 'typical' investor would then have only one or two ties and could return for longer periods but anything over 90 days would create a new 'tie' once again, so should probably be avoided.

In short, most property investors seeking to avoid UK Capital Gains Tax through emigration should probably limit return visits to a maximum of 90 days in each UK tax year, and no more than 45 days in each of the first two UK tax years after departure where they have a spouse, partner or minor child in the UK.

In some cases, however, return visits will need to be limited to no more than 15 days per tax year for the first three years and no more than 45 days per tax year thereafter: especially where the 'work tie' may apply.

Longer visits will be possible in some cases but detailed professional advice is essential!

Earlier Years

For 2012/13 and earlier years, the general rules on return visits were:

- They could not exceed 182 days in any one UK tax year
- They had to average less than 91 days per year

However, this was only one aspect of the situation and must be regarded as the minimum criterion for maintaining non-resident status. In practice, HM Revenue and Customs looked at many other factors and the more links that the individual maintained with the UK, the more likely they were to continue to be UK resident, and hence still liable for UK Capital Gains Tax.

Which Days Must Be Counted in a Visit?

The general rule is that any day on which you are present in the UK at midnight is counted for the purpose of the above tests.

This is subject to exclusions for:

- Days of arrival, when you are merely in transit from one foreign country to another, you leave the UK the next day, and you do not carry out any other activities whilst in the UK.
- Days when you are prevented from leaving the UK due to exceptional circumstances beyond your control (up to a maximum of 60 such days in a tax year).

From 2013/14 onwards, any individual who has been UK resident in any of the previous three tax years and who has three or more 'ties' (see above) must also count any other days when they are present in the UK at **any time** – subject to an exclusion for the first 30 such days. (These days count as part of the individual's return visits but do not count towards the '90-day tie'.)

Special Circumstances

As explained above, there are many other factors to be taken into account. In addition to the rules on return visits, there are special rules for:

- The year of death
- Individuals working full-time in the UK (who will usually be UK resident)
- Individuals working full-time abroad (who will usually be non-UK resident)
- Individuals who retain a home in the UK

The last point is particularly important. Under certain circumstances, an individual who is present at their UK home at any time on 30 or more days in a UK tax year may be automatically treated as UK resident for that year.

8.33 PLANNING FOR NON-RESIDENTS & THOSE INTENDING TO EMIGRATE IN THE FUTURE

The Government proposes to begin taxing non-UK residents on gains arising on residential property in the UK. Only the part of the gain arising after 5ᵗ April 2015 is to be taxed so, for those with large existing capital gains in their portfolio, emigration remains a good way to avoid Capital Gains Tax.

Example

Yvonne has a large portfolio of UK residential property. At 5ᵗ April 2015, the total gains on her portfolio amount to around £2m. Selling her portfolio whilst still a UK resident would give her a Capital Gains Tax bill of up to £560,000.

Instead, Yvonne emigrates, becoming non-UK resident for tax purposes. She sells her portfolio a short time later, when her total gains amount to £2,150,000.

Yvonne is only subject to UK Capital Gains Tax on the £150,000 of additional gains arising after 5ᵗ April 2015. After deducting her 2015/16 annual exemption of £11,100, she has taxable gains of £138,900, giving her a maximum tax bill of just £38,892 – not bad for a portfolio with over £2m of gains in it!

See Section 8.32 for a detailed examination of some of the crucial points to bear in mind when considering emigrating for tax purposes.

Other Planning Issues

The proposal to begin taxing non-UK residents on gains on UK residential property will reduce the effectiveness of emigration as a Capital Gains Tax planning strategy in the future, but those with large existing gains like Yvonne could still benefit.

In our example above, Yvonne sold her portfolio fairly soon after emigrating, so her tax bill was not too large. Let us now suppose instead, however, that she waits several years and eventually sells her portfolio at a total gain of £3m. Her UK Capital Gains Tax bill would now be 28% of the £1m gain arising after 5ᵗ April 2015 – a total of £280,000 (ignoring her annual exemption). Is there anything she could have done to reduce this burden?

To begin with, there are simple steps which Yvonne could take, like selling one property in each UK tax year to maximise the savings produced by her annual exemptions, or putting properties into joint names with a spouse or civil partner to enable the couple to benefit from two annual exemptions.

Those who are already non-UK resident before 5ᵗʰ April 2015 could also consider putting UK residential property into joint names with another non-UK resident person (such as an unmarried partner or an adult child) before that date. The transfer would not be subject to UK Capital Gains Tax and two annual exemptions would be available on future disposals.

Another simple step being considered by many property investors who are already non-UK resident, or who are considering emigration in the future, is to have their UK residential property portfolio valued at 5ᵗʰ April 2015. A good robust valuation carried out at the time may be extremely useful in the future when the issue of the property's value at that date becomes critical. By obtaining professional valuations at the relevant time, they will carry more weight in the future and are less likely to be challenged.

In Yvonne's case, we saw that her portfolio had gains of 'around £2m' at 5ᵗʰ April 2015. If valuations as at that date are only carried out several years later, this rough figure may well prevail. If, instead, she has the valuations carried out on or near to 5ᵗʰ April 2015, she might find these indicate that the existing gains at that date are actually greater. Every additional £10,000 of value at 5ᵗʰ April 2015 indicated by her valuations will eventually save her £2,800 in UK Capital Gains Tax.

It is also worth bearing in mind that the proposed new Capital Gains Tax charges arising from 5ᵗʰ April 2015 only apply to UK residential property.

Hence, an investor like Yvonne might benefit by selling off her UK residential property portfolio and reinvesting the proceeds in either:

a)   Overseas property, or
b)   Commercial property in the UK

Naturally, Yvonne should wait until she is non-UK resident before she begins this process: unless she has some properties which she can sell with little or no Capital Gains Tax liability at the moment (e.g. a property with a small gain which is covered by her annual exemption).

Those who are already non-UK resident may benefit by starting a similar process now, with a view to disposing of all UK residential property before 5ᵗʰ April 2015.

Another potential strategy may be to transfer UK residential properties into a company: before 5ᵗʰ April 2015 for those who are already non-UK resident; or shortly after emigration for those who are currently still UK resident.

This is unlikely to eliminate UK tax on the properties altogether, but may reduce it significantly. Properties worth over £500,000 which are not being rented out as part of a property rental business should generally be excluded from such a transfer, however, due to the additional 'Mansion Taxes' described in Section 7.15.

Careful Planning Required

Many of the strategies described above have additional tax implications, and it is also essential to consider the overseas tax implications arising in the investor's country of residence, nationality, and the country where properties are located. Hence, professional advice is essential!

Nonetheless, some careful planning should enable many property investors to significantly reduce the impact of the Government's proposals.

8.34 THE GENERAL ANTI-ABUSE RULE

The general anti-abuse rule (or 'GAAR' for short) was introduced with effect from 16ᵗʰ July 2013.

The GAAR is intended to be targeted at 'artificial' and 'abusive' or 'aggressive' tax avoidance schemes which go beyond the scope of normal tax planning and which use loopholes in the tax legislation in a way that was not intended by Parliament.

We are being told that 'normal' tax planning will not be affected.

Where the GAAR applies, any tax advantage gained through the use of the 'abusive' scheme will be reversed.

Personally, I would not regard any tax planning strategies discussed in this guide as being 'abusive' and I believe that most professional tax advisors would agree with me. I would thus hope that none of the techniques discussed in this guide will be affected by the GAAR.

Nonetheless, at present, it is way too early to tell just exactly how HM Revenue and Customs will apply the GAAR in practice. It is therefore possible that some more advanced planning strategies could be at risk of being targeted under the GAAR.

Chapter 9

Planning With More Complex Structures

9.1 USING A PROPERTY COMPANY TO SAVE TAX

In recent years, many UK property investors have been drawn towards the idea of running their property business through a limited company.

This is due, in part, to the fact that Corporation Tax rates are considerably lower than higher rate Income Tax, thus providing the opportunity to make huge annual tax savings on rental profits.

Another major benefit is the ability to set interest on funds borrowed for a company's property investments against other income or capital gains within the company or even the investor's own income.

Companies also continue to be eligible for indexation relief on their capital gains.

Conversely, however, a company is not entitled to many of the other reliefs available to individuals under the Capital Gains Tax regime and is not entitled to principal private residence relief, private letting relief or an annual exemption.

Furthermore, there is a significant 'catch' which lies in the fact that further tax costs will often arise when extracting profits or sale proceeds from the company.

All of these conflicting factors combine to make the decision whether or not to use a company a highly complex issue. Nevertheless, despite its complexity, it is well worth reviewing your own circumstances to see whether you have scope to make the substantial tax savings which are available under the right conditions.

A detailed examination of the tax benefits and pitfalls of using a company to invest in property is contained in the Taxcafe.co.uk Guide 'Using a Property Company to Save Tax'.

In this guide, we show how a property investor using the favourable Corporation Tax regime can sometimes achieve a significantly higher income than a personal investor.

9.2 PARTNERSHIPS

Some of the legal background to property partnerships was covered in Section 2.13. Most of the tax rules outlined throughout this guide apply equally to partnerships, including any individual members of corporate or limited partnerships.

Wealth Warning

From 2014/15 onwards, profit shares attributed to a member of a partnership which is not subject to UK Income Tax (typically a company) may, under certain circumstances, be allocated to the individual members of the partnership for tax purposes.

In many ways, a property partnership simply combines joint ownership with a more sophisticated profit sharing agreement.

However, a partnership is considerably more flexible, as, subject to the terms of the partnership agreement, partners may join, leave or change their profit share at any time.

Each partner is taxed on his or her share of rental income, trading profits or capital gains, as allocated according to the partnership agreement (subject to the 'Wealth Warning' above).

There are, however, restrictions on any 'non-active' partners claiming relief for their share of partnership trading losses. Broadly speaking, a partner is usually classed as 'non-active' if they spend an average of less than ten hours per week engaged in the partnership's trading activities.

Firstly, the total cumulative amount of loss which a non-active partner may claim is restricted to the amount of capital which they have invested in the partnership. Capital contributed after 1· March 2007 may be excluded from this calculation if the investment was made primarily to secure extra loss relief.

Secondly, there is an annual limit of £25,000 on claims for partnership trading loss relief by non-active partners. This limit applies to the total claims made by any individual each tax year in respect of all partnerships in which they are a non-active partner and any trade in which they are a so-called 'non-active sole trader' (see Section 5.10).

The restriction of relief for partnership trading losses is of particular concern to 'husband and wife' property trading partnerships where one spouse is not actively involved.

Getting the less active spouse to work in the business for at least ten hours a week may therefore be advisable.

Stamp Duty Land Tax

A major drawback to property investment partnerships is the danger of incurring Stamp Duty Land Tax charges at frequent intervals. Stamp Duty Land Tax is payable whenever a partner:

a)   Introduces property into a partnership,
b)   Takes property out of a partnership, or
c)   Changes their profit share.

Furthermore, Stamp Duty Land Tax may also be charged on partners withdrawing capital from a partnership within three years of introducing property.

Example Part 1

Dave has been in a property investment partnership with four friends, Dozy, Beaky, Mick and Tich, for several years. The five friends each have a 20% profit share. Dave would now like to retire and wishes to leave the partnership. The partners agree that, by way of consideration for giving up his partnership share, Dave should take the property known as 'Dee Towers' with him. Dee Towers is worth £1,000,000.

Dave already had a 20% share in Dee Towers through the partnership so he is treated as acquiring an 80% share, worth £800,000, when he leaves the partnership. He will therefore face a Stamp Duty Land Tax charge of £32,000! (4% x £800,000)

Example Part 2

A short time later, Mick inherits £1,000,000 from his great aunt Shirley. He decides that he would like to invest this in the partnership. At the same time, Tich has decided that he would like to retire and wishes to sell his partnership share. Mick therefore buys Tich's 25% partnership share for £1,000,000, thus increasing his own share from 25% to 50%.

Immediately prior to Mick's new investment, the partnership had a commercial property portfolio with a total gross value of £20,000,000 and borrowings of £16,000,000.

Whilst the partnership's net assets are only £4,000,000, however, the Stamp Duty Land Tax charge is based on its property portfolio's gross value.

Mick has increased his profit share from 25% to 50%. He is therefore treated as having acquired a 25% interest in commercial property worth £20,000,000. Hence, Mick will be faced with a Stamp Duty Land Tax bill of £200,000! (25% of £20,000,000 charged at 4%)

By and large, therefore, anyone using a property investment partnership should try to get their profit shares right in the first place and do their utmost to avoid changing them at a later stage.

Note, however, that a straightforward cash investment into the partnership will not incur any Stamp Duty Land Tax charge if there is no change in the partnership profit shares. Hence, if Mick had simply put £1,000,000 into the partnership, rather than buying out Tich's share, he could have avoided the Stamp Duty Land Tax charge.

Note also that the amount which Mick paid for Tich's share has no bearing on the amount of Stamp Duty Land Tax payable which is based instead on the gross value of the partnership's property portfolio.

It is worth contrasting this with the position which would have existed if the five friends had set up a property investment company instead.

Subject to some anti-avoidance rules, the shares in a property investment company can change hands for a Stamp Duty charge of only 0.5%, which represents a considerable saving compared to the rather draconian 4% which often applies to property investment partnerships. Furthermore, the charge on company shares would be based on the actual consideration paid for those shares and not on the gross value of the underlying properties.

Example Revisited

As above, Mick is investing £1,000,000 in a property investment business which owns a property portfolio with a gross value of £20,000,000 but has net assets of only £4,000,000. This time, however, he is purchasing shares in a property investment company. His Stamp Duty liability will therefore be just £5,000.

The lesson here is clear – if you and your colleagues are likely to change profit shares with any degree of frequency whatsoever, a company is likely to be much better than a partnership.

Other Partnerships Holding Property

There is no Stamp Duty Land Tax charge on the purchase of profit share in most trading partnerships, including a property management partnership.

Sadly, however, this relaxation does not apply to property investment, property development or property dealing partnerships.

The other charges described above continue to apply to all partnerships.

Wealth Warning

HM Revenue and Customs interprets the Stamp Duty Land Tax rules for partnerships as applying not only to property held by the partnership, but also to property held by an individual partner for use in the partnership business.

The Annual Investment Allowance

In most cases, the annual investment allowance is available to partnerships in the same way as any other business entity (see Section 3.10).

However, where one or more of the members of the partnership is a company, the annual investment allowance will not be available.

9.3   LIMITED LIABILITY PARTNERSHIPS

Since the year 2000, a new legal entity has been available throughout the UK – a Limited Liability Partnership, or 'LLP' for short. Like a Scottish partnership, an LLP is a legal person and may own property directly.

All of the rules described in the previous section apply equally to limited liability partnerships, subject to the 'Wealth Warning' below.

Wealth Warning

From 6ᵗʰ April 2014 onwards, members of a limited liability partnership whose profit share is mostly fixed without reference to the overall performance of the business may, under certain circumstances, have to be treated as employees for Income Tax and National Insurance purposes.

A further important point to note is that interest on funds borrowed to invest in, or lend to, a property investment LLP is not eligible for Income Tax relief.

9.4   PROPERTY SYNDICATES AND SPECIAL PURPOSE VEHICLES

The term 'syndicate' is a very loose one. When you join a property syndicate, you may, in fact, be investing through any one of a number of structures (or 'Special Purpose Vehicles' as they are often called), including those which I have already outlined above, Unit Trusts (either UK or Offshore) or a much more loosely defined Joint Venture agreement.

The best that I can say is that you should find out exactly how your syndicate is structured and take your own independent legal and tax advice on it. As with any other kind of investment, you need to be very careful who you trust with your money!

9.5   PENSION SCHEMES

Self-Invested Personal Pension Schemes (often known as SIPPs) are prohibited from investing directly in residential property. They may, however, invest in:

- Commercial property
- Real Estate Investment Trusts
- Property Unit Trusts
- Property Authorised Investment Funds
- Dedicated student halls of residence (but not individual student flats)
- Hotels (including hotel rooms and other holiday accommodation bought under 'leaseback' schemes)
- Residential care homes
- Residential property syndicates of 11 or more people

The last point is probably the closest that investors are going to be able to get to the original ideal of investing their pension funds directly into a residential property portfolio.

The Self-Invested Personal Pension Scheme will be regarded as investing in the syndicate rather than the property and this means that the syndicate will be able to borrow up to 85% of the value of its property investments – a vast improvement on the 50% of net value rule applying to the Self-Invested Personal Pension Scheme itself.

No syndicate member may hold 10% or more of the syndicate and personal use of any syndicate property by any member of the syndicate is strictly prohibited.

Where hotel rooms or other holiday accommodation are bought under a 'leaseback' scheme by a Self-Invested Personal Pension Scheme, any personal use of the property by a member of the pension scheme is also strictly prohibited and heavy penalties apply for any transgression.

Self-Invested Personal Pension Schemes can also invest in Real Estate Investment Trusts, Property Authorised Investment Funds or Property Unit Trusts and these provide other indirect methods for investing pension funds into residential property.

Investment through a Self-Invested Personal Pension Scheme can provide some advantages, as income and gains within the Pension Scheme are tax free. The difficulty for many property investors, however, is that without 'earnings', their net contributions to the Self-Invested Personal Pension Scheme eligible for tax relief are limited to a paltry £2,880 per tax year.

9.6 OTHER WAYS TO INVEST IN PROPERTY

Other ways to invest in property indirectly include:

- Real Estate Investment Trusts, which may invest in both commercial and residential property. Dividends paid out by the Real Estate Investment Trust are treated as property income, like rent, in the hands of the investor. Sadly, however, it is not possible to set off any rental losses which the investor has on their own property portfolio.

- Property Authorised Investment Funds – up to 100% of the fund can now be invested in property.

- Authorised Collective Schemes – investments in these schemes which, in turn, invest in property, may now be included within both Individual Savings Accounts and Child Trust Funds.

Appendix A

UK Tax Rates and Allowances: 2013/14 to 2015/16

	Rates	2013/14	2014/15	2015/16
		£	£	£
Income Tax				
Personal allowance		9,440	10,000	10,500
Basic rate band	20%	32,010	31,865	31,785
Higher rate/Threshold	40%	41,450	41,865	42,285
Personal allowance withdrawal				
Effective rate/From	60%	100,000	100,000	100,000
To		118,880	120,000	121,000
Super tax rate/Threshold	45%	150,000	150,000	150,000
Starting rate band applying to interest and other savings income only				
	10%	2,790	2,880	
	0%			5,000
National Insurance				
Primary threshold	9%/12%	7,755	7,956	8,164*
Upper earnings limit	2%	41,450	41,865	42,285
Secondary threshold	13.8%	7,696	7,956	8,164*
Employment allowance		n/a	2,000	2,000
Class 2 – per week		2.70	2.75	2.85*
Small earnings exception		5,725	5,885	6,005*
Class 3 – per week		13.55	13.90	14.20
Pension Contributions				
Annual allowance		50,000	40,000	40,000
Lifetime allowance		1.5m	1.25m	1.25m
Capital Gains Tax				
Annual exemption		10,900	11,000	11,100
Entrepreneurs' relief				
Rate/Lifetime limit	10%	10m	10m	10m
Inheritance Tax				
Nil Rate Band		325,000	325,000	325,000
Annual Exemption		3,000	3,000	3,000

Age-related Allowances, etc.

Age allowance: lower (1)	10,500	10,500	n/a
Age allowance: higher (2)	10,660	10,660	10,660
MCA: born before 6/4/1935 (3)	7,915	8,165	8,395*
MCA minimum	3,040	3,140	3,230*
Income limit	26,100	27,000	27,800*
Blind Person's Allowance	2,160	2,230	2,300*

* - Estimated, based on RPI/CPI inflation at rates of 2.8%/2.0% respectively

Notes
1. Available to individuals born between 6ᵗʰ April 1938 and 5ᵗʰ April 1948
2. Available to individuals born before 6ᵗʰ April 1938
3. The Married Couples Allowance, 'MCA', is given at a rate of 10%

Indexation Relief Rates

(See Section 6.11 for details of the continuing application of this relief in certain circumstances)

Percentages applying to disposals made by individuals between 1 April 1998 and 5 April 2008 of assets acquired (or enhancement expenditure incurred) during:

Month	Rate	Month	Rate	Month	Rate
Mar-82	104.7%	Mar-85	75.2%	Mar-88	56.2%
Apr-82	100.6%	Apr-85	71.6%	Apr-88	54.5%
May-82	99.2%	May-85	70.8%	May-88	53.1%
Jun-82	98.7%	Jun-85	70.4%	Jun-88	52.5%
Jul-82	98.6%	Jul-85	70.7%	Jul-88	52.4%
Aug-82	98.5%	Aug-85	70.3%	Aug-88	50.7%
Sep-82	98.7%	Sep-85	70.4%	Sep-88	50.0%
Oct-82	97.7%	Oct-85	70.1%	Oct-88	48.5%
Nov-82	96.7%	Nov-85	69.5%	Nov-88	47.8%
Dec-82	97.1%	Dec-85	69.3%	Dec-88	47.4%
Jan-83	96.8%	Jan-86	68.9%	Jan-89	46.5%
Feb-83	96.0%	Feb-86	68.3%	Feb-89	45.4%
Mar-83	95.6%	Mar-86	68.1%	Mar-89	44.8%
Apr-83	92.9%	Apr-86	66.5%	Apr-89	42.3%
May-83	92.1%	May-86	66.2%	May-89	41.4%
Jun-83	91.7%	Jun-86	66.3%	Jun-89	40.9%
Jul-83	90.6%	Jul-86	66.7%	Jul-89	40.8%
Aug-83	89.8%	Aug-86	67.1%	Aug-89	40.4%
Sep-83	88.9%	Sep-86	65.4%	Sep-89	39.5%
Oct-83	88.3%	Oct-86	65.2%	Oct-89	38.4%
Nov-83	87.6%	Nov-86	63.8%	Nov-89	37.2%
Dec-83	87.1%	Dec-86	63.2%	Dec-89	36.9%
Jan-84	87.2%	Jan-87	62.6%	Jan-90	36.1%
Feb-84	86.5%	Feb-87	62.0%	Feb-90	35.3%
Mar-84	85.9%	Mar-87	61.6%	Mar-90	33.9%
Apr-84	83.4%	Apr-87	59.7%	Apr-90	30.0%
May-84	82.8%	May-87	59.6%	May-90	28.8%
Jun-84	82.3%	Jun-87	59.6%	Jun-90	28.3%
Jul-84	82.5%	Jul-87	59.7%	Jul-90	28.2%
Aug-84	80.8%	Aug-87	59.3%	Aug-90	26.9%
Sep-84	80.4%	Sep-87	58.8%	Sep-90	25.8%
Oct-84	79.3%	Oct-87	58.0%	Oct-90	24.8%
Nov-84	78.8%	Nov-87	57.3%	Nov-90	25.1%
Dec-84	78.9%	Dec-87	57.4%	Dec-90	25.2%
Jan-85	78.3%	Jan-88	57.4%	Jan-91	24.9%
Feb-85	76.9%	Feb-88	56.8%	Feb-91	24.2%

Appendix B (cont'd)

Month	Rate	Month	Rate	Month	Rate
Mar-91	23.7%	Aug-93	15.1%	Jan-96	8.3%
Apr-91	22.2%	Sep-93	14.6%	Feb-96	7.8%
May-91	21.8%	Oct-93	14.7%	Mar-96	7.3%
Jun-91	21.3%	Nov-93	14.8%	Apr-96	6.6%
Jul-91	21.5%	Dec-93	14.6%	May-96	6.3%
Aug-91	21.3%	Jan-94	15.1%	Jun-96	6.3%
Sep-91	20.8%	Feb-94	14.4%	Jul-96	6.7%
Oct-91	20.4%	Mar-94	14.1%	Aug-96	6.2%
Nov-91	19.9%	Apr-94	12.8%	Sep-96	5.7%
Dec-91	19.8%	May-94	12.4%	Oct-96	5.7%
Jan-92	19.9%	Jun-94	12.4%	Nov-96	5.7%
Feb-92	19.3%	Jul-94	12.9%	Dec-96	5.3%
Mar-92	18.9%	Aug-94	12.4%	Jan-97	5.3%
Apr-92	17.1%	Sep-94	12.1%	Feb-97	4.9%
May-92	16.7%	Oct-94	12.0%	Mar-97	4.6%
Jun-92	16.7%	Nov-94	11.9%	Apr-97	4.0%
Jul-92	17.1%	Dec-94	11.4%	May-97	3.6%
Aug-92	17.1%	Jan-95	11.4%	Jun-97	3.2%
Sep-92	16.6%	Feb-95	10.7%	Jul-97	3.2%
Oct-92	16.2%	Mar-95	10.2%	Aug-97	2.6%
Nov-92	16.4%	Apr-95	9.1%	Sep-97	2.1%
Dec-92	16.8%	May-95	8.7%	Oct-97	1.9%
Jan-93	17.9%	Jun-95	8.5%	Nov-97	1.9%
Feb-93	17.1%	Jul-95	9.1%	Dec-97	1.6%
Mar-93	16.7%	Aug-95	8.5%	Jan-98	1.9%
Apr-93	15.6%	Sep-95	8.0%	Feb-98	1.4%
May-93	15.2%	Oct-95	8.5%	Mar-98	1.1%
Jun-93	15.3%	Nov-95	8.5%	Apr-98	
Jul-93	15.6%	Dec-95	7.9%	or later	0.0%

Short Leases

(See Section 6.34)

Proportion of the original cost of a lease of 50 or more years' duration allowed as a deduction for Capital Gains Tax purposes on a disposal of that lease.

Years Remaining	%	Years Remaining	%
50	100	25	81.100
49	99.657	24	79.622
48	99.289	23	78.055
47	98.902	22	76.399
46	98.490	21	74.635
45	98.059	20	72.770
44	97.595	19	70.791
43	97.107	18	68.697
42	96.593	17	66.470
41	96.041	16	64.116
40	95.457	15	61.617
39	94.842	14	58.971
38	94.189	13	56.167
37	93.497	12	53.191
36	92.761	11	50.038
35	91.981	10	46.695
34	91.156	9	43.154
33	90.280	8	39.399
32	89.354	7	35.414
31	88.371	6	31.195
30	87.330	5	26.722
29	86.226	4	21.983
28	85.053	3	16.959
27	83.816	2	11.629
26	82.496	1	5.983

Appendix D

The European Union &
The European Economic Area

The European Union

The 28 member states of the European Union are:

Austria	admitted 1 January 1995
Belgium	founding member
Bulgaria	admitted 1 January 2007
Croatia	admitted 1 July 2013
Cyprus	admitted 1 May 2004
Czech Republic	admitted 1 May 2004
Denmark	admitted 1 January 1973
Estonia	admitted 1 May 2004
Finland	admitted 1 January 1995
France	founding member
Germany	founding member
Greece	admitted 1 January 1981
Hungary	admitted 1 May 2004
Irish Republic	admitted 1 January 1973
Italy	founding member
Latvia	admitted 1 May 2004
Lithuania	admitted 1 May 2004
Luxembourg	founding member
Malta	admitted 1 May 2004
Netherlands	founding member
Poland	admitted 1 May 2004
Portugal	admitted 1 January 1986
Romania	admitted 1 January 2007
Slovakia	admitted 1 May 2004
Slovenia	admitted 1 May 2004
Spain	admitted 1 January 1986
Sweden	admitted 1 January 1995
United Kingdom	admitted 1 January 1973

The European Economic Area comprises the 28 member states of the European Union plus Iceland, Liechtenstein and Norway.